CARING FOR THE SOUL
IN A POSTMODERN AGE

CARING FOR THE SOUL IN A POSTMODERN AGE

Politics and Phenomenology in the Thought of Jan Patočka

Edward F. Findlay

STATE UNIVERSITY OF NEW YORK PRESS

Published by
State University of New York Press, Albany

© 2002 State University of New York

Printed in the United States of America

For information, address State University of New York Press,
90 State Street, Suite 700, Albany, NY 12207

Production by Cathleen Collins
Marketing by Fran Keneston

Library of Congress Cataloging in Publication Data

Findlay, Edward F. 1965–
    Caring for the soul in a postmodern age : politics and phenomenology in the
    thought of Jan Patočka / Edward F. Findlay.
        p. cm.
    Includes bibliographical references and index.
    ISBN 0–7914–5485–1 (alk. paper) — ISBN 0–7914–5486–X (pbk. : alk. paper)
    1. Patočka, Jan, 1907–1977. I. Title.

B4805.P384.F56 2002
199′.437—dc21

                                                                2002021241

10 9 8 7 6 5 4 3 2 1

Contents

Acknowledgments

This book would have been impossible without the help of a number of individuals and organizations, and I would like to extend my sincere gratitude to them all. I am grateful, first of all, to Professors G. Ellis Sandoz and Cecil Eubanks of the Department of Political Science at Louisiana State University for their invaluable support and assistance. Intellectual encouragement also came from Professors Robert Faulkner and Christopher Bruell of the Political Science Department at Boston College, where I benefited immensely from a postdoctoral fellowship. The research and writing of the book took place primarily in Prague, however, and I am indebted to the Center for Theoretical Study of Charles University and the Academy of Sciences in the Czech Republic, for hosting and facilitating my research. I would particularly like to thank Ivan Chvatík for his support and his critical perspective, and Ivan Havel for permitting me to make valuable use of the facilities at CTS. I would also like to acknowledge the support of the William J. Fulbright Commission of the United States and the Fulbright Committee in Prague, which made my overseas experience possible. I want to thank, as well, the Institute for Human Sciences in Vienna, Austria, which has also supported my work and involved me in additional projects on the intellectual legacy of Jan Patočka. Last, but most important, I want to thank my wife, Alžběta, and my father, Edward J., for their constant encouragement and sage advice. Without you, there is nothing. This book is, above all else, for you both.

1

Introduction

The Czech philosopher Jan Patočka died in a Prague hospital on March 13, 1977, at age sixty-nine. The cause of death was a brain hemorrhage, brought on by a series of exhausting interrogations at the hands of the StB, the Czechoslovak secret police. Patočka had been under interrogation for his involvement in a protest, in the name of human rights, against the deceitful rule of the communist government in Czechoslovakia. This protest took the form of a document called Charter 77. Its purpose was, in Socratic style, to inform the regime publicly of its own hypocrisy, of its failure to abide by the international Helsinki agreement to which it was a signatory. The Charter admirably accomplished this task, gaining in the process worldwide respect and launching the dissident career of the young playwright Václav Havel who, just over a decade later, would assume the presidency of the newly democratic Czechoslovak republic. Without Patočka's involvement as a spokesman, it is doubtful whether the Charter would have been as effective. The philosopher was explicit in stating, shortly before his death, that there are things worth suffering for.[1] In choosing to speak for the Charter, he chose to speak the truth, not merely in private, but in the public realm. In acting politically, in speaking truthfully before his own Athenian Senate knowing full well the cost involved, Jan Patočka, like his model Socrates, signaled that there was an unbreakable relationship between politics and philosophy, between truth and the realm of our social being. Through his actions and words, Patočka declared that we should not be content with a passive awareness of this relationship; we must act according to it. In the work that follows I will pursue the nature of this relationship as it is uniquely developed in the work of the late Czech philosopher Jan Patočka.

Jan Patočka spoke in one moment as a dedicated classicist, in another as a thorough postmodernist. It is conceivable, depending on the texts on which you choose to focus, to defend his work from either perspective. This is a temptation for the contemporary reader. One might read him, for example, as a moral Platonist who is enough of a contemporary to pay attention to postmodern theory or, alternately, as a committed postmodern

1

who is willing to pay lip service to the classics. Such readings should be avoided, however. With this study I will show that the voice of Jan Patočka is a distinctive one in contemporary philosophy, that his work deserves recognition not merely as an alternative reading of already established bodies of work, but as a unique contribution to philosophy and to political theory.

A Czech in the midst of the twentieth century, Patočka was literally surrounded by German influence, in politics as well as in education. It is not surprising, therefore, that the context of his work is largely determined by German philosophy. Patočka naturally came under the influence of the towering philosophical figures of the time and place, Edmund Husserl and Martin Heidegger. It is Husserl and Heidegger, above all others, who account for the specific direction of his work. Yet as a doctoral student in the twenties and thirties, Patočka was also well read in the works of, among others, Brentano, Bergson, Scheler, Koyré, Radl, and Ingarden.[2]

Although of the age when political developments forced many of his contemporaries to emigrate, Patočka chose to remain in Czechoslovakia for the duration of the periods of National Socialist and Communist rule. Among those Central European philosophical contemporaries who did emigrate, the names of Arendt, Strauss, and Voegelin come to mind. Patočka shares a great deal with these thinkers and can be properly situated in the broad context of the themes that they pursue. He speaks directly, in addition, to contemporary thinkers such as Maurice Merleau-Ponty and Paul Ricoeur, as well as Richard Rorty and Jacques Derrida. Methodologically, what ties Patočka to these thinkers is his engagement with phenomenology and ontology, with philosophy pursued through direct, experiential evidence illuminated by analysis of the structures inherent to the human being. Thematically, he shares with many of these individuals an interest in the classical philosophy and politics of ancient Athens combined with a postmodern interest in the problem of metaphysics and the source, the foundation, of the shared sense of meaningfulness that underlies Western civilization. Yet Patočka's work belongs to the context of these other thinkers not only from the perspective of method and theme; he belongs with them as well because of the significance and relevance of what he has to say. This is a point to be established in the course of this study, however.

Patočka's work is inspired by the goal expressed by Edmund Husserl in his last major work, the *Crisis of European Sciences*. As a reaction to this "crisis," the crisis of rationality accompanying the rise of positivism and its subordination of the question of relevance to one of method or objectivity, Husserl sought a renewal of the spirit that was at the heart of Western culture, the spirit of reason.[3] As Husserl's student during the period when this theme was formulated, Patočka took on himself the task of pursuing and clarifying this strand of Husserl's thought—a strand that fully occupied the German phenomenologist only at the end of his life. What Patočka realized was that Husserl's transcendental phenomenology, while it proceeded from unimpeachable insight about the importance of the direct experience of phenomena (as opposed to the more indirect experience of phenomena perceived through the anticipatory lenses of theory or ideology), was in many ways inappropriate to the task. Husserl's understanding of reason was still anchored in Enlightenment thinking, while Patočka wished to renew an ancient understanding of reason by subjecting it to a contemporary critique that was critical of Enlightenment thought.

Patočka chose, therefore, not to pursue the problem along Husserlian lines, as a search for a universal philosophy in the Cartesian tradition. He felt that rationality primarily indicated a mode of living, of examining reality, modeled on the dialectical activity of Socrates. His was a concrete question, a question of the being of man in the world and in history. For the development of this insight Patočka looked to the work of Martin Heidegger, who was particularly important in two ways: first, he brought to Patočka a thematic exploration of human being, and second, he stressed the importance of history, of understanding humanity as situated temporally, or historically.

Husserl had pointed to rationality, the Greek "insight," as the underlying principle of European civilization. Patočka wanted to renew it as a principle not by disregarding the contemporary and returning to the ancient, but by reexamining the ancient with the help of contemporary thought. Reason had to be re-understood phenomenologically and ontologically, and this meant understanding it—following Heidegger's critique of metaphysics—in a nonmetaphysical sense.[4]

Husserl and Heidegger, then, profoundly influenced the political thought of Jan Patočka. The importance of their work to contemporary thought leads many political theorists to attempt to locate a coherent theory of politics in their work directly. It is generally true, however, that these attempts have not had great success. The fact is that neither Husserl nor Heidegger lends himself readily to political theory. Yet their work is crucial to the contemporary critique of the Western theory that political theorists look to as justification for their normative political stances. What is perhaps needed, then, is not an attempt to read Husserl or Heidegger as political thought, but an attempt to write political thought in light of their work. This is an appropriate description of Patočka's task; while true that he tries to remain faithful to the insight of his German teachers, he nevertheless moves to develop a politically relevant philosophy that draws on them yet is independent of their particular frameworks.

German philosophy was not the only influence that made a decisive impression. Patočka lived in a time and place of great upheaval and conflict.

Czechoslovak hopes for political freedom were crushed repeatedly during the course of his life: first at Munich in 1938 and the resulting occupation by the Third Reich, once again with the Communist takeover after World War II, and finally in 1968 with the Soviet-led invasion in the wake of the Prague Spring. It is no exaggeration, then, to remark as Josef Novák did that "Patočka's bibliography is inseparable from his biography."[5] To note and take account of the influence of history, however, is something substantially different from drawing the conclusion that Patočka's work is determined by that history, that he is essentially, for example, a "dissident" philosopher. To make such a charge is to imply that it is the dissident experience that is substantive, and not the philosophy. Patočka is not, in this sense, a dissident philosopher. His work does not depend on his historical experience with dissidence; instead, it is the dissident experience that is made additionally meaningful through his political philosophy.

Rather than a simple response to external events, Patočka's political theory is philosophy in the truest sense of the term. It realizes first of all that philosophy, like all human achievements, is a historical one, and second, that new philosophies do not simply replace older ones but are continuous with them. To take these principles seriously is to accept the challenge offered by Patočka—the challenge to reveal the dialogue and the continuity between the ancient and the new, between the classical and the postmodern.

Before approaching the question of the significance of this material a few more words need to be said about the disparate nature of much of Patočka's work. As a result of the reality of communism, Jan Patočka was only for very short periods able to work and conduct research as a university professor. He was also unable to publish much of what he did produce. Though he wrote a vast amount in his lifetime, relatively little of it is in the form of significant texts to which one can authoritatively point as reflecting a center of the philosopher's canon. As Josef Moural put it in a short essay on this topic, "[t]here is too little of finished big works, and too much of sketches, fragments, lectures for various levels of listeners."[6] Even among works that can be called major, a great variety of topics are considered. In addition to his attention to phenomenology, Patočka was also a philosopher of history and, some would also say, a historian of philosophy.[7]

There is a question, therefore, about the existence of a genuine center in the philosopher's work. At least one Czech commentator, Moural notes, has argued that there is no "core" to Patočka's work, no "project" in any systematic sense. In this view, Patočka's greatness lies in his ability to interpret other philosophers.[8] In defense of this position, a former student, the Czech philosopher Ladislav Hejdánek, maintains that Patočka did not genuinely pursue phenomenology as the centerpiece of his philosophizing. There are others, though, who make the opposite claim. Moural also points to a perspective that holds that phenomenology—particularly the unfinished projects of an "asubjective" phenomenology and the theory of three movements of human existence—was in fact the "center of gravity" that determined a basic unity in this work.[9]

While both viewpoints can be adequately defended, Moural appropriately notes a third element, "one that is more difficult to identify and describe."[10] This is the theme that the editors of Patočka's *Collected Works* have chosen to title "Care for the Soul." As those editors, Ivan Chvatík and Pavel Kouba, put it, this title indicates "the works that concern the position of human beings in the world and in history: from the moral and religious questions of the individual through the attitudes towards current social and political events up to general reflections on the philosophy of history."[11] These texts, which contain political as well as historical reflections, are highlighted by the one work that most would agree to call a *magnum opus*: the *Heretical Essays in the Philosophy of History*. In pointing toward these works, Moural correctly implies that here, in this as yet fully unexplored theme in Patočka's work, may be the core, the most significant project, of a lifetime of philosophy. It is Moural's contention, indeed, that the theme of "care for the soul," which "emphasizes the necessity of radical self-clarification to be achieved through historical enquiry,"[12] may be viewed as encompassing, and not standing in contrast to, the interest in phenomenology.

Moural places the question of care for the soul within the broader confines of an inquiry into historicity, and in this he is at least partly correct. In addition to history, I maintain that Patočka is also inquiring into the nature of politics and the political model conducive to human freedom. Philosophy, he argued, is the care for the soul that takes place within the "care for the *polis*, for the optimal state."[13] In his brief essay, Moural leaves the reader with a challenge to undertake an examination of Patočka's work in light of the theme of history; this is a challenge that leads to what I consider the "core" of Patočka's work: the question of the "*social being* of humans."[14] With this interest, not solely in *being* but in *social being*, the Czech philosopher incorporates into his study of Husserl and Heidegger a Platonically inspired devotion to the reality of human beings in community—in other words, to politics.

It is this part of Patočka's work that belongs under the heading of "care for the soul," and it is the central focus of this study. It leads, not inward into the methodological questions of phenomenology, but outward into the world of human social life, the world of political and historical activity. Yet phenomenology remains a crucial part of the equation, for Patočka argued that "the question of human social being is also in the first place a *phenomenological* question."[15] Thus to get at the philosophy of history and politics that is at the center of Patočka's work, one must first work through the implications of the phenomenology and ontology of Husserl and Heidegger. Only when this is done is the question of history, that "domain of changing social being of humans," fully illuminated. It is only in history, Patočka concludes, that the "*social being* of humans can manifest itself as *essentially free*."[16]

Care for the soul thus implies care for the social being of humans; it is the political theme at the center of the philosophy of Jan Patočka. Directed toward the social reality of human beings, this work is naturally relevant to the sciences that study that reality. Thus it is, in his series of phenomenological lectures entitled *Body, Community, Language, World* that Patočka stresses the need of a philosophical justification for the social sciences. "[F]or all social sciences," he writes, "the point at which they become genuine sciences is penetration through self-illusions, self-deceptions, our idols of ourselves. Providing a philosophical foundation for actual human scientific disciplines demands that we find access to this situation, not an empirical, but a foundational, justifying one."[17]

Thus setting out his own goal, Patočka brings us to the question of the significance of his achievement. As a student of Heidegger, it is correct to assume that when Patočka speaks about a philosophical "foundation," he is not referring to the type of "metaphysical" foundation of which Heidegger was so critical.[18] Since the critique offered by Heidegger and, before him, Nietzsche, the question of the foundation has been at the center of contemporary thought. It is a fundamental question, and in many ways a dilemma, of postmodernism. The notion that theory and philosophy should be pursued on the basis of an objectively transcendental foundation has been discredited. It is in light of this that Patočka maintains, along Heideggerean lines, that we are in a "postmetaphysical" era or, as others would say, an age of postmodernism.

The contours of the postmodern dilemma take form as the question is raised of a justification for political and ethical values or norms. Without a solid foundation on which to construct arguments and base conclusions, questions as fundamental as those of morality and justice lose their anchor. It is a loss that cannot be replaced through scientific method; the most elaborate arguments of utilitarianism notwithstanding, social problems inevitably require answers from the realm of morality. The "postmetaphysical" world, Patočka argues, is grounded in nihilism, in a fundamental meaninglessness; its apparent options are to commit to a stance of ethical relativism, the relativism of all meaning, or to seek a renewal of metaphysics through anthropocentric substitutes for transcendental certainty, such as are offered by teleological philosophies of history or eschatological political movements.

This postmodern dilemma is centered, then, in the question of meaning. If one rejects objective, metaphysical meaning, there seems to be no recourse but to commit to meaning that is merely relative, meaning as a function of the will of humans. Jan Patočka is a postmodern philosopher in the sense that he denies the "simply given meaning" of grand narratives and metaphysical systems. Meaning or knowledge taken from an objectively transcendent source, disconnected from human reality in the world, is meaning naively received. It is meaning that seeks to end the need for questioning, not to encourage it. Patočka is not satisfied merely to critique metaphysics, however. He sees human life as absolutely meaningful, and in a nonrelativistic way.

His work seeks to respond to this problem of meaning, of the foundation of meaningfulness in human life. Because he does not conceive of the individual as an independent, disconnected being, but as one integrated into historical relationships with the world and with other beings in a social setting, it is a question that cannot be abstracted from its political or historical context. Meaning, and the sense of a ground on which humans can build continuity, is a factor of our living truthfully in the world and of our relating to the world, not as a collection of objects, but as a whole. What Patočka describes under the rubric of care for the soul is a foundation for politics and ethics in the contemporary world—a foundation that is itself nonmetaphysical.

In terms of its value for political philosophy, Patočka's work is outstanding in its attempt to develop an approach to philosophy and politics that is nonfoundational in the traditional sense, yet does not abandon ethical insight, such as that offered in classical thought by Plato and Aristotle and, in the modern period, by philosophical politicians such as the first Czech president T. G. Masaryk. It is this region between the two poles of a rejection of a simply given, absolute reality on one hand, and the refusal to descend into an amoral nihilism on the other, that must be explored by political theory. An evaluation of Patočka's work is therefore crucial to contemporary political thought.

What Patočka offers, though, is not a "solution" to the problem of meaning or to history. To the contrary, he demands recognition that meaning is not an objective constant in human life, that it is problematic. What is constant, what is "absolute," is the "possibility" inherent in human being. By virtue of an ontological reality noted by Heidegger—that as humans we take an interest in our own being—we have the possibility to pursue this interest toward an intensification, a growth of that being. For Patočka, this can best be done through an understanding of our social being and the possibilities available to it—the possibilities of freedom and of historical action. Here, then, are the concepts that emerge from Patočka's philosophy of history and politics. It is through active freedom in a social and political setting inspired by the model of the Greek polis—that is, a model grounded in the fragile consistency of a community that accepts the conflict and uncertainty natural to free and equal beings—that human life is most fully open to a nonrelativistic meaningfulness.

With this study of the political thought in the philosophy of Jan Patočka, I intend to illuminate and evaluate this argument for a retheoretization of the ground, of the foundations, of Western thought. What is at stake is more than an intellectual exercise, for as Patočka clearly points out, the contemporary world, particularly in regard to its political realities, is mired in a crisis. We exist in an age, with all the characteristics of a technological "supercivilization," that is unable to break its search for meaning free from entanglement with the metaphysical remnants of past theoretical endeavors. Modern civilization searches for meaning by seeking a solution to the problem of history. It seeks to solve history by mastering it—through a political or a philosophical system so perfect as to preclude the possibility of an insoluble problem. To do so is to seek to end history. "Yet the problem of history," Patočka is adamant, "may not be resolved, it must be preserved as a problem."[19]

In order to illuminate the problematic conception of history and politics that makes sense of this enigmatic statement, to illuminate the sense of caring for the soul as a primary function of the polis, I present five substantive chapters of analysis, appended to which is a brief review of the literature on Patočka. Chapter 2, immediately following this introduction, focuses on reading Patočka as an interpreter of Edmund Husserl and Martin Heidegger. Here I discuss the way in which phenomenology, Husserl's methodology for studying reality "as it appears to the ordinary observer or as we encounter it in direct, immediate experience,"[20] forms a basis for Patočka's approach to philosophy. I also trace the influence of the later Husserl, and particularly his *Crisis of European Sciences*, on the young Patočka's view of history and the spirit of the European world. Husserl, however, is only a part of the story. Patočka is not a follower of phenomenology so much as an interpreter of it, and this interpretation is primarily indebted to the ontological insight of Martin Heidegger. Heidegger's influence is also considered, then, as well as the way in which Patočka takes a consciously different path from Heidegger, a path that leads directly to the realm of politics, and not away from it. Last, in chapter 2, I discuss Patočka's own phenomenological contribution: a phenomenology of three movements in human life that becomes the theoretical basis for his work in philosophy of history.

The influence of Husserl and Heidegger is crucial, but it is not in contemporary theory that Patočka finds his greatest inspiration. Consciously departing from Heidegger in this regard, Patočka looks to Plato or, more particularly, to Socrates as epitomizing the approach to philosophy he wishes to emulate. This Socratic approach, however, is viewed through Heideggerean eyes. In chapter 3 I consider the philosopher's relation to Greek philosophy. Here a number of important texts stand out. First is the series of lectures entitled *Plato and Europe*, which present the thesis that the care for the soul, as Patočka understands it, is the "spirit" of European life, a spirit that has been made progressively opaque in the course of Western history. In the same vein is the important essay "Negative Platonism," which gives a clear account of Patočka's reading of Socratic activity as nonmetaphysical and develops a distinction between the figure of Socrates and the later work of Plato. This chapter is important, therefore, for establishing the feasibility of the attempt to, in effect, combine classical theory and symbolism with contemporary critique.

The fourth chapter shifts to the philosophy of history that, as Josef Moural pointed out, belongs within the context of the theme of caring for the soul. Patočka's philosophy of history is presented in the first three of his *Heretical Essays in the Philosophy of History*. I discuss these chapters with the aim of uncovering both the controversial nature and the intent of the contention that history can be said to have a particular beginning, coinciding with the origin of philosophy and politics in Greek antiquity. This review of the meaning of history in Patočka's work leads naturally to a discussion of the site of historical activity (the polis) and its characteristics (freedom and a recognition of problematicity). This chapter concludes, then, with an introduction of the theme of politics.

I turn, in the fifth chapter, directly to a consideration of politics, starting with a review of some of Patočka's other political texts and concluding with an examination of the final two of the *Heretical Essays*, in which the social and political reality of the contemporary world is subject to critique. The aim of chapter 5, entitled "Politics and Ethics in the Twentieth Century," is threefold. First, it is to bring out the details of Patočka's analysis of contemporary civilization and its technological character. This analysis culminates in the striking and controversial essay "Wars of the Twentieth Century and the Twentieth Century as War," with which Patočka concludes his *Heretical Essays*. I try to demonstrate, with a look at not only this essay but also a number of lesser-known essays written at the same time, that there is a fundamental consistency in Patočka's writings, even as those writings are marked by drastic shifts in tone and metaphor. The point to be stressed is that, even as Patočka shifts from a Platonic stress on care for the soul to a more Nietzschean idiom in his discussion of war and conflict, no major change in philosophy is taking place. The challenge for readers, as I noted earlier, is not to read this thinker as you wish him to be, as, for example, a Platonic moralist whose talk of conflict is inexplicable. Patočka occupies a nontraditional space in philosophy.

His understanding of care for the soul does not lead to a transcendental harmony; care for the soul is, rather, a difficult process that involves conflict and requires a willingness to sacrifice.

The second aim of this chapter is to illuminate the attributes of the individual who is genuinely able to care for his soul, the individual who exemplifies the self-understanding characteristic of a historical and political actor. This individual, or "spiritual person,"[21] is neither a typical politician nor a "Guardian" in the sense of Plato's *Republic*. He or she may be a member of any profession. What is important is the person's willingness to accept a "problematic" life and to speak truthfully in the public realm. In this way, Patočka emphasizes, the "spiritual person" of whatever profession is nonetheless political.

My third aim, in chapter 5, is to introduce an essential element of Patočkan politics: the element of ethics and morality. Patočka's final writings, which came in defense of Charter 77, stress the "moral attitude" of the spiritual person and of the political state to which he belongs. Moral sentiment, it is argued, is sovereign over both the individual and the state. Patočka's political thought thus culminates in a commitment to a certain unconditionality of ethical comportment. Yet this position leads to a potential objection. How is it possible to require an unconditional ethics if one is committed to a critique of metaphysics? Can postmodern critique be applied to political theory without dissolving into ethical relativism?

With these questions I return to the central theme of this study and of Patočka's political theory, the problem of the foundation. I conclude with a sixth chapter that explores this theme. It is, in Patočka's terms, a problem of the meaningfulness of human reality. The world as a whole is the meaningful context of our lives, yet it is not an abstract, metaphysical objectification. To the degree that this can be demonstrated persuasively, and Patočka attempts to do so using phenomenological analysis, then the ground of politics and ethics takes on an alternate form, one that contrasts distinctly with the variety of forms given to it in the technological, as well as the pretechnological, eras.

Patočka's philosophy, I contend, is an internally consistent and convincing alternative to political theory that styles itself as either "postmodern" or "classical." It most certainly belongs in the canon of contemporary theory. It is not, however, without its shortcomings, and I discuss the project in chapter 6 with a critical eye, noting the limits of its perspective and the opposition it may provoke. As an appendix to this study, I also include a review of the primary literature on Jan Patočka in English. As a scholar whose ability to work and publish was suppressed by an authoritarian state, Patočka has not been the subject of a significant literature outside his native land. This has begun to change in the last decade but, as I note in the appendix, the literature is still limited and inconsistent. I hope to address this deficiency with this study.

In concluding this introduction, it will be pertinent to note a few of the biographical details of Jan Patočka's life.[22] Patočka was born in 1907 in the town of Turnov, in what was then the Czech part of the Austro-Hungarian Empire. He was the third of four boys in a family of modest means but superior education. Patočka's father was a well-known classical philologist with a wide-ranging interest in the literary arts, and his mother was trained in opera. Although the family was forced to live modestly due to the elder Patočka's ill health, it is certain that the children were not at a loss for education.

The young Patočka began a course of study in philosophy at Prague's ancient Charles University in 1925 and was able to gain a stipend, four years later, to study in Paris. It was here, at the Sorbonne, that Patočka attended a series of lectures given by Edmund Husserl, the *Paris Lectures*, which were to develop into the *Cartesian Meditations*. This exposure undoubtedly influenced the Czech philosophy student, although it would be several more years before he would work directly with the German phenomenologist.

After completing his degree from Charles University, Patočka again sought an international fellowship, this time ending up in Freiburg to study directly under Husserl and his assistant Eugen Fink, and also to attend the lectures of Martin Heidegger. It was in fact Fink with whom Patočka worked most closely in Freiburg, and it was arguably Fink's direct influence that was most important in determining the course that Patočka's interest in phenomenology would take.[23] Fink's influence was particularly important in his encouragement of the critical perspective toward Husserl's methodology that would come to be central to Patočka's work.

Patočka also pursued a relationship with Husserl, however, and he was to some degree rewarded. Back in Prague in the mid-1930s, Patočka was instrumental in bringing the renowned phenomenologist to the Czech capital to lecture. These "Prague lectures," from November of 1935, became the basis for Husserl's last major work, the *Crisis of European Sciences*, which had an inordinate influence on the direction of Patočka's career.

In the years that followed, Patočka's world was to fall apart. Following the Munich Diktat and the Nazi invasion of Czechoslovakia in 1938, non-German universities were closed and life became extraordinarily trying. As a result of the occupation, however, Czechoslovakia was spared major battles or destruction during the war. Patočka was thus able to continue to write occasional articles; this despite being forced to work, as he was in 1944, as a tunneler. This last job, for which his academic inclinations did not well prepare him, fortunately did not last long. By 1945 the war came to an end and the philosopher was able to take up a position at Charles University as a full professor.

Once again, however, international political forces were to intrude decisively on his career. His return to the university, where he immediately began to fill the needs of a student population starved for instruction, was only short-lived. By 1948 the Communist Party was in control of the government and the forty years of Czechoslovak communism had begun. Patočka was again dismissed from the university, and this time effectively barred from print. For the next fifteen years—when he was in his prime— Patočka could only manage to find work in archives. While his years in the Komenský (Comenius) archive were extraordinarily productive—he wrote extensively on Komenský and the history of ideas—he was forced to set aside most of his own philosophical research.[24] He was, however, able to avoid all involvement with the political regime and remain faithful to his convictions.

It was not until the late 1960s that the regime began to liberalize and Patočka was able to return to the university. His career took on a second wind and a number of his most significant lecture series, such as the *Body, Community, Language, World* lectures, were delivered to appreciative students during this period. The liberalization of the Prague Spring was also short-lived, however; the Soviet-led invasion of 1968 crushed the hopes and dreams of open-minded Czechs in a devastating fashion. The blow to the psyche of Czech intellectuals was unimaginable. Many had genuinely believed they were entering a period that would be truly free and just. Their bitterness and inner conflict was intense, and some of it is reflected in the tone of the underground "apartment seminars" that Patočka held during the 1970s.

The invasion eventually meant the end of Patočka's career at the university. He was retired against his will in 1972 and again barred from print. But this did not stop him, now that he was a retiree, from pursuing his philosophical and pedagogic ambitions. Patočka continued to lecture to students in the 1970s, but this time illegally in underground seminars held surreptitiously in the private apartments of willing individuals. The *Heretical Essays in the Philosophy of History* were written during this period and published privately as *samizdat*, with carefully guarded copies typed, retyped, and circulated for eager students.

For Patočka, these activities meant that he was engaged in the two activities that mattered most to him: philosophy and education. For the authorities, however, it meant dissidence. Many of Patočka's students or admirers during this time, such as the young playwright Václav Havel, were willing to voice opposition to the regime and take the consequences for it. Thus it was in 1977 that Havel, along with a number of other dissident intellectuals, decided to issue a protest under the name of Charter 77. For the document to carry weight, however, they needed the support of a recognized and respected figure. Although he was hesitant, Jan Patočka, at the age of 69, accepted that role. It was to be the role that brought him international fame, and cost him his life. It was, however, a role entirely in keeping with his political philosophy.

2

"Concrete Humans in Their Corporeal World"

An Interpretation of Husserl and Heidegger

For those familiar with the philosophical traditions associated with Edmund Husserl and Martin Heidegger, the first inclination on encountering Jan Patočka is to view his work as a modification of their, more original, theses. To some extent this is justifiable, for the Czech philosopher is most definitely a student of Husserl and Heidegger, and his work is built on conceptualizations worked out by these two thinkers. Yet to conceive of Patočka as primarily a "Husserlian" or, alternately, a "Heideggerean" thinker is to miss the main thrust of his thought, the most original aspect of his philosophy. Patočka's approach to philosophy is not determined, in the end, by the methodology of either thinker—neither by strict attention to phenomenological method nor by complete immersion in the ontology of being and understanding. Patočka wants to emphasize an area that is not served particularly well either by Husserl or Heidegger. Through his philosophy, he wants to illuminate human social and political reality. Patočka's interpretation is geared toward uncovering a ground for the being of humans in society. As a result, it is necessarily disloyal to the thought of his teachers. While drawing insight from both, he purposefully chooses not to follow either too closely.

Patočka's intent is to bring the insights of Husserl and Heidegger into direct contact with the social sciences. This requires, as he admits with reference to his philosophy of history, a bit of heresy. An examination of Patočka's reliance on these two thinkers will demonstrate that he does not apply their work so much as he interprets it. Developing a philosophy that speaks to being in its concrete, social activity means that Patočka cannot simply follow the framework of either thinker. He pursues phenomenology on the level of its insight, rather than on the level of its method. This means, for instance, that he engages with the whole Heidegger, both the early analyst of *Being and Time* and the later thinker who looks to poetry, world, and earth. This is not a quirk in Patočka's approach but a necessity.

As a starting point for this study of Jan Patočka's political theory, it is important to clarify the nature of his relationship with the two contemporary figures on whom his work relies most heavily. I wish to show how Patočka is able to develop a philosophy that brings their work to bear on an understanding of contemporary political reality. As Patočka understood his task, he was taking their work in a direction that it was meant to go—although neither philosopher took it very far in that direction himself. Though Patočka is a phenomenologist and an adherent of many of the ontological insights explicated by Heidegger, he is more of a critic of the two philosophers than a follower. He does not deny the validity of their insights, but refines their thought and takes it in directions to which it, as originally presented, was not appropriate. That Patočka is neither simply a Husserlian nor a Heideggerean thinker makes his work politically relevant where theirs has largely failed to be.

The basic logic of Patočka's critique of Husserl and Heidegger concerns the being of humans *in* the world, that is, the relation of humans not only to their consciousness, but to their bodies, their communities, and their world. As Patočka himself describes it, he is interested in "concrete humans in their corporeal world."[1] This is a world in which human movement is "shared" movement and the being of humans is historical and social—and thus, political. Patočka's "phenomenological philosophy,"[2] seen in this light, forms a consistent and coherent basis for his more explicitly political writings.

HUSSERL

The story of Patočka's philosophical achievement begins with his association with Edmund Husserl. His first encounter with the German phenomenologist came in 1929 when, as a student concluding his studies at the philosophical faculty of Charles University in Prague, he was able to spend a year on an exchange program at the Sorbonne in Paris. Husserl, at the time, was at the Sorbonne to deliver his *Paris Lectures*, which became the basis for his famous *Cartesian Meditations*. It was during this lecture series that the two were first introduced, albeit only briefly.

The association with Husserl began in earnest in 1933, however, after Patočka had completed his doctoral work and was in Berlin on a grant from the Humboldt Foundation. While studying Greek thought in Berlin under Jacob Klein, the suggestion was put to him to relocate to Freiburg, where he might be closer to Husserl and might also hear Martin Heidegger, with whom Klein had studied. Patočka promptly addressed a letter to Husserl in Freiburg asking to be sponsored and, to his surprise, received a warm invitation. Husserl let Patočka know that he thought of him as a fellow countryman—Husserl had been born in Moravia, in the present-day Czech Republic—and conditioned the invitation only with the requirement that Patočka come free of "preconceived philosophical convictions."[3]

The experience of 1933 in Freiburg was singularly influential in terms of the development of Patočka's phenomenological philosophy. Here his working relationship with Husserl began, and it was here as well that Patočka was first able to hear Heidegger, who was at the height of his fame after the publication of *Being and Time*. Patočka worked most closely in 1933 with Husserl's assistant, Eugen Fink; he developed, during this period, both a deep appreciation for the aims and methods of Husserlian phenomenology and a critical stance toward many of the presumptions on which it rested. Fink, also of independent mind when it came to the philosophy of his teacher, seems to have encouraged the younger Czech in the latter, even encouraging him to consider Heidegger's critique of phenomenology.[4] Ultimately, Patočka did just that and it was, as Ivan Blecha has described it, "[p]recisely this location between Husserl and Heidegger and the attempt at a specific synthesis of the motives of both sides that later helped Patočka to find a distinctive place in phenomenology."[5]

Despite his working mainly with Fink, a relationship between the young Czech and the elder Husserl developed. This relationship advanced in the years following the Freiburg stay, with Patočka receiving an invitation to spend Christmas with the Husserls in 1934. More important for Patočka's philosophy, however, was the progression of their professional relationship. The high point of the association undoubtedly occurred in 1934–1935, when Husserl was laying the groundwork for his last major work, *The Crisis of European Sciences and Transcendental Phenomenology*. It was the content of this work that was to act as a springboard for Patočka's lifelong pursuit of philosophy. Husserl's first public expression of the themes of the *Crisis* came in a letter he sent—in lieu of a personal appearance—to the World Philosophical Congress of 1934, held in Prague. At Husserl's request, the letter was read to the Congress by Jan Patočka, and it represented Husserl's answer to the request of the Congress for comment on "the mission of philosophy in our time."[6]

A more significant presentation of the themes of the *Crisis*, however, took place a year later, also in Prague, and also as a result of action by Patočka. In November of 1935, he hosted Husserl for a series of lectures to the Prague Circle, the *Cercle philosophique de Prague pour les recherches sur l'entendement humain*. The content of these lectures, entitled "The Crisis of European Sciences and Psychology," became the basis for the larger work, the first parts of which were published a year later in 1936.[7] The more well-known "Vienna Lecture" was actually a precursor to the Prague lectures, taking place in May of 1935.

The Crisis of European Sciences

While Patočka is a critic of many of the assumptions on which Husserl bases his phenomenological texts, his philosophical career was nonetheless significantly determined by the themes outlined in *Crisis*.[8] Patočka was strongly influenced by his close association with Husserl in the mid-1930s, which provided him with a raison d'être for his philosophical career. Husserl's *Crisis* was an incomplete work, an introduction to a new expression of the phenomenological outlook. Nevertheless, Patočka found in it themes that resonated, that had the potential, if correctly analyzed, to lead philosophy back to itself, that is, back to a consideration of existence as it is concretely experienced. Patočka's career is, to a large degree, a detailed critique, elaboration, and exploration of themes that were of concern to Husserl at the end of his life.

Primary among these themes is that of the "crisis" of European rationality. The perception of a sense of crisis in Europe at this time was reflected in the increased popularity of early existentialism, particularly the *Existenzphilosophie* of Jaspers and Heidegger.[9] Husserl strongly opposed this movement as a solution to the problem—considering it a form of antirationalism; and yet he did admit, in the words of David Carr, that *Existenzphilosophie* had "given needed expression to something real: a deeply felt lack of direction for man's existence as a whole, a sense of the emptiness of Europe's cultural values, a feeling of crisis and breakdown, the demand that philosophy be relevant to life."[10]

Accepting the relevance of this diagnosis, Husserl proposed a philosophical approach to the problem that seemed quite unlike his earlier work: he proposed a historical analysis that sought to uncover the guiding principle behind philosophy itself. This was not an antirationalistic endeavor, he emphasized—it was its opposite. It was an attempt to rescue rationalism from the decline to which it had been subject with the rise of natural science methodology during and after the Enlightenment.

The argument, encompassing a critique of scientism and positivism, claims that the stunning advances in the natural sciences led to the summary dismissal of the methods of the humanistic sciences as mere subjective reflections on the "unconditionally universal elements and laws" of nature itself, which could only be truly accessed by the development of the exact sciences.[11] The methods of the exact sciences, then, came to be seen as the exclusive mode of access to what became the new basis of reality—the "unconditionally universal" idealizations of the hard sciences. In this situation, lived experience is merely a subjective reflection of that reality, often distorted and inaccurate. This transfer of ontological validity to the constructs of science is at the root of what Husserl called the crisis of Western rationality.[12] Rationality in the West had gone astray, but this did not demand an antirational solution. As Husserl put it in his Vienna lecture,

> I too am certain that the European crisis has its roots in a misguided rationalism. But we must not take this to mean that rationality as such is evil or that it is of only subordinate significance for mankind's existence as a whole. Rationality, in that high and genuine sense of which alone we are speaking, the primordial Greek sense . . . still requires, to be sure, much clarification through self-reflection; but it is called in its mature form to guide [our] development. On the other hand we readily admit (and German Idealism preceded us long ago in this insight) that the stage of development of *ratio* represented by the rationalism of the Age of Enlightenment was a mistake, though certainly an understandable one.[13]

A renewal of reason called for an examination of its origin and its status as the guiding principle of European life. This examination needed to proceed historically, and it needed to refer directly to the origin of philosophy in Greek antiquity.

In order to understand the crisis of Europe, Husserl wrote, the very concept of "Europe" must first be understood. Europe is indistinguishable from its spiritual *telos*.[14] It is "*the historical teleology of the infinite goals of reason*," and it has its birthplace in ancient Greece. In other words, Europe begins with and is defined by philosophy, in the original sense of the word. As the "primal phenomenon of spiritual Europe," philosophy is distinct from what is found in other civilizations by virtue of important differences.[15] "[O]nly in the Greeks do we have a universal ("cosmological") life-interest in the essentially new form of a purely "theoretical" attitude, and this as a communal form."[16] In distinguishing this "theoretical" attitude as something new, he contrasts it to a "natural" attitude that is prior to the theoretical.[17] With the concept of the "natural" attitude, Husserl is describing a pretheoretical, or prephilosophical perspective on life in which things are accepted as simply given. The breakthrough came with the Greek adoption of a theoretical attitude toward human existence amounting to a skeptical interrogation of simply given knowledge. This was the beginning of explicit self-reflection in Western thought and the essence of rationalism. The downfall of Europe has been a result of its estrangement from this essence, its hope for escape from the crisis contingent on its ability to renew this "spirit of philosophy."[18]

Like Husserl, Patočka was convinced of the reality of a crisis, or degradation, of European rationalism. He saw Husserl's diagnosis of the problem as relatively sound; the German philosopher's prescription for solving it, however, was not. The centrality of the theme of the crisis to Patočka's philosophy, as well as his certainty as to the inappropriateness of the Husserlian approach, are clearly demonstrated in two quite distinct texts— one from the beginning and the other from the end of his career. The first text, "Masaryk's and Husserl's Conception of the Spiritual Crisis of European Humanity," comes from 1936, when Husserl was still involved in the writing of *Crisis* and Patočka was in close contact with him. The second text represents a lecture given in Warsaw in 1971 entitled "Edmund Husserl's Philosophy of the Crisis of the Sciences and His Conception of a Phenomenology of the *Life-World*." Despite the gap of thirty-five years, both texts reveal a similar critique: a fundamental disconnectedness in Husserl from the substantiality of the concrete world, which is a world of action and a world of "good and evil" represented, in the earlier article, by the Czech philosopher-president T. G. Masaryk.

In this first essay, Patočka notes that both Masaryk, a "civilizer and an organizer," and Husserl, a "contemplator," are convinced of the debilitating effect on European society of a "protracted spiritual crisis."[19] Though they share a common perception of the problem, their approaches to its solution are drastically different. The young Patočka is inspired by both, yet he sees the need for a third approach that avoids their mistakes. Masaryk's failure stems from his theology, grounded in an "objectivistic conception of God" and appended to an understanding of philosophy based on Descartes. Although Patočka could not agree with Masaryk's combination of theology and Cartesianism, he was nevertheless an adherent of the solidity of Masaryk's ethical and political stances, the practical application of his thought.[20] The intellectual foundations were untenable, but the goals were consistent with human reality; the chore was thus to uncover the authentic foundations for the moral and political posture exemplified by T. G. Masaryk.

Husserl, in contrast, follows "a purely theoretical path"—"that of analysis and reflection, without regard for practical questions, striving solely for clarity and precision of philosophical results."[21] This theoretical philosophy, pursued with exacting rigor, is Husserl's prescription for a solution to the crisis of rationality—a return to philosophy in its essence, guided by phenomenology. As Patočka points out, however, there is a certain weakness in this disregard for the practical, just as there is intellectual weakness in Masaryk's adherence to a practical religiosity:

A man of action, like Masaryk, expresses himself in his active conception of faith; a man of uncompromising intellectual consistency, like Husserl, might find that it interferes with his work. Perhaps we might say, paraphrasing one of Masaryk's well-known sayings, that the German is weak in his strength, the Czech is strong in his weakness.[22]

The Masarykan stress on individual action, on "personal decision which does not follow from theories or rest on arguments," is an attempt to provide answers to genuine problems of human existence, problems which Husserl's philosophy does not address, "though it can perhaps serve as the ground on which such answers can be built."[23] In this early article, Jan Patočka is convinced of two things: the need for a solution to the crisis of European humanity is indeed real, and the best approach to such a solution will draw on a synthesis of practical and theoretical considerations.

By 1971 and the time of the Warsaw lecture, the critique of the Husserlian approach had been elaborated in detail; the basic insight of 1936, however, remained intact. Patočka is even more convinced, after the passage of three and a half decades, of the relevance of Husserl's "diagnosis" of the root of the modern condition as the ascendency of scientific method over all else. The foci remain rationality and responsibility: as the essential ingredients of philosophy, these make up the core of a "life in truth," the symbolic goal of Patočka's philosophy. He neatly summarizes, in the Warsaw lecture, the ground of Husserl's concerns:

> We might formulate Husserl's thoughts on philosophy, science and rationality roughly as follows. Science is genuinely a science—rationally grounded and internally clear knowledge—only as long as it remains in close contact with philosophy, which is its starting point and its foundation. Philosophy is nothing other than a life (dedicated to thought) which responds to the call for a fully responsible thought. An attitude of responsibility is one which makes its opinions conform to its intuitions of the matters themselves, not inversely. We can see that only such a responsible attitude makes possible the *life in truth* which is the essence of philosophy and of every science that has not lost touch with it. Life in truth, in turn, is rationality. This life in truth, as the characteristic *bios*, is what the ancient Greeks had founded as an ongoing tradition whose meaning is always capable of being rediscovered and of being renewed and enriched thanks precisely to the possibility of being rediscovered.[24]

Modern science's abandonment of responsibility coincided with its proposal of a universal systematization of scientific method. The result has been the "crisis" of rational civilization. The same science that increasingly makes life possible "at the same time strips life of all higher reasons for living, leaving us alone in the face of the chaos of instincts and of traditions devoid of any but merely factual cohesion."[25] The granting of special status to the methods of natural science has facilitated a debasement of the spiritual aspects of life, rendering it increasingly empty.

Despite the perspicacity of the diagnosis, the solution proposed was not persuasive. The basis of Patočka's critique concerned the degree to which Husserl's "natural" world was a purely theoretical construction, disconnected from the concreteness of practical human action. As Husserl described this "natural" world, it led to a "metaphysical outcome" that was "unsatisfactory" and "in the end disappointing."[26] Husserl described it not as a substantial world, but rather in terms of an immense transcendental intersubjectivity, meaning that the world could only be conceived of as a collection of all of the subjective perceptions of individual consciousnesses. The end result was a world deprived of all independence of being. This necessitated a detailed critique and a thorough revision of the concept.

Husserl's approach to philosophy, which sought a "postulate of philosophy as an absolutely apodictic science,"[27] revealed that his conception of rationality, or reason, was determined not so much by the Greek understanding of reason to which he appealed—expressed in the differentiation of the concept of "intelligence," or *nous*[28]—but by a more modern, Cartesian vision of reason and knowledge. Patočka knew that reason did not lead to apodicticity, to certainty, and so he took over Husserl's goal by shifting the direction of its inquiry. He was to examine, in his career, not only the ontological work of Martin Heidegger, but also the Platonic theme of rationality as a component of caring for the development of the human soul. In this way, Patočka not only moved beyond Husserl, he also managed to remain faithful to the understanding of reason expressed by the Greeks over that characteristic of the moderns.

Nevertheless, Patočka's close contact with Husserl during the decade of the 1930s was critical in determining the direction of his philosophical career. Husserl's basic goal from *The Crisis of European Sciences*—a resuscitation of the concept of reason via a turn to history and a reconsideration of the origin of philosophy in ancient Greece—was taken on as a central aim by Patočka as well. Yet Patočka did not simply follow his teacher in an application of the principles he had laid down. He sought a more complete understanding of the content of reason than that offered by Husserl. This led him, in the end, to secure his own place in philosophy by moving away from Husserl and developing a phenomenological and ontological philosophy that took up many of the insights of Heidegger and applied them to the social being of man.

The Insight of Phenomenology

Prior to developing his ontology Patočka was a dedicated student—and critic—of phenomenology. His commentary on Husserl is not limited to his writings about the *Crisis*; he also wrote extensively on phenomenology and the phenomenological method, writings which in themselves justify Patočka's inclusion on a list of the century's significant philosophers.[29] Though a critic of many aspects of Husserlian phenomenology, Patočka nonetheless considered himself a phenomenologist.

He agreed with Husserl that the goal of phenomenology was to grasp phenomena without distortion, to attempt to see things as they are. This did not mean seeing and describing things as they are ideally, or "in themselves," but rather as they genuinely appear to us in our experience; only in this way could we avoid the mistake of perceiving things as we believe them to be, rather than as they are. As he wrote, "For Husserl the reflection on phenomena means delving into the way things present themselves to us in our ordinary experience."[30] This is not something obvious, as Patočka explains, paraphrasing Husserl: The difficulty "is that we frequently think we see and know what in reality we only think, that we do not know how to see what we see, that intermediate links insinuate themselves between the seen and our knowing and must be systematically removed."[31] This task of seeing things as they genuinely appear, undistortedly, is the broad goal of phenomenology; it is the goal of reflecting on the world and on human affairs as they truly are, rather than as we may perceive them abstractly, or as we may wish them to be.

In the academic year 1968–1969, Jan Patočka delivered a series of lectures at Charles University in Prague that belong among his most original contributions to the study of phenomenology. Entitled *Body, Community, Language, World*, this text (compiled from notes taken by his students and translated into English by Erazim Kohák) offers a clear and coherent picture of his revision of the approaches of Husserl and Heidegger. Patočka begins the lectures by making it clear that the philosophical course he is pursuing is phenomenological, rather than metaphysical. He argues that metaphysics, "which constructs philosophy as a special scientific system," is the very opposite of phenomenology. "Phenomenology examines the experiential content of such theses; in every abstract thought it seeks to uncover what is hidden in it, how we arrive at it, what seen and lived reality underlies it."[32] For philosophy to claim intellectual validity, it must resist the temptation of the scientific system and remain committed to human experience.

The phenomenology pursued by Patočka is not to be confused with a repetition of the technique of Husserl, however. "By phenomenology we shall not mean the teachings of Husserl," he writes at the start of *Body, Community, Language, World.* "What we have defined as phenomenology—learning to think and see precisely (how to read, how to articulate what we see)—is always present in philosophy."³³ Patočka's approach to philosophy is not primarily a method. It is rather a thematic attempt to clarify its experiential essence. Phenomenology as Patočka pursues it is a means to place distance between the art of human self-reflection and the metaphysical baggage that has accumulated around philosophy as practiced in Europe for more than two thousand years. This interpretation, which rejects the subjective element of Husserl's work and instead pursues problems related to the corporeality of the body and the "movements" of human beings within the world, is less an abstract theoretical venture than an application of theoretical insight to the concreteness of human experience. This, he was convinced, also was characteristic of the Socratic pursuit of truth. It is in this sense that ontological phenomenology, meaning primarily the insights of Husserl and Heidegger taken together, is inherently linked to the world of ancient philosophy.

> Phenomenology left the greater part of the whole modern tradition behind, but this ontological phenomenology goes to the very beginnings of our European tradition of thought, because it shows that ancient philosophy is already ontology which hinges on the problem of truth—but this was not taken sufficiently deeply by it.³⁴

Patočka sought to pursue phenomenology in a different way than either Husserl or Heidegger. He called it a process of doing phenomenology over again from its very roots.³⁵

All of this is not meant to imply that Patočka ignored Husserl's methodology—to the contrary. Patočka wrote extensively on Husserl and took his early work with the utmost seriousness. His numerous publications and scripta on this topic stand by themselves within the narrower field of phenomenological studies. A thorough examination of these texts, however, is beyond the scope of this study. Here I must be content with only a brief overview of his critique of Husserl, and that primarily within the scope of the broader theme: the degree to which Patočka's phenomenology is a form of political philosophy.

The Critique of Husserl and the Concept of the "World as a Whole"

The phenomenologist Erazim Kohák has characterized Jan Patočka's *Introduction to Husserl's Phenomenology* as a "major philosophical achievement."[36] This book, also derived from a lecture series delivered at Charles University at the end of the 1960s, is, as Kohák points out, more of an in-depth interpretation of Husserl than an introduction. In it, Patočka offers a detailed review and critique of the methods of Husserlian phenomenology; in his other lecture series of that time, *Body, Community, Language, World,* he presents an outline of his own revision of that phenomenology. Of the elements of phenomenology Patočka chooses to revise or reconceive, none are more central than the concepts of the "natural world" and the "world as a whole."[37]

Patočka's first philosophical work, presented in 1936 for habilitation as full University Professor and entitled "The Natural World as a Philosophical Problem," begins with the following sentence: "The problem of philosophy is the world as a whole."[38] This problem does not concern the physical world, the planet, but rather the whole that is our context, the constant backdrop of our lives and experience. The question of our understanding and relationship to this whole is key to the philosophical undertaking, for no human action or experience can take place absent the world. Following Husserl, Patočka was convinced that "[o]ur individual experience always presupposes a context preceding it."[39] This context, this prior whole, determines the meaningfulness of the particularities which are contained within it, for particulars become meaningful only in the context of the whole which defines them.[40] What Patočka calls the "world as a whole" is a concept crucial to phenomenological philosophy. His conception of this world, however, is distinctly different from Husserl's. To get at the heart of this difference, and to grasp Patočka's understanding of our perception of the world, I must first review certain elements of Husserl's understanding. Here Erazim Kohák's explanation in his "Philosophical Biography" is helpful.

For both Husserl and Patočka, human perception is more than the mere noting of particulars with which we come into daily contact. When we perceive an object, we may do so not merely as we see it, from one side or from a certain angle, but as we know it to be. We also perceive it categorically, as a complete whole and an invariant structure greater than what we see from the limited access of our particular perspective—this is what Husserl refers to as "eidetic intuition" and Patočka translates as "perception of the universal."[41] In effect, then, we are able to perceive more than is actually present before us. Patočka describes this experience when he notes that "far more is present to me as real than what is actually given: whatever stands in some relation to the self-given is also actual. Things beyond our senses are present to us."[42] For Patočka, significantly, the perception of things "beyond our senses" is not an abstraction. Such things are also experiential, they are actual. We are not limited, in our ability to perceive reality, to what is directly given.

Husserl's approach to our experience of objects as reality focuses on the act of experiencing in the human consciousness, the mode in which the object is given to us in consciousness. As we consider objects, we can never forget that we are experiencing them in a particular, perspectival manner. Husserl concludes from this that, in fact, no objects are truly independent of our experiencing of them in our consciousness. The very existence of objects, and of the world itself, is relative to the positing of them by the subjective consciousness. This, in simplified form, is the achievement of Husserl's early work: the grounding of objectivity in the subject.[43] Husserl is seeking to demonstrate with his phenomenology "that the objectivity of the object is thinkable only if we start out from the subjectivity of the subject."[44] It is here that Patočka centers his critique of Husserlian phenomenology.

For Husserl, not only are individual objects of perception grounded in the subject's relation to them, so also is the collective totality of those objects—the world. As Kohák explains, "the world of material objects [in Husserl] is no more than a product of acts of synthesis of perspectival views, and so always dubitable, contingent, not absolute."[45] For Patočka, however, this is entirely insufficient; not only the objects of the world but also the world as a whole are indubitably actual and irreducible to subjective consciousness. While he agrees with Husserl that the world should be understood not metaphysically but phenomenologically—as "a phenomenologically given universal rather than a constructed, abstract one"[46]—he is unable to accept Husserl's derivation of that universal from human subjectivity. Patočka recognizes the world as a whole as fundamentally autonomous, as an element of reality with which the human being must interact in a dialectical relationship. Whereas with Husserl the drama of perception proceeds within the human consciousness, for Patočka we must admit to a certain autonomy for the world as a whole that precedes the particularities of perception. The world itself can never be perceived as a particular, it exists via a nonperceptual givenness that is itself a condition for the perception of particulars. The recognition of the world as a whole is also a condition for a type of human action that bases itself, not on the particular needs of a given moment, but on the overall situation of human being within the cosmos. As he describes it:

> The nonperceptual, prevenient givenness of the whole is then the basis of special modes of human comportment not directed at particulars, at the resolution of particular situations or at one-sidedly oriented measures within the world, but of modes in which man comports himself with respect to the whole as such.[47]

These modes of comportment, as we shall see, are essential to the conduct of life in philosophical and political truthfulness—what Patočka calls "life in truth."

Patočka thus borrows from Husserl's original conceptualization of the world as a phenomenologically given universal, but rejects the reduction of that world to the subjective consciousness. Patočka's construction is less a matter of pure phenomenology in the Husserlian sense, and more relative to a broader, philosophical perspective on the situation of man in his concrete context, his culture, his community, his history. Yet Patočka remains committed to avoiding the trap of abstracting a world, he wishes to proceed along phenomenological lines. He also wishes, as we have seen, to proceed *asubjectively*, that is, to avoid Husserl's reliance on subjectivity as the ultimate "ground of certainty."[48] What, then, of the concept of the "world as a whole"? How is it delimited, and how does it rely on phenomenology to avoid a fall into abstract metaphysics?

In the early chapters of *Body, Community, Language, World*, Patočka offers a description of the world of humans that differentiates it further, beyond the simplicity of the world as a basic "context." In fact, the context description is more appropriate for animals than for humans. Animals live in immediate relation to their context, to what interests and affects them immediately. Humans, by contrast, constantly place themselves into situations beyond the immediately given—they project into the past, the future, into imagination, into possibility. They do this, however, without escaping from their corporeal situation in the present. "For us humans, what is immediately present in each moment is also a focus of other possibilities, of partial worlds, and so on. What is characteristic of us is our variety of possibilities, a freedom from the present, from the immediately given."[49] Human orientation is not limited to its immediate context, as it is for animals. Our living, Patočka writes, with its ability to transcend the immediate, is a living in a world, not simply in a context. In our experience, the human world is not a subjective entity; it is autonomous and concrete. Yet this does not imply that it is limited to our given physical surroundings. The world is both a concrete reality and the setting for our projection into possibility beyond the limitations of the given.

Although the whole is conceived as a unity it is necessary that there exist variety within it, a variety of different landscapes within which the human being can project himself and pursue possibilities. Patočka designates these landscapes using the phenomenological concept, or metaphor, of "horizons."[50] They represent a way in which the unity of the whole is preserved while permitting the exploration of particular possibilities, of variety, within it. The horizon, as Patočka defines it, "is something that circumscribes all the particulars of a given landscape, its visual part, but transcends it."[51] It is that which we cannot see yet know to be present at the edges of that which we can see—the ultimate context of our perceptual landscape. It is the presence of that which is not directly present before us, but which is only anticipated, suggested by experience.[52]

Human beings do not live only among things immediately present. They also live in horizons, "amid possibilities as if they were realities." Life in horizons is not directed inwardly, but outwardly. Man does not live directed toward himself; instead, he aims toward horizons, toward possibility and, as Patočka wants to emphasize, toward the world. To live in this way is to "broaden actuality immensely," and it is "typically human."[53] Horizons, which demarcate the particular landscapes of the world, do not imply an escape into a metaphysically transcendent reality. To the contrary, they point to our living, not in ourselves, but among things—they point toward our living in the world. "The projection into the world never ceases, we never live in ourselves, we always live among things, there where our work is, living in horizons outside ourselves, not within."[54]

With his explication of human consciousness as horizonal, of humans as beings that project outward from themselves into the world and its possibilities, Patočka begins to sketch out his revision of phenomenology. Already the direction of this revision is clear. It is toward the concrete and experiential elements of human life and action *in concreto*, in the world. The thrust of Patočka's critique is to suggest that philosophy, if it hopes to remain consistent with experience, cannot avoid the fundamental situatedness of humans within a concrete world and, as we shall see, a concrete community. It is what Erazim Kohák has demarcated as potentially Patočka's "great contribution to phenomenology": the recognition of what Patočka termed the "hardness of reality."[55] The movement indicated here is from philosophy as a theoretical venture toward philosophy in the concrete context of human life in the world, of human political life.

There remains to consider the concept of the world as Patočka presents it. In what way is it to be understood, if neither as an objective entity nor an abstract metaphysical construction? Patočka's explanation is again phenomenological; the world can be described only as it manifests itself to us. This is to say that it cannot be described as a "thing." It appears, rather, as a framework, anticipated as a whole, and "in this anticipation it is not given as a reality, it does not appear, it is not itself a phenomenon: it is what phenomenalizes."[56] In this sense it can be understood neither as a reality relative to my subjectivity, nor as objective reality; it is rather in the form of an interval, something "in-between" the two that "cannot be understood in terms of things themselves."[57]

In the final analysis, the whole will resist concrete definition because it does not manifest itself as a thing whose limits or boundaries can be firmly grasped. The whole as Patočka wishes to express it is the reality of our being, and as such is only available to us in glimpses, in particulars. "Reality is never revealed to us as a whole," Patočka writes. "In understanding the whole we encounter particulars but the understanding of the whole, of being, conceals itself in understanding particulars."[58] Patočka's conception of being, here, is inherently connected to human striving within the world and influenced, as we shall see, by Heidegger. Thus the limitations of the Husserlian framework are, in the end, dissatisfying. Husserl's approach by means of the phenomenological reduction is overly speculative, rather than reflective.[59] For Patočka, human striving within the world is grounded in the "vital act" of reflection; human existence is "an existence on the way to itself, seeking itself, understanding itself, that is, understanding its possibilities."[60]

Understood in this way, the Husserlian reduction is less relevant, while the concept of the whole becomes even more important. The whole is the context of this human striving; it is, in a sense, its ground. Though it cannot be wholly grasped analytically, it clearly exists experientially, as the foundational constant supporting the myriad possibilities and directions of human lives. Patočka goes so far as to say that it provides us with an "objectival meaning," though, he would wish to be clear, not in the meta-physical sense of a supreme being or Idea:

> Even though we might not be able to analyze the structure of this antecedent whole, set it clearly before us, it is present in the func-tioning references, in the phases of dealing with things. It leads us from moment to moment, it allows us to deal with the same, to have before us *an objectival meaning constant in diverse opera-tions* (emphasis mine).[61]

Here the whole is understood in terms of its ontological significance: it is the necessary backdrop for our individual reality. The diverse operations that individuate us, and through which we come to understand reality, are united in their common participation in the whole. Humans belong to this whole, but in a special mode, that of human beings, who are uniquely capa-ble of comprehending its presence as the backdrop of their existence and of relating to it in their actions and understanding of particulars. This is in fact definitive of our being as humans:

> It means that humans by their living single themselves out of the whole in an explicit relation to it and that their most intrinsically human possibility—that of existing in a human way—lies in their understanding this specific trait, that humans are capable of encountering being as things are not.[62]

In this relation to the whole, this "openness" to being, lies our humanity and the font of our ability to pursue possibility.

Patočka has replicated, to some degree, an ancient conception of humanity as existing within a cosmoslike[63] whole comprehensible in its order though not graspable in its entirety. We exist within it as individual beings, united in our singular ability to grasp the uniqueness of our situation, and defined as human by our pursuit of such understanding, by our vital reflection. Though the conception of the whole is by no means new, Patočka pursues an approach to it that can justifiably claim to be. It is an approach grounded in phenomenological experience, pursued not along the lines of Husserlian subjectivism, but rather with an emphasis on our concrete surrounding—the world, both in its particularities and as a whole. The world as a whole is not an objective entity. It does, however, exist as an experiential constant in human life. In this sense it can be said to make up part of the ground of human existence. It is not a metaphysical foundation for human life, however, for it is neither posited as objective nor as an ethical guidepost for our human decision-making. Patočka wishes, above all, to avoid constructing a foundation in metaphysics. The question of ethics and decision making is a relevant one, though, and demands investigation. The concluding chapters of this study, therefore, explore ethics and politics and their relation to the theme of the "world as a whole" as a nonmetaphysical ground for a life of *praxis*.

The *"Natural"* World

Whereas most phenomenologists seem to focus on Husserl's earlier, explicitly phenomenological work, I have already noted that it was the concerns of the later Husserl that most strongly influenced Patočka, namely, the themes of the *Crisis* texts. In these writings, Husserl aimed toward a resuscitation of European rationalism by turning back to the very beginnings of that rationalism: to the pretheoretical "natural attitude" of what he called the *Lebenswelt*, or life-world, and to the development of the "theoretical attitude" in philosophical thought. Understanding the life-world was crucial to the task of recovery from the "crisis" wrought by the progressive and unreflective domination of the methods of natural science over human life. Patočka's interest in a life-world, or what he called the "natural" world, stemmed from these sources in Husserl.[64] As Patočka put it in his 1967 article, "The 'Natural' World and Phenomenology," the philosophical concern with the "natural" world "is the effort to render problematic once more the unquestioned way in which we are governed by the metaphysics of science and technology (or, better, of technoscience). The purpose of that problematization of the obvious is to liberate our vision."[65]

For Husserl, the life-world was something of an abstract conceptualization. It was the "pregiven world," the world in which objects were "straightforwardly intuited"; it was the world as it would have been prior to the arrival of science.[66] Patočka once again appreciated Husserl's insight, but felt that the concept as it was worked out was untenable. He spent a considerable amount of time on the idea of the "natural" world, both in his early work (e.g., in his habilitation thesis) and again in the last decade of his life. Patočka lays out the details of his revision of the "natural" world in two articles from his later period, "Edmund Husserl's Philosophy of the Crisis of the Sciences and His Conception of a Phenomenology of the 'Life-World,'" his Warsaw Lecture from 1971, and "The 'Natural' World and Phenomenology" from 1967.

The thrust of Patočka's critique of the life-world follows the pattern of his other critique. Husserl's conception is overly theoretical, divorced from the tactile realities of human existence in the world. Husserl conceives of his life-world in terms of pure intuition of objects while Patočka sees it as the setting for human life in its concreteness, in its activity.[67] In his Warsaw Lecture, Patočka refers to Husserl's concept as a form of "phenomenological metaphysics" that is "in the end disappointing." It is, he continues, conceived as "a product of the common achievements (*Leistungen*) of subjectivities for whom this world is nothing but a common link devoid of any genuine substantiality."[68] A conceptualization of this kind might, he admits, be appropriate as a means of analyzing certain aspects of scientific inquiry. But what of actual human practice, of human politics and life in community, for example? Can Husserlian subjectivity "show us a positive way for reason to follow so that it could found not only a new science or a new foundation for science, but a genuine human *praxis?*"[69] To this end, Patočka is convinced, is required a more human conception of the "natural" world, a conception grounded in the world in which we live.

The problem with Husserl's life-world is that it is abstractly posited as a quasi-metaphysical entity, a site independent of the "historical contingencies" of human development. Patočka, however, is clear to recognize that human beings are at all times historical beings, even in those cases where they choose to act ahistorically. The thematic exploration of the "natural" world in Patočka's work is not to be understood as a search for a hypothetical "state of nature," but rather for the mode of self-understanding that governs when we live simply and without reflection. It is not a search for humanity prior to or abstracted from civilization, but simply prior to the development of self-reflective theory, of self-interpretation as the basis for community. The "natural" world reflects the most elemental movement of human existence; it is a cornerstone of our self-understanding.

For Patočka, this must be a world of an active order, a world in which one could say that humans *live*. This is the crux of his disagreement with Husserl. As he explains it in his Warsaw Lecture, Husserl's life-world focuses on the "perception" or "observation" of objects by intuition;[70] the fundamental concept is that of perception. For Patočka, on the other hand, the world as an active order is centered more around an "I can" than an "I perceive." It is based on this understanding that the "natural" world can justifiably be called a world of good (and of evil.) Experientially, the world comes to us in these terms, not in terms of intuition of objects.[71]

> From this viewpoint, the "natural" world can be understood entirely naturally: it is a world where we can live, live in a community in which we can find a place and be accepted, enjoying the protection which enables us to take on the concrete tasks of defense and of struggle against what threatens us in the context of humans and of things alike. It is the world of embodied living beings who work and struggle, who approach each other and draw back, living in mutual respect; who communicate with the world of others by word and understanding; who relate to this existence in its totality and so also to the world as such.[72]

With this analysis, Patočka transforms the Husserlian "natural" world from an abstraction into a concrete conceptualization of a basic, prereflective mode of human existence that can be applied to human history. Patočka's view of the "natural" world becomes, as we shall see, a key component of his phenomenology of three human "movements" as well as his philosophy of history.

THE INFLUENCE OF HEIDEGGER

The profound influence of the work of Martin Heidegger on Patočka's philosophy is undeniable. Though his association with Heidegger was negligible—he attended a few of his lectures in Freiburg in 1933, but never studied directly under him—Patočka felt that the German philosopher's ontological perspective was one of the great accomplishments of the twentieth-century. The controversy surrounding Heidegger's politics has doubtlessly contributed to the eagerness with which many interpreters of twentieth century philosophy use the labels "Heideggerean" or "anti-Heideggerean" to describe contemporary perspectives. This tendency is certainly present in interpretive work on Patočka, whose texts are replete with Heideggerean concepts. Analysts think it important to demonstrate that Patočka is or is not a Heideggerean thinker.[73] I disagree with this approach. Patočka is a student of both Husserl and Heidegger who draws on many of their conceptualizations; yet he is also a critic in both cases, making it inaccurate to call him simply a Husserlian or a Heideggerean. I start from the assumption that he is neither "type" of thinker, but an independent mind whose variations on the themes of German phenomenological and ontological philosophy take it in an innovative direction.

As with Husserl, Patočka's critique of Heidegger leads toward a self-understanding of human existence as political existence, as solidly grounded in the concreteness of life in the world and in community. It is, Patočka makes clear, a critique arising from the contention that Heidegger's philosophy is not fully appropriate to an understanding of man in his concrete, corporeal existence—an existence that relates not only to his self-understanding, but also to the realities of his body, his community, his language, and his world. It is only this broader understanding, which emphasizes rather than sunders its ties to classical Greek philosophy, that will enable the development of a conception of man relative to his pursuit of life in a political community, a polis.

The previous paragraph notwithstanding, it is clear that Patočka felt that the insights of Heidegger's ontological philosophy were necessary, although perhaps not entirely sufficient, to the development of a philosophical understanding of the existence of "concrete humans in their corporeal world."[74] In many crucial respects, they proved for him far more appropriate than Husserl's insights. Not the least of those respects was the emphasis Heidegger placed on the importance of history, and the role of freedom and responsibility therein. Patočka also considered history to be essential to the proper pursuit of phenomenological analysis. Husserlian methodology was insufficient, in this regard, as it relied on the concept of an ahistorical, disinterested spectator (as the locus of perception).[75] Heidegger, however, rejected Husserl's ahistorical subjectivity and concerned himself instead with the relationship of man to his being, an inherently historical relationship that manifests itself in human freedom and responsibility. As Patočka writes in his *Heretical Essays on the Philosophy of History*: "Heidegger is a philosopher of the primacy of freedom and in his view history is not a drama which unfolds before our eyes but a responsible realization of the relation which humans are. History is not a perception but a responsibility."[76] Here, but not only here, the historico-ontological work of Heidegger provided a way for Patočka to get closer to his goal of understanding human existence not in the abstract, but in the concrete.

Primarily, however, it was the relationship of man to his own being, as Heidegger pursued and elucidated it, that most captured and held Patočka's attention. Patočka's movement in the direction of Heideggerean ontology cannot easily be traced chronologically. Though his use of language inspired by Heidegger is more apparent at certain times than at others, his overall concern is to integrate it with themes drawn from Husserl. Patočka pursues such an independent direction, and he consciously attempts, not a synthesis of Husserl and Heidegger, a straightforward combination of their work, but an interpretative variation that stands apart from the work of either German philosopher. Thus there is no trepidation in admixing Heideggerean concepts into a Husserlian phenomenological framework. Judged strictly from the perspective of either elder philosopher, this attempt may seem at times untenable. But to appraise in this way is to fail to appreciate the Czech philosopher's attempt at a unique perspective—one informed by a radically different set of cultural and political circumstances than in the case of Husserl or Heidegger.

The Ontological Insight

It is in the *Body, Community, Language, World* lectures that Jan Patočka makes his most concerted effort to elaborate an original interpretation of phenomenological philosophy. It is an interpretation specifically directed toward application to the human, or social, sciences. To this end, the ontological insight of Heidegger, the sense that man is "interested" in his own being and accomplishes that being rather than simply lives it, is an essential component. This insight is the heart of a perspective on human existence as an activity rather than an entity or a thing. For Heidegger, the basic question of philosophy is the ontological question, the question of our being. Humanity is uniquely constituted in that it alone takes an interest in its own being, and it is this phenomenon that prompts the revival of the ontological question originally asked by the pre-Socratic philosophers. This nonindifference to our own being, as Patočka writes in his *Heretical Essays*, is both the starting point and the condition for understanding the phenomenon of being; it is the condition for "the right understanding of the significance of phenomenology in general."[77]

A proper phenomenological approach to human existence, then, requires an appreciation for its interestedness, for its acting, not objectively, but interestedly. "Such a being [as man], concerned with its own being, cannot in principle be grasped in its distinctiveness by observation. A mere observing look can never capture this active nature of our being for ourselves, its interestedness, its interest in itself."[78] Implicit here is a prioritization of this aspect of the Heideggerean approach over the Husserlian approach, and Patočka borrows explicitly from *Being and Time* to do so.[79] He reiterates the basic Heideggerean standpoint when he asks whether "human experience by its very nature [is] something essentially different from what can be given in object experience? That is a question which Husserl never raised."[80] We can come to understand our own being, not through object experience, but only through an examination of how we live that being, how we create it. "[L]iving means accomplishing our being. So it is not the case that we first are and then do something; our being takes place entirely in that doing."[81] Our mode of access to being is thus relative to the way in which we live, not to the way in which we understand ourselves theoretically.

Patočka is not satisfied with the theoretical posture of a "disinterested spectator," and Heidegger is helpful in this regard. The theoretical nature of Husserl's work and his background in mathematics and Cartesianism make his methodology suitable to a philosophical foundation for the hard sciences. Patočka, however, is interested in a philosophical foundation for the social sciences, including politics, and to this end the ontological themes of Heidegger are invaluable. An approach to the social sciences cannot rest on the empirical, on the simply observable:

> Husserl's phenomenology would do as a philosophical foundation for the natural sciences. . . . Social sciences, though, are sciences because they uncover something about personal and social reality that we cannot learn by simple introspection. Social sciences normally appeal to mere empirical data. However, they need also a philosophical foundation in order to locate their fundamental problem.[82]

The study of humanity, the subject of the social sciences, is not marked by the clarity which the empiricist assumes. Human being, human existence in the world, is not a clear and transparent phenomenon, and this represents a problem for those who would study it.

> The problem itself arises in the human disciplines as we penetrate to a certain aspect of ourself which is clear to us in one sense and not in another. For that reason, for all social sciences, the point at which they become genuine sciences is penetration through self-illusions, self-deceptions, our idols of ourselves. Providing a philosophical foundation for actual human scientific disciplines demands that we find access to this situation, not an empirical but a foundational, justifying one.[83]

It is by a phenomenological philosophy, founded not on Cartesian principles but on ontology and geared toward an understanding of human movement in the world, that Patočka hopes to penetrate through the delusions that confound our scientific attempts to grasp social and political reality. One of the greatest of those delusions is the belief that man is an objective creature whose motivating impulses are clearly evident in his outward bearing. It was Heidegger rather than Husserl who resisted this presumption, arguing that there is an element of "concealment" that must be considered. By taking up this phenomenon thematically, Heidegger's work had an advantage over Husserl's and so became a model for Patočka's pursuit. "In virtue of that," Patočka wrote, Heidegger's phenomenology "can become the philosophical foundation of human science."[84]

The subject of Patočka's debt to and interpretation of Heidegger is a vast one. Here I will limit myself to a few, basic points. Patočka is convinced that human existence requires consideration of man's interaction with his world, the things in it, and the multitude of possibilities created by that interaction. This interaction is definitive of not merely man's life, but of his very being. The being of humans, which Heidegger denotes as *Dasein*, is distinguished from other beings not only because it takes a thematic interest it itself, in its own being, but also because it is self-constitutive via its pursuit of the possibilities open to it. Patočka seeks to explore the possibilities of being human in a way that is not speculative or abstract. "When Heidegger says that existence is something that in its very being relates to its being," he writes, "it sounds metaphysical and speculative. We shall show, however, that it is something that can be exhibited descriptively."[85] Patočka takes on this descriptive task in his interpretation of Heidegger's ontology.

In fact, Patočka proceeds in this way in his interpretation of both Husserl and Heidegger, taking philosophical constructs and judging their validity against the experience of human beings living in a historical world. In this sense Patočka explicates his philosophy in a different way than did either of the two German philosophers—the specter of the concreteness of our lives, of the world and its objects, of human relations and politics, is always present.

Finitude and Other Heideggerean Themes

Patočka appears to follow Heidegger directly in his particular focus on the finitude of human life. The Heideggerean notion of finitude, of "being-toward-death,"[86] is a central theme in Patočka's writings. As he uses this theme, however, it takes on a different significance; the resulting concept is applicable, not only to the self-understanding of the existential individual, but also to the community, to actual political and historical life.

Patočka was strongly influenced by what he called Heidegger's "phenomenology of finitude." In contrast to Husserl, in whom even the finitude of our relation to the world can be suspended, the Heideggerean view claims that finitude "penetrate[s] the very content of our being so deeply that it constitutes the fundamental content of our being in all its moments and expressions."[87] It is not simply that humans are finite, for all living beings share that trait; it is rather in our awareness of and relation to our own death that humans exhibit a certain uniqueness. We have noted that Patočka has set for himself the task of exhibiting phenomenological and ontological concepts descriptively and experientially. This requires that he discuss them in terms of their effect on human life. He does this with the concept of finitude in his *Body, Community, Language, World* lectures:

Finitude is not easily described though we can say what must belong to it. Human beings are always threatened; in all their acts they deal with their limitations. Humans are not delimited like stones or like animals who are not aware of their own perishing, humans know their limitations, are constantly relating to their own finitude as to their own being, caring for and looking after their needs.[88]

Our awareness of our finitude, and our acceptance of it, directly colors our pursuit of the activities and possibilities of life. Heidegger even grounded the definitive activity of reflection in the finitude of being human.[89]

The crucial element in Patočka's application of this concept to social being is his contention that the Heideggerean stress on finitude shares something with the Platonic *meletē thanatou*, the "learning to die" of the *Phaedo*. Socrates *and* Heidegger tell us that, in order to care for life, to live authentically, one must care for death and not attempt to evade it. In Heidegger, Patočka finds particularly relevant the discussion of the attitude of "everydayness" that characterizes "they" who effectively deny the certainty of death. Denying death, of course, is tantamount to fleeing from it; the Platonic philosopher, in contrast, "overcame death fundamentally by not fleeing from it but by facing up to it. This philosophy was *meletē thanatou*, care for death; care for the soul is inseparable from care for death that becomes the true care for life."[90] The Platonic conception of "care for the soul" as the base component of the truthful life is thereby brought into direct relation to the insight of Heidegger. Patočka places the Socratic "care for the soul" on the same page with Heidegger's "being-toward-death." In doing so, he brings Heidegger into contact with the Platonic focus on the construction of community.

This merging of two conceptions of finitude does not exhaust Patočka's use of the theme, nor his application of it beyond the limits of the Heideggerean analysis. In the *Heretical Essays*, Patočka makes the theme central to his analysis of the politics of war prevalent in the twentieth century. Here, in the final essay entitled "Wars of the Twentieth Century and the Twentieth Century as War," the near-continual warfare of the first half of this century is analyzed in terms of finitude. Resistance to human finitude, in the form of the promise that victory in war will protect us from death, becomes a means to justify ideological warfare. Life becomes the highest value, so much so that humans are objectified and their deaths rendered anonymous in its pursuit. The target here is political ideology, the systematization of life in the name of an idea, as, for example, the idea that mere life is more significant than free life. The refusal to face death, to care for it, to understand its function as a pole of life that determines our existence, all of this Patočka finds immediately present in the political conflagrations of the twentieth century. A solution to these crises, as with the crisis of modern science noted by Husserl, lies in the ability to see human life as a whole, and that requires a recognition of death as the ultimate possibility of that life. As he explains it, "We relate to death as the ultimate possibility, the possibility of a radical impossibility of being. That impossibility casts a shadow over our whole life yet at the same time *makes it possible, enables it to be a whole.*" Relating to death "does not mean thinking about death. It means, rather, rejecting that way of life which would live at any price and takes *mere life* as its measure."[91] Patočka's explication of finitude has laid a Platonic stress on a Heideggerean theme and applied it directly to human social being, exhibiting its effect descriptively, in terms of its concrete effect on human life.

The theme of finitude has been examined in some detail because it is fundamental to Patočka's work, and because it shows how the Czech philosopher applies the work of Heidegger. The use of Heideggerean themes, however, is determined by the fact that Patočka is not, in the end, a Heideggerean. This is exemplified in that, while the Czech strongly felt the intimate connection between philosophy and politics, Heidegger, at least after his disastrous foray into politics in the 1930s, completely abandoned it. Before examining the basis of Patočka's critique in more detail, let me first note a few of the other Patočkan themes that draw from Heidegger.

Patočka makes use of another theme central to *Being and Time* when he speaks of "care." For Heidegger, the notion of "care" (*Sorge*) is definitive of the being of *Dasein* and implies a concern and solicitude in terms of our relations to beings in the world.[92] Patočka embraces the Heideggerean analysis, but attempts to add to it the sense of care present in the Socratic dialogues—that of caring for the soul by nurturing it and attuning it toward the eternal. Implied in the Socratic version is the necessity of choice—the individual choice of whether to pursue care for the soul or whether to deny it. Yet Patočka is not consciously abandoning the Heideggerean for the Socratic here, he feels that the two concepts are related. Heidegger's use of care, as Jacques Derrida has noted, invokes something of the concern and solicitude signified by the Platonic *meletē thanatou.*[93]

In appealing to the Socratic sense of care, Patočka is nevertheless trying to remain faithful to another Heideggerean theme, the critique of metaphysics. Socrates, as he argues in the essay "Negative Platonism," acts in such a way as to reject metaphysical knowledge, even as he speaks in metaphysical symbols. Patočka is with Heidegger in excluding metaphysics, but he does not agree to exclude the wisdom of Socrates in the process.

Other Heideggerean themes figuring in Patočka's philosophy include the question of the essence of technology—directly related to the dominance of metaphysics over Western civilization—and the Heraclitian notion of conflict, or *polemos*, as not only a unifying factor in human existence, but one with a certain ontological priority. With each of these themes, Patočka draws directly on Heidegger. Yet in each case, the emphasis and application is distinctly different, pointing to a political philosophy that is primarily concerned with being human, not in existential abstraction, but in the concrete context of life with other beings, life in community.

The Critique of Heidegger

To complete this overview of the importance of Heidegger to the thought of Jan Patočka, I have to clarify what so far has only been implied—the critique of Heidegger in Patočka's work. Although Patočka makes significant use of concepts pioneered by Heidegger, he does so with a view toward a different picture of human existence. He questions openly whether the "fundamental ontology" of Heidegger is, in itself, appropriate to that which Patočka seeks: an understanding of man in his relation to community and to history. He asks, for instance in "Cartesianism and Phenomenology," whether the Heideggerean approach to human existence via an exploration of *Dasein*, is "also adequate to serving as an ontological projection of a science or sciences of man?" He continues:

> Certainly a fundamental ontology makes possible an understanding of human life both in its fall into nonhumanity and in its moral outreach; but is what it offers a sufficient basis for a philosophy of man in community, in language and custom, in his essential generativeness, his tradition, and his historicity?[94]

Patočka concludes that, in and of itself, it is not. Though Heidegger took the philosophical study of humanity in directions previously unexplored by modern thinkers, there is nonetheless a sense of reductiveness in his work. He is so deeply immersed in ontology that the experience of humans in the world is often eclipsed. This perception is summarized succinctly in a short essay entitled simply "Heidegger," in which the respective faults of both Heidegger and Husserl are compared.

> Perhaps it's possible to say that Heidegger's philosophy suffers from the opposite sickness than the philosophy of Husserl. The latter lacked the understanding of the ontological sphere, it was however able to analyze the mass of ontic phenomena, which revived great interest in psychology, sociology, etc. of the post-war period. Heidegger's philosophy distinguishes anew the ontological sphere, however it doesn't find its way back to anthropology.[95]

For Patočka, an authentic philosophy of mankind must examine "all of that to which human life has access," all aspects of life given to humans in the form of experience.[96]

Thus broadly characterized, I can briefly examine several specific points of contention with the Heideggerean focus, discussed in *Body, Community, Language, World*. Here, Patočka stresses the need for phenomenology to take account of our corporeity, meaning not only the simple fact of our existing in a body, but also the connection it implies between humans and objects within and of the world. This marks a point of contention with the Heidegger of *Being and Time*, for whom everything is centered in our relation to ourselves. "Existential philosophy, for instance the early Heidegger," Patočka writes, "defines existence in terms of self-relatedness."[97] It is an account that stresses our relation to our own being, rather than our relation to the things around us. Yet the things around us are inherently relative to our being. The simple fact that we exist in a corporeal body means that we relate to things, and that relation is not insignificant. It is, rather, analogous to our self-relation. Patočka explains as follows:

> What is characteristic of Heidegger's analysis of being in the world is how little space is devoted to the concrete phenomena involved, for instance to the phenomenon of corporeity. Heidegger's entire analysis takes place in the dimension of the moral struggle of humans for their own autonomy. Only by the way does Heidegger recognize that the struggling being is a corporeal one, without explicating it. Yet precisely in the course of that explication does it become apparent that our relation to things is fully analogous to our self-relation, that it is a continuation of our life in the body. It is not something sharply different from the way we live in our body, relating to ourselves.[98]

Our relation to ourselves, our self-understanding as autonomous entities, is therefore not the sole factor constitutive of our being. Because of our corporeity and the nature of our lives as played out in communities, we relate to other beings, both objects and persons, and we relate to the world that is their context. These relations are part of our being, they enable our successful self-relation. In order to actualize that self-relation, Patočka writes, our personal being "must go round about through another being. We relate to ourselves by relating to the other, to more and more things and ultimately to the universe as such, so locating ourselves in the world."[99]

This relating to the world and its contents is characteristic of all living beings, even those not imbued with self-understanding. It is characteristic not only of adult humans, but of children and of animals as well—all relate to the world in a similarly harmonious way; this is a fact of their living. In

Heidegger, however, the focus is exclusively laid on the mode of self-understanding, as if it were exhaustive of our existence. Here, Patočka argues, "Heidegger is leaving something out, setting it aside. . . the elementary protofact of *harmony with the world* is the same for humans, children, animals. That can only mean that in human living not everything is given solely by understanding, as Heidegger would have it."[100] In the adult human the mode of understanding may be dominant, but this does not mean that the modes of humanity that are prior to understanding simply cease to be of importance. In fact, human activity may partake of different levels of being, including the animal's and the child's prelinguistic mode, relating simply and directly to the world. "[O]ur human existence in a (working, pragmatic) world," Patočka writes, "presupposes the existence of the childish and of the animal-like within us."[101] Thus the mode of understanding pursued by Heidegger does not exhaust human reality. The direct relation to the world of the child and the animal belongs to what Patočka calls the first movement of being human, and is contrasted with modes of human movement through work and philosophy.

I have already noted that what is characteristic of humans is the variety of possibilities present to them. The location of the self in the world, the world of objects and the world of human beings, is largely determinative of the extent of these possibilities. We become aware of our possibilities not as we delve deeper into ourselves, but as we become involved in other things, as we interact with other beings. Our becoming involved in the world "is at the same time the movement in which we become embodied in something other than ourselves, become involved, become objective. This becoming involved in what originally we are not but what we become reveals our possibilities to us."[102]

For Patočka, the realm of our involvement with the world in this particular sense, that is, in the sense of involvement with other beings and with the situations presented by this interaction, is the political realm. Our *politics*—our understanding and organization of our relations with and among the community, and our relations to the objects of the community such as laws—can never be a matter of indifference to the philosopher. Our being is, as Patočka notes, a "shared being," and it is on this point that Heidegger's analysis is insufficient: "For Heidegger the dimension of shared being (that the thrust toward the world always involves being with others) plays a minor role; it is mentioned but not adequately analyzed and made concrete."[103]

The final point of criticism addresses the way in which Heidegger portrays our relation to the world. For Patočka, it is a fundamentally positive relation. It is for us to understand, not to escape. And this, Patočka notes, is distinctly different from the Heideggerean conception of our relation to the world as a "fall."

Heidegger understands the relation of existence as a *fall* into the world. Existence must fight its way out of the world, must be liberated from it by carrying out a certain 'purification.' The fall consists of the important phenomenon that we fall into things, devote ourselves to them, and thereby objectify ourselves. . . . Liberation from the fall into the world is a liberation from this objectification, a return to existing in the strong sense, as distinct from mere being.[104]

The possibility of human objectification is real for Patočka as well, but he does not consider it to be an inevitable result of our "fall into things." Our existence in the world, in human community, can be the source of our self-understanding, not only of our self-alienation. "Herein our conception is fundamentally different" from Heidegger's, Patočka continues, "The relation of humans to the world is not negative in that way but rather positive, it is not a self-loss but the condition of the possibility of self-discovery."[105] The thrust into the world is for humans the opening up of possibility, of the possibility for positive development, but also for negative alienation and distortion. Thus the proper understanding of human action in the world, via the human or social sciences, is directly relevant to our philosophical understanding of our existence.

A PHENOMENOLOGY OF MOVEMENT

Beyond his pursuit of an "asubjective" phenomenology focused on corporeity, Patočka makes his most original contribution to phenomenological philosophy by developing an understanding of human existence in terms of movement. Though an approach to philosophy via movement is nothing new, two things contribute to the uniqueness of Patočka's attempt. First, it is understood "independently of the dichotomy between subject and object,"[106] and second, it represents an attempt to combine the Aristotelian concept of *dynamis* with the modern analysis of existence that understands life "as possibilities in a process of realization."[107] While the first factor refers to the insufficiency of modern attempts at interpreting human movement in objective terms as simple locomotion (the foundation of technology), or in subjective terms via the psychological approach of Bergson, it is the second that is closer to the core of Patočka's philosophy.

It is the focus on the corporeity of our existence that leads Patočka to movement, for our awareness of ourselves as bodily is an awareness of our mobility. Our experience is that of corporeal beings, and thus of beings in motion. We live in the world by engaging with it, by involving ourselves and by realizing our possibilities through our actions. "We realize possibilities only by moving, by being physical. Every realization takes place ulti-mately through movement."[108] This understanding of human movement is not of something that we carry out, that we choose to do when it suits us. It is rather that we are movement, it defines us in the world. Like Aristotelian *energeia*, this movement "is a realization of remaining possibilities."[109]

Patočka takes the Aristotelian conception of life as movement and the realization of potential as his starting point and inspiration, but he does not accept it unqualifiedly. It is Aristotle's objectification of movement, his "making it into something that requires an objective bearer to make its dynamic aspect possible," that is problematic. Patočka discards the notion of an "unmoved object," presupposed in Aristotle's account as the founda-tion for human movement and unity, as metaphysical.[110] Instead, the hope is to understand existence nonmetaphysically. In this way Patočka is led again to Heidegger, and to the similarity between Aristotle's *dynamis* as the realization of potentialities, and Heidegger's view of life in terms of the realization of possibilities. "Let us try to compare this Aristotelian concep-tion of movement with the modern conception of existence. Let us try to understand existence as a movement, from the standpoint of movement."[111] The key, as we have noted, is our "lived corporeity," the notion that human life is a bodily existence as well as a noetic one. Life is a process that is inte-grated into the world itself; it is not only in the world, it is *of* the world. Heidegger's understanding of existence, therefore, does not exhaust the possibilities of existence. "To understand existence as movement means to grasp humans as beings in and of the world. They are beings that not only are in the world, as Heidegger tells us (in the sense of understanding the world), but rather are themselves a part of the world process."[112]

In addition to being as active and in motion, Patočka adopts a hierar-chy of being from Aristotle. This is the notion that being, understood and expressed in terms of its activities and its motion, has a hierarchical struc-ture, with activities such as comprehension, understanding and knowledge at the highest level. This is not to say that these represent the highest human values as such, but that their pursuit by humans is the highest form of human activity, the most fully human activity. The insight is crucial to the diagram of human existence that Patočka presents—one composed of three movements or "vital lines" of human life. These movements are arranged hierarchically, but not as a ladder of values. Rather, all are move-ments in which humans participate naturally. The primary possibility of human life, though, the possibility to achieve understanding and truth, is to participate most fully in the highest level, the authentically human move-ment of existence.

Though Patočka sets off from Aristotelian philosophy, relying on a concept of movement, the tripartite framework of existence he now presents rests on a Heideggerean foundation. The structure that Heidegger presents in his analysis of existence, as Patočka understands it, is the structure of care: "a *project* in a given *situation* which brings us into *contact* with things." The threefold structure of care implies a situation that encompasses the past, a projection into the future, and a presence in our contact with things. In this way "the things with which we deal and which we modify are revealed." This basic structure of three divisions serves as a model for Patočka's own interpretation of three movements. He does not understand the structure, however, as a "trinity of undifferentiated moments but rather as a trinity of *movements* in which our life unfolds."[113] He thus proposes three movements of human life that effectively represent an Aristotelian hierarchy of being—one structured, however, around activities drawn from the insights of Heideggerean philosophy. In the *Body, Community, Language, World* lectures the three movements are described as follows:

1. the movement of sinking roots, of anchoring—an instinctive-affective movement of our existence;
2. the movement of self-sustenance, of self-projection—the movement of our coming to terms with the reality we handle, a movement carried out in the region of human work;
3. the movement of existence in the narrower sense of the word, which typically seeks to bestow a global closure and meaning on the regions and rhythms of the first and second movement.[114]

In the *Heretical Essays*, the three movements are described in a more metaphorical, less Husserlian manner: there they are referred to as the movements of acceptance, of defense (of life), and of truth.

Patočka argues that human existence partakes in each of these three movements, although to varying degrees. Our life "takes place in a polyphony of three voices."[115] While characteristics of one movement may appear in another, it is more broadly the case that the assumption of one movement suppresses the previous. The most fundamental movement, the one common to all humans, which acts as a center for human life, is the first movement. This is the movement in which humans simply accept their situation, are in harmony with the world, and anchor themselves in it by accepting it as given. It is, Patočka writes, the acceptance of the entire world as if it were a mother's lap—an instinctual, prereflective acceptance.[116] In this movement we sink roots into our surroundings, and we accept our dependence on another for safety and warmth. It is an instinctive-affective movement that provides us with our center in life.

The affective movement does not submerge us into the world as into a purposive, practical milieu but rather as into an all-embracing context of landscapes which address us in a certain wholeness and a priori make it possible for humans to have a world, not only individual entities . . . it bears within it a central vital core, a core of vital warmth which is not only an addition to the being of what surrounds us but a condition of the being of our life.[117]

This movement reflects an acceptance of the cosmos without reflection; we are at home in it but it is necessarily characterized by a lack of self-understanding.[118] It is also a situation in which humans do not exert control over their situation. They are, therefore, completely subject to contingency, to chance and fortune.

This mode is broken up by the second movement of life, however. This is the movement in which we come into contact, and come to terms, with the things present in our world. Here we extend our existing into things and work to preserve and reproduce our lives. With this movement we ensure our physical continuity: "This is the sphere in which we primarily live."[119] This is also the sphere of what Patočka calls self-surrender, for when we work we surrender ourselves to the burden of living, the necessity of prolonging life via our labor. Here, and particularly in the contrast between this movement and the third, the work of another contemporary philosopher comes directly into play. Hannah Arendt's work on the movement from the sphere of the household to the sphere of the polis in *The Human Condition* provided Patočka with a thesis on which he based much of the philosophy of history presented in his *Heretical Essays*.[120] As I have argued, Patočka's approach to phenomenology and to Husserl and Heidegger was influenced by his desire to broaden the scope of this philosophy to encompass humanity in its communal and political activities. Thus the phenomenological interpretation of existence as movement draws on a fundamental distinction first noted by Arendt between the movement of labor and the movement of freedom in the polis. This second movement of existence is the movement in which we defend our lives by accepting the burden of work. Here we bind ourselves to that life and to the Earth that provides us with the opportunity to work.[121] "This is a realm," Patočka writes, "of the average, of anonymity, of social roles in which people are not themselves, are not existence in the full sense (an existence which sees itself as existence), are reduced to their roles."[122]

In the first two movements, humans do not exist in the fullness of their potential because they are bound to the Earth. The third movement, in contrast, "is an attempt to break through our earthliness."[123] It is the human movement through which we achieve some distance from all particulars and so attain a view of that which we could not see before, a view of the whole. The third movement is the movement of truth and of existence in the true sense. In the first two movements we are bound to life and so our finitude cannot be considered reflectively and taken into account. We see life, not as a whole, but as a series of moments, lacking an overall conception. Shaking our bondage to the Earth, to things, and coming to terms with our finitude in the third movement leaves us free to see our life as a whole. "The Earth preoccupies us too much, leading us to live within our individual preoccupations, so that ultimately we would not need to see our finitude, our life as a whole. Therein precisely consists the rule of the Earth over us."[124] By pointing to the desire to shake this rule, to disturb it, Patočka is not implying an attempt to escape our human limitations. It is not an attempt to rise above our humanity and dominate it as a superman, it is rather the opposite—to recognize our finitude and to come to understand that our existence is not exhausted by its material aspect. In doing so, we pursue a fundamentally different movement of life, a movement of truth, a "living in truth." The third movement is an attempt at breaking free, but "[w]e do not conceive of the attempt at breaking free as a grasp at mastery, at seizing power, it is not a will to domination but an attempt to gain clarity concerning our situation, to accept the situation and, by that clarity, to transform it."[125] Patočka finds historical examples of this "breaking free" of the bondage of the Earth, interestingly, in the Buddhist metaphor of the quenching of thirst and in the Christian attack on self-centeredness.[126]

With his phenomenology of movement, Patočka has approached philosophy from a perspective grounded in the simple conviction that the essence of human reality cannot be abstracted from its concrete elements, namely, our existence as corporeal beings, objective creatures in an objective world. On the basis of this understanding Patočka was able to interpret existence as a series of movements, of three vital lines that, in addition to describing the ways in which humans exist, also help to define the actual *content* of that existence: human history. History and politics are never far removed in Patočka's writings, and this for good reason. His approach to philosophy, as I have tried to show in this overview of his phenomenology, attempts to demonstrate its connectedness to history and politics. The pursuit of a phenomenology of movement via a combination of ancient and modern philosophy serves to illuminate this fundamental connectedness.[127] The three movements of being human can lead us to greater historical and political understanding, as I shall discuss in the following chapters. Patočka writes:

> Only by starting out from these three fundamental lines, from understanding how they presuppose and negate each other mutually, can we, after analysis, achieve a certain insight into the way

in which these three strands (two movements governed by the Earth, a third breaking free of it) make up the overarching human movement we call history.[128]

Though its subject is phenomenology, *Body, Community, Language, World* also contains an explicit appeal to history.

History and politics, in the end, are to be interpreted in terms of living in truth. This concept has its foundation in phenomenology, in Patočka's understanding of the way in which people encounter and perceive the world. The essence of this encounter is the perception of the world, not merely as a collection of particular entities, but as a whole in itself. In this sense Patočka sees his understanding of the world as more radical than Heidegger's because it focuses not only on our encounter with particulars, but also on our encounter with and interest in the world as a whole. It is only through this conscious encounter, Patočka argues, that people are able to live in truth.

> Humans are the only beings which, because they are not indifferent to themselves and to their being, can live in truth, can choose between life in the anxiety of its roles and needs and life in a relation to the world, not to existing entities only.[129]

Seeing beyond the particular, the attachment of our lives to the material, is the most basic element of the movement of truth. Only in the light of this distance do things appear as they are. Nowhere is this more true than in the realm of politics, an argument made explicit in the *Heretical Essays in the Philosophy of History*.

Patočka further demonstrates his concern with the movement of human history by concluding *Body, Community, Language, World* with something of a political critique. He notes that phenomenology, as he has pursued it, touches on "something that all modern humanism neglected, what that humanism lacks."[130] This is the notion of "nonindifference to being," that we become human only insofar as we perceive our being as something to which we must pay attention, something that challenges us as it presents itself to us as not simply given. Being is approachable via a movement (the third) that we can attain only through that nonindifference, only by responding to the challenge, the responsibility of accomplishing our being. Humanism, by contrast, "thrives on the idea that humans are in some sense the heirs of the absolute," of a reality that is given as a gift rather than achieved. The result is the belief that humans "have a license to subjugate all reality, to appropriate it and to exploit it with no obligation to give anything in return, constraining and disciplining ourselves."[131] Here Patočka provides a link to his analysis of metaphysics and its role in the development of Western civilization, and in doing so connects his phenomenological work with his political concerns.

CONCLUSION

Patočka's phenomenological work calls for a more extensive and in-depth analysis than the scope of this work allows; it is an attempt to transform contemporary phenomenological philosophy, and that not simply by a *synthesis* of Husserl and Heidegger. He aims to be faithful to the core assumptions of phenomenology, and yet to take account of human existence in its active, corporeal, and communal aspects. The phenomenology that I have described here is the ground from which this philosophy will proceed as it engages contemporary history, politics, and the question of the *telos* of European civilization.

Husserl and Heidegger are criticized for a lack of applicability to the human sciences, to the sciences of concrete human activity. The reality of the world and our understanding of it can be reduced neither to the subjective consciousness nor to Heideggerean ontology. The world and our existence within it—existing not only in the world but as part of its vital processes—are also determinative of our being and cannot be left out of any investigation of reality. This is the foundation on which the process of achieving our potential, our being, takes place. It is also the basis for Patočka's objections to Husserl and Heidegger.

The social sciences, because they deal with humans interested in their own being, are distinct from the natural sciences. Our understanding of ourselves is neither clear nor objectively accessible. It is obscure, and is only uncovered as we participate in life actively and as we reflectively examine ourselves and the way in which we live.

> The point is the essential primacy of *practice*. At the very proto-foundation of consciousness, of thought, of the subject, there is acting, not mere seeing. That explains why there is so much opaque, obscure, in our clarity. Such a being, concerned with its own being, cannot in principle be grasped in its distinctiveness by observation.[132]

As an approach to social science, then, Heidegger's philosophy had a distinct advantage over Husserl's by reason of its assumption of nonobjectivity and self-concealment.[133] Yet this assumption, this ontological perspective, did not sufficiently pursue the human relation to things that is analogous to our relation to ourselves. Being human implies an interaction of the interested human, not only with his own being, but with the objective world, the world of individual objects, and the world as a whole.

I have argued in this chapter that Patočka's work is marked by an interpretive application of the work of Husserl and Heidegger to problems that superseded the scope of their own philosophical visions. This interpretive approach to the German philosophers is not only unique, it also blunts the edge of the most likely criticism to be levied against Patočka by followers of Husserl or Heidegger—the question of consistency. While Patočka's negative analysis of the shortcomings of the work of Husserl and Heidegger is relatively clear, several aspects of his positive application of their thought are much less so. Foremost among these is the use of this contemporary German philosophy to analyze the classical thought and symbolism of Plato and Socrates. Patočka emulates the Socratic while proceeding along the lines of the Husserlian and Heideggerean. He is convinced of the compatibility of not only Heidegger and Husserl, but also of Heidegger and Socrates.

The specific relationship to Greek philosophy will be dealt with in succeeding chapters, so I need only note here that the relationship, the belief in the relevance of Plato, was basic to Patočka's thought. His interest in the whole of reality led to an unwillingness, an inability, to overly restrict himself methodologically or theoretically. To portray adequately the reality of man in community, Patočka *had* to draw on Socratic metaphor and insight, just as he had to approach Husserl, or the early and the late Heidegger, in a way that some will find inconsistent or questionable.

There is little sense, then, in trying to judge whether in the end he is most fundamentally with Husserl or Heidegger or Plato or Socrates. He uses all of them in ways that could be arguably inconsistent if one were to judge from the standpoint of the particular conclusions reached by any one of these philosophers. In terms of the difference between the early Heidegger of *Being and Time* and the later Heidegger—the well-known *Kehre* or "turn" in his work—Patočka's attitude is revealing. He mixes an insightful understanding of the change in Heidegger's thought with a refusal to respect that change as fundamental, as effectively requiring the reader to choose between two Heideggers.[134] Instead, Patočka draws on both the early and the late Heidegger, placing analytical concepts drawn from *Being and Time* next to the metaphorical and poetic language of the later, postwar Heidegger. Patočka's focus, as I have noted, is not with ontology as an exclusive science. Both sides of Heidegger's corpus, his rigorous analysis of being along with his poetic emulation of the "saving power" that is attendant to the essence of technology,[135] are relevant to the degree that the philosophy reflects human reality and can be "exhibited descriptively," can be described in terms of our experience of that reality.

This approach, for students of philosophy committed to methodological consistency, has been perceived as lacking. Erazim Kohák and James Dodd, for example, the translator and editor of the editions of Patočka's works in English who both approach Patočka from the perspective of phenomenology, have spoken of what they see as inconsistency. Kohák, largely because he reads the Czech philosopher as Husserlian, sees an "evident tension in Patočka's thought between his Husserlian and his Heideggerean heritages."[136] James Dodd, in his introduction to *Body, Community, Language, World*, sees a similar problem. The phenomenology, he points out, is problematic for the philosopher grounded in methodology; it asks of the reader a willingness to set aside prejudices born of an analytical heritage. As Dodd puts it,

> There is too much of a sense that the conceptual ground has not been prepared enough, that the force of these descriptions of human life rely too much on the commitment of the readers (and, originally, the listeners) to engage faithfully in the effort of "seeing" what it is that Patočka is endeavoring to put into words.[137]

Dodd is correct here; Patočka is convinced that human experience may exceed our analytical abilities. The resort to evocative forms of symbolization is thus not merely acceptable, it is necessary. Yet for a Husserlian, Patočka's phenomenology will remain problematic on methodological grounds. Kohák and Dodd, for instance, argue that he has not completely succeeded in his task, that the tensions have not been ironed out, the contradictions cleared up, the "conceptual ground" fully explicated.

Conclusions such as these, however, may prevent rather than assist us in seeing the full relevance of this body of work. The story of Patočka's philosophy does not end with his interpretation of phenomenology and Heideggerean ontology. It is to Greek philosophy and Socrates that I now turn in order to understand not only Patočka's broader philosophical aims, but also to illuminate the ground for the connection between philosophy and politics.

3

Philosophy After the Death of Metaphysics

Patočka and Greek Thought

As an interpreter of Husserl and Heidegger, Jan Patočka takes up the Husserlian goal of a renewal of rationality in the West and considers it alongside his commitment to Heidegger's critique of metaphysical philosophy. He wants to recover the insight of the classical conception of reason, in other words, but without becoming entangled in traditionally metaphysical formulations. Contemporary philosophy, particularly as expressed by Heidegger, has made a facile reliance on metaphysical thought impossible. Neither Husserl nor Heidegger, for example, focuses on the traditional content of Greek thought. Yet Patočka does not find the twilight of metaphysics to signal a need to abandon classical theory. To the contrary, his work is distinguished by its direct engagement with and emulation of the political theory of Plato. The notion is one of classical philosophy minus the explicit element of metaphysics. It is an interpretation of classical thought as something other than the positing of a metaphysical reality and the development of a means of grasping it through the pursuit of dialectical reasoning. In this chapter I pursue the question that distinguishes Patočka's work from Husserl's and Heidegger's: the question of a nonmetaphysical interpretation of Socrates and Plato. To the extent that the legacy of Nietzsche and Heidegger requires that Platonic thought be abandoned, there would seem to be little hope for a genuine philosophy of politics and ethics. As Patočka interprets it, however, the essence of classical thought is not defined in contrast to contemporary critique, but integrated into it.

As much as he relies on the phenomenological thought of Husserl and Heidegger, the center of gravity in Patočka's work is the figure of Socrates. His philosophy, therefore, is not *primarily* directed toward a revision of twentieth-century phenomenology. It attempts such a revision, but as a methodological means toward a larger goal, a goal that is as much political and historical as it is philosophical. Rather than discard classical thought as hopelessly metaphysical, Patočka examines it anew; he puts its spirituality and metaphysical formulations to the test of contemporary critique. These formulations, particularly the Socratic injunction to "care for the soul," continue to be relevant in the postmetaphysical age precisely because their essence does not impel us to seek a metaphysical foundation for our scientific inquiry into the nature of reality.

Patočka's hope is to recover what Husserl sought in his later years, the "insight" of Western rationality that epitomizes the European ideal of civilization. This is an insight, though, an understanding of reason, that became progressively deformed as it was subject to attempts at metaphysical systemization over the past several millennia. Plato himself took the first step on this road when he expressed the human potential in terms of transcending the apparent images of our experience, via the dialectic, and reaching the real, the ideal forms of reality.[1] What Plato offered in merely symbolic form, however, tempered by an assertion of the limits of human striving, reached a culmination in the modern world with the claims of science, inspired by the aspirations of the metaphysical quest, to be the final "key that unlocks all doors."[2] This scientific self-certainty, of course, is emblematic of the "crisis" in the West that Husserl hoped to reverse by looking to the origin of Western rationality.

Patočka is convinced, in contrast to Heidegger, that the insight on which Europe is founded is embodied in the figure of Socrates and represents the greatest achievement of Western civilization. Yet since Plato—and here he is with Heidegger—philosophy has been in decline, its insight corrupted. Drawing on phenomenology, Patočka begins a reinterpretation of Platonic philosophy. He starts with reason, the anchor of Western civilization, describing it not as a static concept but as an active mode of living and questioning, a phenomenological movement. Yet to symbolize this movement, this fundamental and defining activity central to the history of the West, he abandons the language of twentieth-century phenomenology and returns to an elemental Socratic injunction: the requirement to "care for the soul."[3]

Patočka's response to the Husserlian perception of a crisis, of a dissolution of the center of Western civilization, is not a new philosophy, but a reconsideration of our existing philosophical heritage. The task he sets for himself is to examine the contribution of classical Greek thought to Europe using the analytical tools provided by Husserl and Heidegger. The task of this chapter is to analyze the character of this reinterpretation of classical thought. The underlying question is whether the classical and the postmetaphysical are compatible, and whether a coherent conception of politics and ethics might result from an attempt at synthesis. Patočka answers both questions positively.

The Czech philosopher's extensive writings on Plato, Europe, and history are at the heart of his philosophical work; they represent not only the application of his phenomenological interpretation of Husserl and Heidegger, but also his enduring conviction that politics and history, as the material on which civilization is constructed, are inherently connected to philosophy. The initial force behind these writings, most certainly, was the quest for a renewal of reason, Husserl's goal of reclarifying what he considered to be the *telos* of European humanity. Whereas Husserl's career was coming to a close as he developed the thesis of the *Crisis*, making it impossible for him to pursue the problem in any detail, Patočka's was just beginning.

In attempting to reconstruct the dissipated center of Western civilization, Patočka is not simply reinforcing traditional Western philosophy. With Heidegger, he concludes that Western thought has largely taken its lead from a tendency first visible in Plato and Aristotle: the tendency to encapsulate the philosophical insight represented by Socrates in a systematic, quasi-objective form. Philosophers since Plato have generally pursued philosophy as metaphysics, as the objectification of a transcendental, metaphysical reality. It is this objectification, this cessation of the movement and uncertainty of philosophy, this metaphysical systematization criticized by Heidegger,[4] which is itself at the heart of the crisis of rationalism. The recovery of philosophy requires an explication of the nonmetaphysical phenomena at the center of the Western tradition; it will be a recovery that is heretical with regard to traditional thought.

Patočka wrote extensively on Greek philosophy, particularly in his later years, when his banishment from university and professional life ended his career but freed him to concentrate on topics close to his heart yet forbidden by communist censorship. He focused most particularly on the Socratic problem of the mode of life most conducive to truth: life as care for the soul. This is, of course, also a mode of life that reflects the goals of philosophy, and so a characteristically European activity. It has been eclipsed, however, by the progressive domination in Western thought of metaphysics. Among his numerous lectures and texts on ancient thought, three stand out. First and foremost is a series of lectures from 1973 entitled *Plato and Europe*, delivered illegally to dedicated students in private apartments and concentrating specifically on this topic. Nearly simultaneous with the preparation for these lectures was a book-length text written for publication in German and eventually entitled *Europe and the Post-European Age*. Finally, in another series of underground lectures from 1973, entitled "Four Seminars towards the Problem of Europe" and distributed as samizdat, Patočka returned to these topics and, in response to student questions, to their relationship to the later Heidegger.[5] The theme that ties these works together is the notion of "caring for the soul"; this symbol represents the heart of the Greek contribution to European civilization, a foundational contribution that is the basis for any claim it may have to universality.

In the background of each of these later texts is a seminal article from 1952 that also requires a closer look. In "Negative Platonism" Patočka elucidates his thesis of a nonmetaphysical "negative" Platonic philosophy rooted in the Socratic dialogues and the concepts of Socratic ignorance and continual questioning—notions that implicitly reject, according to Patočka, any "positive" or objective ground for human knowledge. Socrates and, for the most part, Plato are characterized as "shakers," as challengers of systematic knowledge not propagators of it.

Patočka's dedication in these works is to the very idea of philosophy itself. Along with Husserl, he defines it narrowly: as the originally European practice of self-reflection pioneered among the philosophers of ancient Greece.[6] Rather than an attempt to discover and map out a preexisting given truth, philosophy is an activity that affects human reality in the course of examining it. Human reality, then, is not a fixed constant. It is variable, dependent largely on the particularities of the situation in which the human being stands. "The situation of man," Patočka writes in *Plato and Europe*, "is something that changes when we become conscious of it. A naive and a conscious situation are two different situations. Our reality is always situational, so that if it is reflected on, it is already different by the fact of our having reflected on it. Of course the question is whether it is in this way better."[7] This last comment, the question of whether we improve reality by reflecting on it, is not meant rhetorically. Reflection is an activity with definite consequences, and Patočka feels that these consequences are and must continue to be positive for human life. He maintains: "Philosophical thought ought to have a different sense, that philosophical thought should somehow help us in our need."[8] Though philosophy is a dangerous undertaking in terms of its challenge to authority, its primary effect is positive: reflection has the effect of introducing clarity: "In every case a reflective situation is—in contrast to a naive situation—to a certain degree clarified, or at least on the path to clarity."[9]

Patočka's understanding of philosophy stresses reflection as the questioning of that which we suppose to be certain, simple, and clear; it is the questioning of knowledge received and accepted without reflection. To the extent it succeeds, it necessarily challenges the everyday certainties of life; it calls them into question. The early pursuit of philosophy in ancient Greece was of this type, Patočka argues, and this is crucial to the concept of reason in Europe. Reason does not naively look to authority for knowledge; it challenges that naïveté.

The process of the conscious breaking through of everyday certainty, everyday mediocrity, which does not ask the question of what man lives for, was most deeply experienced in Greek philosophy, from which all of our philosophy comes, and one of its greatest masters, Plato, urgently described this process for us in his dialogues. He wanted to show that philosophy is not merely the conveying of some doctrine, of certain pieces of information (pieces of information are that which is contained in the sciences), but that philosophizing is motion, a certain internal process in man which is connected in its essence with our rebound from naively natural and limited everydayness.[10]

In this form, philosophy can be described as the pursuit of truth and freedom: two notions that are meaningful only where we actively question knowledge instead of living as if it were given.

The spirit of freedom and truth is the Socratic spirit. Socratic activity, and Patočka clearly considers Socrates a historical figure quite distinct from Plato, exemplifies the phenomenological movement of truth described in *Body, Community, Language, World*. It is what is elsewhere called a "life in truth."[11] Patočka's picture of Socrates does not repeat the traditional understanding, it is drawn instead with the help of Heideggerean insights. We might even call it a Heideggerean Socrates, this despite Heidegger's turn away from Socrates and toward the presocratics in *An Introduction to Metaphysics*.[12] Although the influence of Heidegger is clear, there still remain fundamental differences that point Patočka's philosophy in an explicitly ethical and political direction, in distinct contrast to Heidegger.

Patočka's approach to Socrates and classical thought takes seriously the analysis of Heidegger, yet resists following it too closely. When Patočka contends that freedom is an essential component of truth, for example, a kinship with Heidegger's "On the Essence of Truth" (in which the essence of truth is described as freedom) is evident. Yet Patočka's interpretation of truth as freedom is distinct from the German philosopher's.[13] When Patočka speaks of freedom, he speaks of it in the fullness of its social and political, as well as its phenomenological, implications. Truth is the freedom to "let beings appear," as Heidegger describes it, but it is also a movement of life, a way of living that humans have the potential to achieve and which is characterized by an explicitly ethical side. Truth is the freedom, not only to let beings appear, but also to live freely and humanly, it is the freedom that enables the philosopher to stand and challenge naive faith and simply given knowledge. "Truth . . . is an internal battle of man for his essential, inner freedom, a freedom which man has in his core not factually, but essentially. Truth is a question of the truthfulness of man."[14] Here, truth is as much a matter of the way in which one lives in the long term as it is a product of the authentic disclosure of beings in a particular moment. This is a significant point of contrast, for it emphasizes truth as a mode of being, a way of life with an implicit moral element.

PLATO AND EUROPE

In *Plato and Europe*, the work most often held up as emblematic of Patočka's abiding morality, the following claim is made: "I believe that it is perhaps possible," Patočka writes, "to venture to put forward the thesis that *Europe* . . . arose out of *care for the soul*, TES PSYCHES EMPIMELEISTHAI. This is the embryo out of which grew that which Europe was."[15] This is the thesis of *Plato and Europe*, and it responds directly to the concerns raised by Edmund Husserl in his late writings on the *Crisis of European Sciences*. Yet *Plato and Europe*, which consists of a series of private lectures from the year 1973, is far more than an attempt to respond to Husserl. Along with the *Heretical Essays in the Philosophy of History*, *Plato and Europe* and its accompanying texts represent the high point of the political philosophy that had been progressively developing in Jan Patočka's thought. Here the question is not philosophy in the abstract, but in the concrete setting of its relation to European history and civilization. The problem of Europe, Patočka concludes, is a spiritual problem. It is the problem of the "care for the soul."

The *Plato and Europe* lectures are the centerpiece of the many illegal apartment lectures given by Patočka during the 1970s, via which he was able to continue to philosophize even after he was "retired" from the university by its communist administrators. This was the period of "normalization," a particularly disheartening time in Czechoslovak history as the government ruthlessly snuffed out all trace of the freedoms enjoyed in the reformist period of the late 1960s. *Plato and Europe* responds to this despondent situation as Patočka is explicit in seeking "hope" for the future in his reflections. It would be a mistake, however, to conclude that these lectures were merely dissident texts with the primary aim of offering hope to students discouraged by communism; they were in fact broad philosophical reflections directed toward civilization in the West as a whole. The distorted ideology of Czechoslovak communism was itself a manifestation of the crisis of the West, and Patočka intended to examine the roots of that crisis.

These lectures, as their title suggests, establish a connection between Greek philosophy and European civilization. They claim that Europe is distinctive by virtue of its historical assumption of the standpoint of classical Greek philosophy, the standpoint of reason, as a guiding principle. The decline of Europe, both in the narrower sense of the loss of its geopolitical dominance and in the broader sense of the crisis of reason affecting the West as a whole, is a consequence of its misunderstanding of this principle. Its hope for the future, which is a universal hope to the extent the concept of reason and its manifestations such as political democracy are considered to be applicable to mankind generally, depends on its ability to renew its heritage. Patočka felt that the phenomenological philosophies of Husserl and Heidegger were necessary aids in the pursuit of this goal, although not by themselves sufficient. They were crucial, however, to an understanding of care for the soul in a contemporary context. Interestingly, it was often the case that the students to whom Patočka lectured were more interested in pursuing the Heideggerean and phenomenological details than the Socratic. Yet Patočka made it clear in these lectures that his abiding focus was Western civilization rather than contemporary philosophy, and this focus necessitated an exploration of the concept of "care for the soul." This was, as he stressed, the essence of European reality:

> One thing, however, puzzles me, that all of you have only questions on phenomenology and Heidegger, etc., but not even one question has come having to do with Europe, with that which was my most actual thesis; that European reality, in spite of the two great turning points, consists in that which resumes the whole of antiquity, that is, the concern for and care of the soul and everything that connects with it.[16]

The very reality of European civilization, he argues, is tied up in its "spiritual foundations."[17]

At the heart of these lectures is the sense that an understanding of the European heritage can positively affect human life, both in terms of the self-constitution of the individual and the ordering of the civilization itself. Our Platonic heritage, despite its damaged reputation, still contains the seeds of an authentic life. Those philosophical seeds, however, must be understood in relation, not to dreams of a perfect system, but to what Patočka calls the "hardness of reality."

> [A] further question is whether in that which it would be possible to demarcate as the European heritage, there exists something that could be credible to us to a certain degree, that could affect us in such a way that we could again see hope in a certain perspective, in a certain future, without indulging in illusory dreams and without in some way underestimating the hardness and seriousness of the situation in which we find ourselves.[18]

In accepting the hardness of reality and assuming responsibility for the formation of the soul, humans attest to a mode of living that is truthful, that is constant and of a higher order than material reality. To illuminate the context of this argument, a closer look at Patočka's understanding of Europe and "European reality" is required.

As the dominant geopolitical entity in the world, Patočka argues, Europe has effectively ended, its position destroyed during two wars in the space of thirty years. The world has entered a post-European age and it is the task of philosophy to assist in restoring equilibrium—not by returning Europe to its former position of power, but by seeking to understand the path that Europe traveled and how it failed to take up the challenge presented by its Socratic heritage. This task, it is asserted, is relevant not merely to the relationship of Europeans to their own history, but to humanity in general.

> But the question is, when we go towards the roots of the present disequilibrium, whether we must not go to the very beginnings of Europe and through these beginnings all the way to the very relation between man and his place in the world; whether the disequilibrium that we observe today isn't something that has to do, not only with European man in a particular historical age, but something that today concerns man in general in his relation to the planet. I think that it is necessary to answer this question positively: it concerns man and his relation to the planet. And this is clear precisely today, when Europe has ended. When Europe, that two-thousand-year construction which was able to carry humanity to a quite new level of reflectivity and consciousness, and also power and strength, when this historical reality, which for so long assumed that all of humanity was contained in it, that it was humanity and all else was insignificant, has definitively ended.[19]

Patočka explains the decline of Europe as a result of two main factors: disunity and enormous power. Disunity, the prevalence of numerous sovereign states at varying levels of development without any higher authority, was coupled with enormous power, available as a result of advanced technical and scientific knowledge. Both factors, he notes, are characteristically modern.[20] Europe is not a single state, and Patočka does not propose to make it one, but it does possess a common history and heritage. *Plato and Europe* contends that, more than any other single factor, the recognition and philosophical explication of the heritage of Europe as "care for the soul" has the potential to provide relief from the history of the twentieth century as war.[21]

The lectures of *Plato and Europe* point backward from the contemporary disunity to the Greek polis as the foundational moment in European history. The spiritual core of Europe is in the Greek polis; the Roman Empire, and Christianity following it, both draw on that heritage in their attempts to order European civilization. In arguing for the singular importance of the Greek experience, Patočka must contend that both the Judaic and the Christian traditions are not independent poles of European culture, but derivative poles in that they had first to "travel through" Greek thought in order to become what they did for European civilization.

Judaism, he argues, had to Hellenize itself, whereas Christianity itself is indebted to Athens for the thought of the "other world" of justice and pure good.[22]

What is it that characterizes Greek philosophy in such a distinctive way? Patočka describes it as a conscious decision no longer to accept life and its inevitable decline as simply given. Greek philosophy, he contends, is characterized by a challenge, a refusal to accept the simple fate of a world and a life ever in decline. It resisted the inevitability of decline and, in doing so, discovered human freedom and its relation to the eternal. The battle against the degenerative tendency of the world, the resistance to it, is precisely human freedom; this is what the Greeks called *care for the soul.*

> The philosophical discovery of eternity is a special thing. From the point of view of modern natural science it is naturally incomprehensible. But what is contained in it? It is resistance; it is a battle against that fall, against time, against that entire degenerative tendency of the world and of life. This battle is in a certain sense understandably lost, but in a certain other sense not so, because the situation in which man is, differs according to how he stands in relation to it. And the freedom of man rests—possibly— precisely in this! The Greeks, the Greek philosophers, in whom the Greek spirit is expressed most sharply, expressed human freedom with the term: care for the soul.[23]

With this we have the first hint as to the explicit content of the concept of caring for the soul. Caring for the soul changes the situation in which man stands; it enables him to stand freely, but it demands of him a burdensome responsibility.

In the second chapter of *Plato and Europe*, Patočka shows the relationship of his concern with Greek philosophy and Socrates to his phenomenology. It was through Edmund Husserl that he came to be engaged in the pursuit of the principle on which European life was founded, and it is through Husserlian phenomenology that he wished to demonstrate the relevance of his conclusions. Yet Patočka makes a point of recognizing the differences between his work and Husserl's. He describes his work phenomenologically yet notes a distinction between it and pure phenomenology. In *Plato and Europe*, Patočka pursues what he calls "phenomenological philosophy." This is a purposeful distinction, implying that philosophy properly pursued is inseparable from the social realm, the realm of human interaction with other beings and with the things of the world. "Phenomenological philosophy differs from phenomenology in that it not only wants to distinguish phenomena as such, but it also wants to deduce consequences, it wants to deduce from this *metaphysical consequences*, that means it asks about the relation between phenomena and beings."[24] In other words, Patočka wishes his phenomenological philosophy to have a broader aim than just the distinguishing of phenomena. It is to touch directly on issues consequential to the act of philosophizing itself, issues such as the relation of the philosopher to society and to the concrete world.

An important point, however, that Patočka makes is that phenomenology, as a science of revealing, is still appropriate to his aim. This is because the distinguishing of phenomena is for him no abstract venture. It is tied to human comportment in the world both in terms of the consequences mentioned above, and in relation to the effect on human activity of morality, of the differentiation between good and evil. When we decide how to comport ourselves, when we decide how to act in relation to good and evil, we reveal ourselves. And that which leads us to decide how to act is also revealed:

> Just when man does not want to merely recognize, when he wants at the same time to act, when he orients himself with respect to good and evil, everywhere there something must—this is clear— show itself to him. Precisely that must show itself to him which designates good and evil and, naturally, because good and evil are something that concern us, we must at the same time reveal ourselves to ourselves."[25]

It is in revealing itself that something genuinely becomes a "phenomenon," that is, something distinguished from a mere being. Phenomena are beings that have been revealed, or that manifest themselves. They show themselves in truth.[26]

In the case of the human being, this is a crucial distinction. Man is a being of truth, meaning a being who has the potential to live truthfully, to show himself and view others without distortion. He is unlike other beings in this possibility. Yet this remains only a possibility, not a given characteristic. "Man has, on the basis of the fact that he stands between phenomena and mere being, the possibility to either *capitulate and fall into mere being*, or to realize himself as a *being of truth, a being of phenomena.*"[27] The human situation is in between truth and mere being. Humans can choose to live as if the objects and equations and given knowledge around them are exhaustive of reality, but they also have the choice to open themselves to the possibility that phenomena are more complex than they at first appear. The course of our lives, Patočka contends, is determined by our pursuit of the higher movement or our capitulation to the lower.

The mode of truth, however, the mode of revealing human life as it truly is, does not deliver us of pain and insecurity. In fact, it may do the opposite by revealing the basic problematicity of life. We are in a precarious situation; rather than simple and secure, the human world is fundamentally problematic. Living philosophically, living in truth, does not solve problems so much as it presents them. Our self-recognition as beings of truth damns us to a life of problematicity as it frees us from bondage to the merely material. The consciousness of problematicity is not new to Greek philosophy; it is present in myth as well, in the common notion of our position in the universe as insecure. It was the greatness of the Greek philosophers, Patočka argues, not merely to recognize this problematicity, but to infer from it a "plan of life" that was not a curse, but a form of human greatness. "Everything from insight," is how Patočka describes it.[28] Mankind is not doomed by the precariousness of its existence that shows itself so clearly in, for example, the myth of Oedipus. To the contrary, our insight enables us to rise up from out of our situation of desperation. As a result of insight, human life is shown to be other than as in traditional myth, that is, doomed to a certain futility, to helplessness in the face of fate by virtue of our essential separateness from the realm of the divine.

Insight is the mode by which we apply a philosophical vision to human life. It is the mode by which we order our existence in the world, it is our means to create a just order out of chaos. The solution of Greek philosophy is to show that man, though not divine, is not merely an object among others in the world. He is privileged with the possibility of living on a higher level than other beings of nature, a level approaching the divine. Because of this, the Greeks could see that *man would be able, in certain circumstances, to make of the human world a world of truth and justice. The way in which it is possible to achieve this,"* Patočka concludes, "is precisely the object of caring for the soul."[29]

The "care for the soul" is recognized as the instrument of such an action, an action that would enable us to live, not as mere beings, but as beings of insight. It would enable us to acquire, based on our knowledge of living with other humans, the "moral insight," which is the "sedimentation and codification" of human experience.[30] Patočka believes that Europe is characterized by precisely this call to reflection, for only in Europe did the movement from myth to philosophy occur. European history, broadly speaking, is the history of various attempts to embody institutionally this care for the soul.[31]

CARING FOR THE SOUL

The process of philosophy is that of caring for the soul. Yet as I have attempted to stress, this process is delineated, not through traditional Platonic analysis, but through a set of analytical lenses derived largely from phenomenology and the work of Martin Heidegger. The process must therefore be examined in greater detail, along with its component parts.

In terms of its formulation, we are first faced with the active part of the process, the act of caring. In *Being and Time* "care," or *Sorge*, is described as the being of *Dasein*, as the existential *a priori* that precedes the situations of *Dasein*.[32] Patočka's concept of care, however, is more accurately described, as Jacques Derrida wrote in *The Gift of Death*, as a concept that combines the Platonic meaning of "learning to die," *meletē thanatou* from the *Phaedo*, and Heidegger's *Sorge*.[33] Although the injunction to "care for the soul" comes directly from the Platonic dialogues, it is read negatively, that is, under the influence of the Heideggerean critique of metaphysics. In the *Heretical Essays*, for example, the Platonic *meletē thanatou* bears the imprint of "being-toward-death":

> Another important moment is that the Platonic philosopher over-
> came death by not fleeing from it but by facing up to it. This phi-
> losophy was *meletē thanatou*, care for death; care for the soul is
> inseparable from care for death which becomes the true care for
> life; life (eternal) is born of this direct look at death, of an over-
> coming of death.[34]

Patočka's aim, in responding to the Husserlian call for a phenomenological rediscovery of the European spirit, is to combine in his interpretation of "care for the soul" the traditional concern for ethics integral to Greek philosophy with the liberating aspects of contemporary perspectives. Heideggerean influence is undeniably present in this interpretation; it is also reflected in the attempt to pinpoint the elusive nature of the second component of "care for the soul": the soul itself.

In his discussion of care for the soul, Patočka appears to contradict his own stated aim to avoid metaphysics by making use of concepts that are clearly metaphysical in content, as, for example, the notion of the "soul." In common understanding, the soul seems to be nothing other than an objectification of a transcendental concept—the embodiment of something that is beyond objective reality in order to make our way in the world more secure, more full of answers. Following Heidegger, Patočka would be expected to eschew the use of such terms. Yet he argues emphatically that the adoption of a nonmetaphysical stance with regard to philosophy does not necessitate the abandonment of metaphor and symbolism that is traditionally considered metaphysical—insofar as those symbols reflect human reality. The notion of the soul, or to be more specific, the Greek soul, is an example of such a symbol.

Philosophy, from its Greek beginnings, defines the soul as that in the human being which is capable of truth.[35] And yet this is merely a descriptive definition. It is more instructive to understand the Greek soul in terms of that characteristic also essential to philosophy: human understanding. In a series of seminars dedicated to the problems of *Plato and Europe*, Patočka expands on this theme. He writes:

When thinking begins, the most it is possible to say is that on one side here stands the world, like a collection of everything which is, on the other side stands the philosophizing man with his ability to understand that which is the world. This ability to understand, this is called soul, in the Greek conception. This is the original understanding, that, on the basis of which man has the ability of truth and of individual truths.[36]

The soul is therefore defined in terms of an ability, a human characteristic which, in a sense, transcends the material world.

Soul is the human characteristic that gives us the ability of truth. And truth, as I said in my discussion of phenomenology, is a function of what Patočka calls the "movements" of human life—it is the highest of those movements.[37] In this way it can be said that both the soul and the truth that it effects are directly relative to action, to human movement. This is nowhere more to the point than in considering the activity of human decision-making. In one of his post–World War II lectures on Greek philosophy at Charles University, Patočka noted that the meaning of the soul in ancient Greece changed with Socrates. Human fate came to be seen as an internal phenomenon, relative to our decision making, not an external one over which we have no control. "With Socrates, the soul is also the bearer of fate. But it is inner fate, the inner lot of man. The soul decides for itself and has a power toward this end which is its alone—the recognition of truth, the strength of distinguishing good and evil."[38] The soul acts on us in those moments when we must decide, when we encounter the possibility of exerting control on our own fate by refusing to give in to the weight of events as they come at us. It acts on us by recognizing truth, and by differentiating between good and evil. This, however, is not a given characteristic. It exists for us as an inherent possibility, one available only if we pursue it. It comes, also, at a price, for the decision to act based on recognition of good and evil is the decision to accept the burden of a life that is no longer simple and instinctive, but problematic.

Why, then, would one choose to care for the soul, why would one choose to distinguish good from evil and thereby problematize life? The answer, Patočka argues, lies in the relationship of the soul, via its movement, to being. It is with a fundamental ontology, not a metaphysics, that this conception of the soul can be understood. To understand the soul in this sense one must not think of it as an entity, a thing, but as the locus of our relationship to our own being. The soul is the center point of a hierarchy of being in Patočka's work. It is defined as the ability to understand our own being, making it a figurative point from which one can progress toward a growth in being (a movement in pursuit of "good"), or fall back toward a loss of being (evil). Care for the soul has its basis in ontology, even as it makes use of metaphysical symbol.

As I remarked in chapter 1, the concept of movement is at the center of Patočka's interpretation of phenomenology. According to Plato, the defining characteristic of the soul is its self-movement; the soul is defined by its motion.[39] But motion toward what? The human ability to recognize truth and good is not a given characteristic but a possibility that the human must pursue in his or her being. The motion of the soul, therefore, its basic function, is tied to the motion of being—a motion that is expressed in terms of either an expansion or a contraction of being. Soul is the movement of our being, care for the soul as an ontological theory is explicable in terms of gain and loss, good and evil:

> In the ontological-cosmological representation of reality care for the soul consequently reveals itself as a theory of motion, like Phaedrus' AUTO HEAUTO KINÚN [that which moves itself]. On the other hand it is possible to formulate care for the soul itself, from this point of view, more precisely: the soul is that which defines itself in the direction of its being and that which consequently directs itself either towards legitimate growth, towards a growth of being, or on the contrary towards decline and a loss of being: the soul is an indicator of the main arteries of being.[40]

The soul differentiates and the arteries of being indicated by it run parallel to the human categories of good and evil. In distinguishing these avenues, the soul helps to distinguish that which is good, for the good exists as that toward which we aim when we develop our being, when we heighten it by the act of reflection.

> In this, then, its most fundamental role is manifested even more markedly. The soul is that which has a sense of good and evil. The soul can exist only when good exists, for its basic motion is motion in the direction of good, but on the other hand good itself has meaning as the goal and vanishing point of everything only at the point where there exists motion. Only insofar as there exists something that can heighten its being by motion towards the good is good operative, meaning it is (exists). The soul thus not only makes possible a conception of the overall hierarchy of being in the sense of good, i.e., a teleological conception, but it is at the same time a justification of good, it gives an answer to the question (which even Nietzsche expressly asked), why choose good and not evil, why truth and not (the possibly more practical) seeming.[41]

We choose good, in this explanation, not because it is an eternal and concrete value in and of itself, something that we can grasp and hold on to, but
because our motion toward it represents a heightening of our being.

For Patočka, good itself is no concrete object, it is neither simple nor
unambiguous. Because it is not a concrete, static category, knowledge of
good (and evil) is also subject to ambiguity, to a lack of clarity. This truth,
Patočka notes, is found even in prephilosophic myth and tragedy.[42]
Oedipus, for instance, represents the painful ambiguity of knowledge of
truth. Through philosophy and myth we try to see the world as a whole, to
see it in truth; in doing so, however, we see that there can be ambiguity in
matters of good and evil. As human, we see the world only in perspectives.
It is revealed to us in parts: "The world is given to us as a whole, but that
doesn't mean that it isn't given to us *perspectively* and that it's given every-
where in its fullness . . . it is a fullness from a certain point of view. The
world . . . is revealed to us *necessarily perspectively*."[43] With this phenomenological argument—it is phenomenology that reveals to us that, because
we encounter objects in a series of (one-sided) perspectives, our access to
them as a whole is not achievable objectively—we cannot but be convinced
of the tenuousness of any claim we have to overall knowledge. Access to
truth is, instead of an objective process, a factor of our reflection and
insight, or what Husserl referred to as intuition.[44] Such is the case, as well,
with the world as a whole, along with the ability to distinguish between
good and evil. "Clarity," Patočka notes in his discussion of Oedipus, "is the
domain of gods. Into it man strayed and in it man wanders."[45] We are not
creatures of divine knowledge. We are ignorant of the most important
things, though we possess the potential for insight, as the Greeks discovered. Our mode of access to knowledge and to good is through our ability
to care for our souls, and so to increase our being, to be more fully human.

Caring for the soul occurs via movement that reveals to us our possibilities, and thereby lays a foundation for our choices, our actions. It is the
movement of European philosophy, Patočka argues, and it reveals that the
soul is in motion between two fundamental possibilities, two levels of
being. The first is the level of *DOXA*, or opinion, the second that of reflective insight. The soul has the possibility to embody either of these two
degrees of being.

> Care for the soul is thus at the same time a discovery of two fun-
> damental possibilities of the soul, two regions in which it moves.
> The soul of everyday intercourse with things and people in
> naively accepted solidarity is the soul of uncertain immediacy, its
> environment is intrusive, binding, but uncertain, diffuse, it wavers
> without solid outlines and limits: it is the soul proper to *DOXA*.

Opposite to this is the soul of questioning examination of the reflective spirit, persisting in solid outlines, purity and exactness.[46]

The movement of the soul is movement between these two possibilities. This, in itself, Patočka argues, is the action of philosophy. It is not an action that is or can be justified objectively, its success is not determined by quantitative results. Rather, its goal is human unity by the formation of the soul in solid outline, a soul that is certain in the consistency of its reflective insight.

> The soul caring for itself is thus in motion from uncertain immediacy to a determining reflection. In this motion is philosophy, and this motion is reality. Philosophy is hence comprehended and achieved by action; there does not exist any "objective" proof of philosophy, as there are objective proofs of mathematical theorems which do not concern our being, do not have an influence on it and are independent of it. In this motion consists, on the other hand, actual philosophizing; for that reason its cause cannot be erected on anything on the earth, nor hanging from the sky, but takes place in the soul in the form of sparks which maintain themselves.[47]

The soul is the locus of the action of philosophizing: philosophy as care for the soul.

Philosophy is thus defined, via Patočka's reading of Plato, not as the custodian of the soul on its journey to a final truth, but as the action of directing its continual movement by a process of thinking via questions, or "thinking questioningly." Here Patočka arrives at the final element of care for the soul: its effect on our activity. One cares for the soul, then, by a philosophical process directed by the interrogation of reality. "Care for the soul generally takes place by *thinking questioningly*."[48] This form of philosophy is one of thought-directed motion, continual and without a concrete goal. It "leads man towards a goal only in the sense that he keeps always in his mind that he continually persist."[49] The goal itself does not exist in any concrete, achievable form. The existence of such a goal would contradict the urge to investigate itself; it would instead become an urge to find. "[I]n the acceptance of investigation," Patočka notes, "is a concomitant certainty that there does not exist any end."[50]

Care for the soul, understood in this way, is the origin of the philosophical idea that is independent of systems.[51] Yet this characterization implies that it could only with great difficulty serve as a stable foundation on which human action and politics could be based. This is, in one sense, true. Philosophy cannot provide the stability and safety of a concrete, consistent and unmoving ground under our feet. But, and this goes to the heart of Patočka's argument for a philosophy of politics, this does not preclude all solidity, all sense of continuity or consistency. The argument for a phenomenological philosophy of movement, based on an interpretation of Socrates as a quasi-heretical figure who aimed to shake the foundations of Greek society rather than set them in concrete, does not condemn the philosophical endeavor to a conclusion that is nihilistic or a form of postmodern relativism. It does not mean that we are unable to speak of ethics as anything other than relative to a situation or to our will. Patočka argues precisely to the contrary.

What this perspective precludes is the summation of life into a simple "truth" based on evidence that is "given" to us in a seemingly self-evident manner.

> The reflecting Socrates, who refutes all those who assume that they have the truth, concentrates his attack especially on those who assume that they can deduce new rules of life from that which is present, from that which is self-evident and given. Just the sort of rules of life, as that which says it is good to care for one's own welfare at all cost.[52]

Yet this Socratic "attack" is not directed toward a critique of all solidity in human life. To the contrary, its exposure of the naive and the unreflective illuminates that which is truly solid and lasting.

In a very real sense, the concept of the soul and our care for it can act as a foundation for human comportment. It gives enduring and unified form to that part of our being that directs our movement and activity. By the thinking that is at the center of Patočka's view of philosophy, we engage in a process of "the inner formation of the soul itself, formation in something uniformly solid and, in this sense, existing—exactly because it is engaged in thinking." Through the process of care:

> the soul first comes to be what it can be, i.e., a unity, not opposing itself, excluding and exorcising all possibility of dispersing in contradiction, and thus does it come to dwell in the end in something that lasts, that is solid. And in the end, everything must be founded on that which is solid. On this is founded our conduct as good men, and on this is also founded our thinking, because only that thinking which reveals what is solid, reveals what is.[53]

The solidity achieved by caring for the soul consists neither of an objectively derived system based on material elements, nor of a simple, divine being on whom we can fall back when we are in doubt. It is, instead, a ground for our conduct based on the formation of our being, its unification, by the process that is most distinctly ours as human beings: the process of "thinking questioningly" that leads to understanding. The soul that does not engage in this inner questioning is at the mercy of the waves of delight and distress that go hand in hand; the soul that does gains a solid form against this fate. Care for the soul is an effort to "stand solidly in the tempest of time," to give to our being a sense of solidity and a connection to that which is not subject to the caprice of fortune and fate. And on this basis, it is an effort to find a consistency in our humanity such that we can direct ourselves in a way that transcends time.

METAPHYSICS AND "NEGATIVE PLATONISM"

Yet to be discussed is perhaps the most important element of Patočka's interpretation of Greek philosophy. This is his critique of metaphysics, the pillar on which he constructs his interpretation of Plato, Europe, and philosophy. The basis of the critique, which he calls a "negative Platonism," is an argument that the Socratic "care for the soul" is something fundamentally different from the metaphysical Platonism from which Western philosophy and science took its lead and to which it has been indebted since Plato. Patočka's critique stems from Heidegger, but whereas the Heideggerean attempt at a postmetaphysical philosophy rejects Platonic writings,—including the ethicopolitical arguments of the Socratic dialogues— Patočka focuses his attention on Socrates. The Socratic dialectic, he argues, represents the motive core of philosophy; it is the living essence of what later became metaphysics. "Negative Platonism" is a postmetaphysical approach to Socrates and Platonism, and it is one of the major achievements of a long career. The thesis of "Negative Platonism" is found in an article of the same name (along with several accompanying texts), stemming from the 1950s.[54] Though these articles were not published during Patočka's lifetime, they represent the philosophical ground on which his later interpretation of Europe, history, and politics was able to proceed.

At the beginning of "Negative Platonism" Patočka notes that there is a consensus in philosophical circles that the "metaphysical phase of philosophy has come to an end." Metaphysics as philosophy is said to be fatally unclear, a "surpassed, obsolete science," and little more than a "secularized theology."[55] If a careful analysis is undertaken, however, it can be shown that those philosophies that trumpet the death of metaphysics most loudly—positivism and Hegelianism, for example—merely take over, they do not dispense with, the fundamental question of metaphysics, the question of the whole. They lead to an integral humanism which, instead of discarding the problem of the whole, absorbs it into its own, anthropocentric perspective on human reality. In spite of all the resistance to the forms that metaphysics traditionally assumed in history, this modern humanism "continues to operate within the matrix set down by this tradition, precisely as a militant opposition to it."[56]

What is metaphysics actually comprised of, then, Patočka is prompted to ask by the shortsightedness of the modern perspective, and how does it relate to philosophy as such? Exactly what it is that is supposed to have died is unclear because the question itself has yet to be posed correctly.[57] An examination of metaphysics begins with the pre-Socratic "protophilosophy," for, though we lack a good history of earliest philosophy, it is clear that here an as yet undifferentiated theory began to take shape. This theory took on a form and distinguished itself from other forms of inquiry in the work of the philosopher whom Patočka calls "the last representative of this primordial form of thought": Socrates.[58] In recognizing Socrates as a "representative" of protophilosophy, Patočka is making an argument that is crucial to distinguishing his work from Heidegger's. Rather than follow Heidegger back to the pre-Socratic thinkers and dismiss the insight of the Platonic dialogues, Patočka argues that Socrates is a distinct figure, one needing to be considered separately from the core Platonic writings. Socrates, whether or not a historical reality, differs in that he represents and personifies the "philosophical protoknowledge" that offers a premetaphysical and ontological insight into reality.[59] Socrates is not to be understood as the tradition sees him, as "a mere introductory chapter of Platonism." Socrates is not a witness for the humanism that ensued from the classical tradition; to the contrary, he is opposed to it.[60]

While separating out Socrates for special consideration, Patočka agrees with Heidegger that Plato is the founder of metaphysics. His thesis departs from Heidegger with its conviction that the Socratic dialogues and their depiction of the polis and the role of the philosopher in it are too insightful to be disregarded. Despite this difference, Patočka claims to remain in basic agreement with the approach to metaphysics of which Heidegger is a representative—termed the "new" critique of metaphysics. Unlike the humanist attempt to negate metaphysics and deny the relevance, as in positivism, of questions about human reality not grounded in quantifiable fact, this "new" critique recognized the deadening effects of metaphysical systematization without negating the experiential reality of the human need to look beyond the given.[61] Patočka's own perspective on metaphysics, notwithstanding its distinctness from the Heideggerean critique, also claims to reflect this approach. As he puts it,

> the purpose of these reflections is now to show that this new way
> of overcoming metaphysics, unlike the older attempts, does not
> limit itself to mere negation and does not impoverish humans by
> taking away any essential aspect of their being. . . . For that very
> reason, this new way can understand even metaphysics itself,

taking from it, in a purified form, its essential philosophical thrust and carrying it on.[62]

It is not a rejection of metaphysics that Patočka is after, but an understanding of its internal history, its experiential essence and subsequent abandonment of that essence.

Plato is the creator of metaphysics, yet still he "remains rooted in this premetaphysical soil"; he shows this through his focus on and description of Socrates.[63] The story of metaphysics that Patočka traces begins with Socratic knowledge, setting it in contrast to the metaphysics later developed in Plato and Aristotle. Socratic knowledge, of course, is also known as Socratic ignorance, or, as Patočka notes, as "learned ignorance, that is, as a question."[64] Socrates continually challenges his interlocutors through questions—questions that skeptically analyze assertions based on finite knowledge. The finite, earthly knowledge of particulars commonly thought to constitute wisdom is shown to be faulty and insufficient. It is knowledge that relates only to things directly present, and as a result it ignores the whole. While the Socratic mode of questioning speaks to human life as a whole, it is unable, in keeping with its skeptical nature, to capture that whole in words. This is a human impossibility, Socrates knows, and he unveils this fact as "one of the fundamental contradictions of being human, that between the relation to the whole, intrinsic to humans, and the inability, the impossibility of expressing this relation in the form of an ordinary finite knowledge."[65] This self-understanding is characteristic of Socrates. Plato, however, went beyond the limits of the Socratic model. He set as his goal, and devised a plan to achieve, the transcendence of this situation of fundamental uncertainty. In doing so, in formulating a conception of ideal forms and considering a means to reach them, Plato laid the groundwork for the development of a type of knowledge that is not uncertain or intangible but objective.

The "premetaphysical soil" in which Socrates remains grounded, in contrast, is far from a secure ground. Through his questioning, Socrates casts into doubt the security of those with whom he speaks; he acts so as to "shake" the simple foundations on which they thought they stood safely. He conceives of life as a question without a simple answer—an inherently unsettling formulation. Metaphysics contrasts distinctly with this approach: "[t]he essence of metaphysics as Plato, Aristotle, and Democritus formulated it consists in offering an answer to the Socratic (or pre-Socratic) question, one which the philosopher seeks to derive from the question itself."[66] Plato, in this description, took that step by portraying philosophy as not only as a movement transcending the sensible, but as one seeking to reach the transcendent Being. It was a movement from the "apparent" to the "real" that took place via a dialectical process, a system by which one sought the unconditional, the indubitable.[67] Patočka locates this movement toward a metaphysics first in the Platonic conceptualization of the Ideas and then in the presentation of a conceptual systematics, a dialectic "that permitted an ascent from the sensible to the suprasensible as well as a descent in the opposite direction."[68] This was, Patočka argues, "the first adumbration of a positive (rationalistic) metaphysics" that not only contributed to a philosophy of metaphysics, but to positive science as well, offering a paradigmatic example of a "conceptual systematics" from which Western science took its lead.[69] It was a movement toward a positive form of knowledge distinct from the negative, skeptical approach of Socrates. What was ignorance became a form of knowing, "a true knowledge more secure than anything on earth and in the heavens."[70]

This development changes the face of the fledgling project of philosophy at its very outset. Both Plato and Aristotle moved from a conception of the Idea as "rigorously transcendent" to a consideration of "mundane, astronomic hierarchies." Patočka sums up the results of this movement toward ideal being in no uncertain terms:

> Finally, human comportment, the meaning of human life, too, receives its formation from ideal being. The integrity of human life is broken. Man becomes one of the beings ruled by ideas; ethics and politics as a grand unity take on the task of discovering the inner ideal law of a humanly perfect life. Thus all these metaphysical disciplines, bequeathed to us by the inspired protooriginators and preserved for us by a long tradition, manifest the fundamental substitution of a transcendent, nonexistent Being for the perennial existents [beings], a substitution bound up with the crucial conception of what-is [beings as a whole] as perennial. Thus the living force of transcendence is replaced by an image of reality which may be harmonious, "spiritual," but is rigid and lifeless; so in place of the living reality of Socrates' struggle against the degeneration of life we now have the imitation of the eternal world of Ideas. The absolute claim of truth now appears guaranteed by an invincible conceptual system and actualized in the form of the perfect state. The Idea, the source of absolute truth, becomes at the same time the source of all that is and of all life within it.[71]

Politics and ethics reflect this substitution of the static for the motive, the concrete for the intangible, as much as does philosophy itself. The striving for the perfect state directly relates to the positing of an eternal realm of Ideas, the notion being that no activity is more worthy of man than the attempt to replicate that perfection.

Despite his critique of Plato, Patočka's goal here is still to illuminate a "Platonism." What Plato has done is conceptualize a ground, a soil from which metaphysical thinking could spring. He did not construct a philosophy that could stand solidly on that ground. There is much in the Platonic corpus to make clear that the metaphysical problem had in no way been resolved. It is for this reason that Patočka shifts much of the responsibility for the project of metaphysics, in the end, onto the shoulders of the more systematic and scientific approach taken by Aristotle. It is Aristotle who becomes the standard, the "philosopher" who inspires Western philosophy as well as science. He is so successful that "the attempt to build a science of the absolute, objective, and positive whole crowds out all other motifs and becomes the point of contention for the next two millennia."[72]

Modern humanist thinking tended to replicate anthropologically the goal of "a global understanding of the whole" embodied in metaphysics even as it decried metaphysics itself. It was not until the relatively recent, twentieth-century attempts to dominate social reality on the basis of a radical humanism, however, that this form of thought, newly emboldened by advances in technology, came to its fully mature form.[73] Modern politics, which Patočka describes as embodying a "rule of Force," is grounded in this anthropocentric transformation of metaphysics.[74]

At the heart of Socratic teaching was an experience of freedom. It began with the oracle's injunction to "know thyself." From a positivist perspective, this would mean looking only to "external experience" to fulfill this requirement. The injunction, however, urges us to understand, not only the experience we have, but the experience we are.[75] In the case of Socrates, the experience that we are is the experience of freedom. Socratic knowledge (or ignorance) is absolutely free; the philosopher frees himself from the material and objective limitations to which his interlocutors remain bound, and he can thus master them in the course of the dialectic.

> He could not be that masterful contestant if he were not wholly free, if he were bound to something finite in heaven or on earth. Socrates' mastery is based on an absolute freedom; he is constantly freeing himself of all the bonds of nature, or tradition, of others' schemata as well as of his own, of all physical and spiritual possessions. That is an immensely audacious philosophy.[76]

It is what Socrates articulates in the dialogues. It is a "negative" philosophy in the sense that, instead of positing some positive content, it takes on "the negative character of a distance, of a remove, of an overcoming of every objectivity." Establishing a distance from the positive objects of the world allows us to view them, for the first time, in the context of the whole.[77] Freedom is a perspective of clarity. In articulating this "negative" experience of transcending the objective realm through freedom, Socrates does not enter into metaphysics.

Patočka contrasts "positive" Platonism with his own interpretation of Socratic freedom, a freedom that presumes a "fundamental separation between Ideas and our reality" that in no way seeks to, or is able to, be bridged. This is his "negative Platonism," an interpretation of Platonic philosophy that paves the way for a more authentic approach to human experience. Negative Platonism bases itself, not on metaphysics, but on the historical experience of human beings:

> The interpretation of our human experience, the experience of historical beings, is something in principle different from metaphysics. While metaphysics discovers a new universe, taking it as its starting point and transcending it, the interpretation of experience discovers, uncovers, sheds light on this, our given life-world, uncovering what had been hidden in it, its concealed meaning, its intrinsic structure, its internal drama.[78]

Negative Platonism, Patočka maintains, is an approach to mankind's historical reality that is neither metaphysical nor an anthropocentric humanism. Yet it does not reject the experience of transcendent reality. To the contrary, Patočka seeks to "preserve" this experience—the abiding essence within metaphysics to which it constantly refers. Humanity's yearning for a transcendent reality is not an irrational folly, and the goal here is to understand this desire and explain its source in human experience. There is a reason why "the human spirit returns to metaphysics ever again, . . . in spite of its being indefensible, even meaningless from the standpoint of objective rationality."[79]

Negative Platonism presents itself as a philosophy in the "precarious position" of not having anything to lean against for support. It is an attempt to understand Western philosophy that affirms the experience of transcendence, but not as a distinct realm with positive contents. It argues that, in a certain sense, humans are subject to both a degree of relativity determined by context, and certainty determined by the truth of man's search for what transcends his own particular objective context.

> [Negative Platonism] preserves for humans the possibility of trusting in a truth that is not relative and mundane, even though it cannot be formulated positively, in terms of contents. It shows how much truth there is in man's perennial metaphysical struggle for something elevated above the natural and the traditional, the struggle for the eternal and the supratemporal, in the struggle, taken up ever again, against a relativism of values and norms— even while agreeing with the idea of a basic historicity of man and

of the relativity of his orientation in his context, of his science and practice, his images of life and the world.[80]

Here we have the outline of an approach, crafted in terms of postmodern presumptions, which still offers the possibility of nonrelativistic and transcendent truth. Negative Platonism interprets and affirms ancient philosophy in light of twentieth-century phenomenology and phenomenological ontology. It responds positively to the dilemmas of the postmetaphysical age without disregarding the insights on which that age rests. This is not a "new" philosophy so much as an attempt to understand the material out of which European civilization is woven.

THE IDEA, THE GOOD, AND THE TRUTH

Despite the appeal to Socrates, Patočka's philosophy proceeds from a contemporary perspective. Yet its reliance on the language of classicism leads one to question whether its antimetaphysical claim can be sustained; it speaks, after all, of a "life in truth" and a movement toward "good." Patočka insists that these symbolizations are intrinsic to philosophy by virtue of their reflection of human experience, yet his own perspective precludes the argument that they refer to objective essences that they are in any way solid or tangible. While contemporary theorists are often willing to dismiss any text that relies on such terminology as hopelessly traditional, Patočka wants to persuade us that the terminology can and must be understood nontraditionally, that is, nonmetaphysically. If he is unable to do so, his own work will not succeed: it will face cursory dismissal by postmodern thinkers at the same time as it is viewed with suspicion by traditionalists for its reliance on Heidegger. Negative Platonism gives us an example of this mode of interpretation with its examination of the concept of the "Idea;" it shows that it can be understood differently than the historical understanding of the Platonic Idea. Along with "Idea," Patočka's use of the concepts of "good" and "truth" needs to be examined.

A specific understanding of Idea, carefully distinguished from the Platonic Idea, is prominent in Patočka's early work. Already in 1946, in an article entitled "Ideology and Life in the Idea," the concept is presented as something fundamentally nonobjective. Significantly, it is inherently connected to politics, with both socialism and fascism described as degradations of the logic of the Idea into ideology. The Idea, Patočka notes in this short essay, is that of human freedom.[81]

It is not until "Negative Platonism" in 1953, however, that a concerted effort is made to explain this conclusion, that is, the conception of the Idea as referring to no tangible object. Heidegger's help is again sought, with the

Greek term *chorismos* from his *An Introduction to Metaphysics* used to refer to a separation between ideas and reality. In Patočka's understanding, which leads to a distinctly different conclusion than Heidegger's, *chorismos* does not refer to the kind of separation or gap one might imagine. It is not a gap between two realms of objects, a gap that begs to be bridged:

> [c]horismos meant originally a separateness without a second object realm. It is a gap that does not separate two realms coordinated or linked by something third that would embrace them both and so would serve as the foundation of both their coordination and their separation. *Chorismos* is a separateness, a distinctness *an sich*, an absolute one, for itself.[82]

Chorismos denotes an insuperable distance between reality as it is directly present to us, as objective and tangible, and transcendent reality. It is, one might say, the sense that we are not limited to the objective, that our being can reach beyond the objects of our present vision and broaden its experience of reality. It implies the sense of *freedom* that is inherent to all spiritual experience:

> The mystery of the *chorismos* is like the experience of freedom, an experience of a distance with respect to real things, of a meaning independent of the objective and the sensory which we reach by inverting the original, "natural" orientation of life, an experience of a rebirth, of a second birth, intrinsic to all spiritual life, familiar to the religious, to the initiates of the arts, and, not least, to philosophers.[83]

Chorismos, then, is a symbol of freedom. It is also the symbol of the Idea, for the Idea is not an object, present or transcendent, but instead the very notion that one can free oneself from the power of objectivity.

The understanding of transcendence as Patočka develops it here is crucial to the contention that man is a historical being. In thinking historically, one projects beyond the present into the past and, perhaps, the future. Historical man escapes the bonds of the present and brings into relevance a present that, so to speak, does not exist because it is past. The historian, as well as man as a historical being, is capable of distinguishing between that which is present and that which is no longer present. This is, Patočka argues, the very power of freeing oneself from the present that is implicit in the Idea. He writes:

> A historical being leans on the past, using it to open up the horizon of the given, with its help overcoming the given and the present. He can do that, however, only if the power of dissociation is available to him, the power of dissociation from mere givenness

and presence, the power of liberation from the purely objective and given—in Platonic usage, that is, the power of the Idea.[84]

The Platonic Idea, then, is akin to the freedom to reach beyond the given to embrace even that which is not there in front of us. This understanding of freedom can be applied politically, as in the aforementioned critique of ideology and, as we shall see in the following chapters, in a broader critique of the pursuit of politics as a technology, as a political program that abandons freedom for the surety achieved when one restricts oneself to manipulating the given.[85]

In phenomenology, a thing in general or "as a whole" is necessarily *transcendent* to its perception.[86] Patočka's philosophy draws directly on this insight; it argues through the lens of classical Greek philosophy that European civilization is, or was, characterized by the recognition that life is fully human only to the extent that it can recognize those values, that sense of the whole, that explicitly transcend the objects of our present perception, our simply given experience. This insight is encapsulated in the notion of the Idea. "Thus the Idea," he writes, "is the pure supraobjective call of transcendence."[87] It is not an object but a "deobjectifying power,"[88] the singular human ability to perceive the transcendental and to act on it, thereby preserving the possibility of a life in truth.

The Idea, I have noted, is a link between philosophy and the social and political realms. The Platonic Idea developed so as to present itself to man positively, as an absolute ideal in which he could participate. It became something obtainable, and mankind, uniquely capable of obtaining it, was challenged to demonstrate this uniqueness by dominating his world. Understood in this way, "positive" Platonism urged man to conceive of himself as a being without limits, a being capable of anything, unrestricted. This is the self-understanding, Patočka argues, that has resulted in a politics of force, in "the twentieth-century as war."[89] Because of its importance, the relevant text deserves to be cited at length:

> The Idea, as we understand it, is not the power of absolute objectification—as the historic Plato's Idea promises to be. As the absolute object, Plato's Idea is a challenge to man to place himself at the center of the *universum* and to dominate it, the way he finally does dominate the entire intelligible and sensible cosmos through the Idea, through participation in the ideal *universum*. This tendency of Platonic metaphysics did not have its full effect and flowering in Plato's own philosophy or in antiquity and the Middle Ages since there it was still blanketed by the overall mythical or theological orientation of the men of the time. Modern metaphysics, however, with its anthropologism and its will to total supremacy of men over object beings, with its naturalism,

constructivism (technicism), and will to power represents the full unfolding of a tendency which is potentially present already here. By contrast, Platonism as we here interpret it shows forth not only man's dignity but also the limits he cannot transcend. It approves the rule humans are instituting over object being but shows that man's calling is not so to rule but to serve. It shows that there is something higher than man, something to which human existence is indissolubly bound and without which the most basic wellsprings of our historical life dry up.[90]

Here, in the early 1950s in a text inspired by a critique of positive metaphysics, we have an example of the very language later used by Patočka to justify the grounds on which the human rights protest Charter 77 was founded—language appealing to something that is "higher" than both man and his government, something that limits man morally and reins in his desire to rule. While in the texts on Charter 77 Patočka appears to be speaking in metaphysical (Kantian) terms, urging the communist government to bow down before an objective morality, here in "Negative Platonism" and throughout his discussion of "care for the soul" he is adamant in declaring that his philosophy is inherently "deobjectifying." This philosophy rejects the notion of a higher objectivity, a higher Being that defines our limits for us. It is instead the power of transcendence that limits us, the power of our ability to transcend the present, objective realm, to see beyond objectivity altogether and thereby take account of the inherently nonobjective world as a whole. With this argument, to which I will return in the following chapters, the groundwork is laid for an explicit approach to human ethics and, indirectly, to politics.

In addition to the concept of the Idea, Patočka's work also does not avoid the terms *good* and *truth*. Yet it is made clear that they, too, are not to be understood as objective values or entities, but rather in terms of the movements of life and openness to the world as a whole. In "Eternity and Historicity," a work from the 1950s belonging to the cycle of "Negative Platonism" texts and only recently published in Czech, Patočka notes that the Socratic question concerns the "good." What is the content of this concept, we have to ask? In asking after the good Socrates is seeking the "single, universal fundamental goal of human life."[91] It is an intense and specific question that has, regrettably, lost its relevance over time. Now it is commonplace to hear one ask in the broadest terms about the meaning of life; but this is a far cry from the question posed by Socrates. How, then, should the original question be understood?

> This question in its original Socratic intensity means: what is the goal in life which is not itself directed as a means to any other goal? Where is the unity to which it is possible to subordinate

one's whole life to the end and without exceptions? And to this question Socrates himself has no positive answer, he rather admits that he does not know.[92]

For the true philosopher, there can be no positive answer. What we receive from Socrates, exemplified in his activity, is "care for the soul." This becomes, then, the Socratic answer to the question of the good, of the goal of life. "Philosophy as the care for the soul is the Socratic answer to the Socratic question."[93]

The good as care for the soul is not a positive answer to the Socratic question, for care for the soul is not a positive, objective thing, but a human movement directed toward a growth in human being itself. There is no reference to an objectivity situated in the heavens or on earth. The good as care for the soul refers instead to a mere possibility in human life, yet it is a possibility that is solid and intrinsic to human existence. As I stated earlier, the existence of the good as the goal of movement is meaningful only insofar as there is such movement, only insofar as, by moving toward the good, something is effecting a heightening of its being.[94] The good can be no solid object or value, existing and unchanging regardless of human attention or indifference to it. It inherently relates to human action, to a movement that is not arbitrary or related to our desires, but is a result of the active nurturing of the soul, the upward formation of our being. This reflects the reality of our soul, that it not only is, but must also be cared for or formed.

This process of caring for the soul, of moving toward the good, is something the human being must undertake in his or her own life. It cannot be encapsulated in a few rules for living; life is not, as the Sophists understood it, a technical problem. It is not possible to live well in the same way as it is possible, say, to be a good shoemaker.[95] And so, "for this reason Socrates also cannot in his own sense preach, as (based on misunderstanding) Xenophon's Socrates does; for Socrates does not have any dogma which he could recommend to people, and no positive moral teachings which could be translated into recipes for life; his work is to wake people to their own being, to their own essence."[96] In traditional metaphysics, the good receives objective form such that it can be translated into dogma or "recipes" for living. For Patočka the good has no such form. It takes shape instead as people are awakened to their possibilities. Socrates moves toward the good as he wakes himself and wakes others to their own being.

Negative Platonism, just as it rejects objectified versions of the Idea and the good, also rejects the objectification of a single, eternal truth. The contours of that "negative" Platonic version of truth are discussed in a companion article to "Negative Platonism" called "The Problem of Truth from the Perspective of Negative Platonism." This essay begins with a description of the problem of truth, said to be "from the beginning the basic question of philosophy," and the various ways in which it has been interpreted in the modern world.[97] It concludes that the problem not only has not been solved, it has not even been adequately framed. In framing the question from the point of view of negative Platonism, Patočka notes that truth is "*finite* truth," in that it is "the truth of a finite being."[98] Finite truth is revealed to finite beings in the course of history, in the problematic process of making sense out of human life.

Though finite, truth is not arbitrary. Its foundation, which is described as "absolute," is contained in our conscious relation to the Idea discussed in "Negative Platonism." That is, our ability for truth is dependent on our ability to distance ourselves, or free ourselves, from the hold of objective beings. The freedom of the Idea is a necessary, and reciprocal, component of truth. "Truth is that which frees man and that which is therefore far from being a work of man, to the contrary, it forms man."[99] Though truth is finite, we do not create it. It is embedded in human freedom, and the call to truth is a call of freedom. Only through free action can we hope to see things clearly and act truthfully toward them. Freedom is no guarantee of truth, but it is its source:

> Freedom, which forever withdraws us from objectivity and by whose power we always exist partially beyond the reach of reality, which is thus at the source of the most varied illusions and errors, is nevertheless also the source of all truth; for without it there is no distance towards reality, and so also clarity about it, except for the immediate functioning of instinctive signals and conformative reactions.[100]

The call to truth, to freedom, also opens us up to the possibility of error. It is an invitation to uncertainty and is therefore grounded in risk. Metaphysical truth, in contrast, provides life with the certainty that it otherwise lacks. It's objective, transcendent foundation acts as a palliative to the anxiety we are heir to as human.[101]

In setting his own perspective in contrast to metaphysics, Patočka further differentiates his understanding of truth. It is not and can never be something solid and simple, requiring neither deliberation nor decision. Truth is not something we can easily get hold of, and even less something that we can carry around with us in security. It is instead an elusive and disproportionate component of our active lives, present when we act in freedom, when we "turn" from error and decline and begin to ascend.

> From the fact that truth is disproportion—that it's never given and, if passively received or spontaneously offered in ready form, can never be other than a treacherous *fata morgana*—results the unstableness and precariousness of truth. It cannot actually

"be"—it is nothing defined, definite (only in the form of its always relative and inadequate expression), but is rather defining. We always lag behind truth, always guiltily, and it exists for us only in the form of a *turn* [my emphasis], an attempt at focusing, in the form of a reaction against the mistake, error, decline, into which we are absorbed in our original passivity.[102]

The truth of metaphysics relies on it being present whether we are active or passive, whether we reach out and seek it or not. Thinking nonmetaphysically, truth is seen to relate to our activity and movement in life, to our seeking to heighten our being. Truth is not constant, but neither is it arbitrary or wholly contingent. Truth, like freedom, forms us.

Patočka's search for good and truth without recourse to metaphysics is an exceptionally difficult, perhaps impossible, task. In the final chapter of this study I will examine the attempt in greater detail. In terms of Patočka's phenomenological treatment of Greek philosophy, however, one important objection must be dealt with immediately: the objection that Socrates cannot and should not be distinguished from the Platonic corpus, that he, too, was engaged in plainly metaphysical speculation about good and truth. The substance of this objection argues that Patočka's "negative" Platonic interpretation of Socrates is misplaced, for Socrates was in fact searching for a new and undiscovered *good* that underlies all relative goods. With his insistence on moral consistency and a "life in truth," Jan Patočka can be said to represent the same metaphysical lineage that he claims to circumnavigate. Focusing on Socrates instead of on Plato as a whole does not acquit one of the charge of being metaphysical, for the line of demarcation between the two is a false one (or at least Patočka does not succeed in drawing it convincingly). Socrates, and so also the Patočkan theory based on his mode of understanding, is engaged in a search for an undiscovered "other world" that must be considered a metaphysical construction.

In response to this critique, Patočka defends Socrates and thereby his own interpretation. Socrates is not engaged, he argues, in an abstract venture. He is concerned not with discovering something new, such as the metaphysical essence of good, but something old: the meaning of the concrete good with which we deal in our daily lives. The critique, Patočka writes, "misses that which Socrates really wants and to which he dedicates his untiring activity. Socrates' question first gets its true meaning at the point when it is not a question seeking after something new, but after the true sense of the old, after the true meaning of all the good which has always occurred in life."[103] Socrates is seeking to understand phenomena that he knows must be transcended in order to be understood. The transcendence is skeptical, it is not a transcendence toward a metaphysical foundation. It is achieved by establishing a certain distance from the particular and material aspects of the phenomena and examining them in that light. In that process, the object of contemplation is viewed freely and without distortion, and so is open to greater human understanding. Socrates does not seek a new good, he seeks the meaning of the good that we encounter in daily life.

The Socratic mode of life leaves us with uncertainty, but it does not leave us aimless. Socrates is not searching for a new certainty in the heavens because he knows that such a search does not increase our self-understanding, it distorts it. He argues that in place of metaphysical certainty there is a human consistency, grounded in the way in which we live and the way in which we interrogate reality. Rejecting metaphysical certainty is a vital act, for it appears to leave us defenseless and insecure, while in fact it offers us a unity and a security of a different, particularly human form.

> Socrates consequently refutes presumed certainty and at the same time invites a persistence, a continuity in this fundamental decision of vital importance. This work points toward an unheard of inner unity and vital concentration: so that even when there isn't a positive, general and content-related answer, still the question itself, if abided to, as untiring activity effects in man that after which he asks.[104]

Rather than destroying continuity, this skeptical mode of being opens us to a life that is truly human, for it is a life that aims toward an ever-increasing understanding of itself and its world, the natural world with which it interacts. And it is this "inner unity" and "continuity" that forms the basis for action geared toward the establishment of ethical and political order in human life, as we shall see in the following chapters.

I have sought to show that the character of Patočka's interpretation of classical philosophy, expressed most directly in his formulations of care for the soul and negative Platonism, offers a compelling, contemporary alternative to the rejection of classicism in much of the thought influenced by Heidegger. Patočka's engagement with Greek thought is a positive engagement, despite its taking place in an antimetaphysical context. It shows that there is a distinct difference between the essence of metaphysics, the impulse to transcend the objective, and the systematization of metaphysics that abandons its own essence and takes on an objective form itself. The figure of Socrates, far from representing the degradation of philosophy, as Nietzsche would have it, epitomizes this difference.

Patočka shows that philosophy is not only possible in the wake of metaphysics, it takes on its full meaning only when it rejects metaphysics and returns to the negative insight and uncertainty of life as care for the soul. This classical symbolism, in turn, is shown to refer to an ontological self-interestedness, to a movement toward a heightening of one's being and a realization of its possibilities. It is a forward movement, yet not a movement toward a particular, transcendental goal. Human movement toward the good is, in Patočka's formulation, movement in ignorance of any final goal. And yet it is characterized by a consistency, a degree of certainty such that the person who lives by examining reality and does not take it for granted will have more, not less, harmony and excellence. As Patočka puts it, "[o]n the basis of this ignorance of the final goal, which explicates itself in continual questioning and examination, there appears the possibility of a just life, harmonious and concentrated; there appears a life with an avoidance of mistakes, a life as it should be, a life with its specific *arete*, its perfection."[105]

In chapters 2 and 3 I have discussed the groundwork on which Patočka bases his engagement with human historical and political existence. It is his interpretation of the phenomenological and ontological work of Husserl and Heidegger, and his application of it to Plato and Socrates, that create the theoretical conditions on which he is able to offer the philosophy of history and politics found in his *Heretical Essays on the Philosophy of History* and other late writings.

4

A Philosophy of History and a Theory of Politics

Despite international renown for his work in phenomenology, Patočka's most influential text is his 1975 collection of *Heretical Essays in the Philosophy of History*. Distinguished by what the French philosopher Paul Ricoeur has called a "sense of grandeur" and a "dense beauty,"[1] the *Heretical Essays* represent the culmination of Patočka's mature philosophy; they aim at an understanding of human reality in which history, philosophy, and politics merge, forming a perspective on being and society that constitutes the Czech philosopher's most important contribution to contemporary political thought.

The *Heretical Essays* coalesce around a philosophy of history and an analysis of European civilization based on two fundamental contentions: first, Patočka argues that the emergence of the Greek polis, and of politics itself, constituted a "breakthrough" in human history, an event that conceptualized human freedom and marked the first time humans confronted the possibility of acting in a truly historical manner. In this period, in this simultaneous rise of politics and philosophy, the spirit of Western civilization was born. It is also Patočka's contention, however, that Western history since the age of the polis is marked by a series of developments that represent the abandonment of the possibility presented by this breakthrough. The present state of the European world, vividly described in his final two essays, is characterized by the prevalence of a desire, not for a genuinely historical life, but for a life that offers a solution to the problematicity and vicissitudes of history—a life geared toward an end of history. With the analysis of history and politics that is the capstone of these essays, Patočka attempts to provide philosophy and politics in the West with an alternative to its present situation; he tries to illuminate a mode of politics that is consistent with the principles of classical political theorizing, even as it is aware of and in conformity with the most perceptive of the insights of contemporary philosophy.

Patočka's analysis of the contemporary world, which I discuss in detail in chapter 5, points above all to difficulties stemming from the void of meaning in human life that has been increasingly predominant since the twilight of traditional forms of metaphysics diagnosed by Nietzsche. We live in a postmetaphysical world yet we remain beings who cannot exist for long in a situation of pervasive meaninglessness. Insofar as the norm of contemporary life in the West is the basically nihilistic worldview of mathematical natural science, it is not surprising for humans to seek options that are meaningful (that is, full of meaning). The twentieth century has been marked by the rise and fall of one such option after another. Politically, the human desire for metaphysical certainty and positive meaning has manifested itself in political or philosophical systems that amounted to secularized and often radical versions of metaphysics "in which humans or humanity step into God's place."[2]

Yet these movements, despite their success in particular regions, have not succeeded in gaining worldwide support. There are also countries, particularly those with liberal democratic traditions, which have been able to resist the urge to transform the realm of politics into a substitute for metaphysical meaning. But this alternative, it is argued, is not a solution to the problem. Political formulations grounded in the nihilistic assumptions of the natural sciences—formulations that order humans as one would material objects—do not satisfy the desire for meaning. The human as self is replaced by the human as role (even "equality" is a role!)[3] So it appears that both the natural meaning of prephilosophical societies and the given meaning of traditional metaphysics have been overcome, and nothing has been left in their place but political radicalism as a substitute for meaning, or the conviction that we can live full and complete lives on the basis of a scientific methodology that views us in neutral, material terms. Neither approach, Patočka contends, responds to the needs of human social being. The politics of radicalism offers humans false meaning, while the scientific approach avoids the question of meaning altogether and thereby prompts people to seek either substitutions for meaning or an "escape" from the question altogether. Theories that discard the question of meaning are as insufficient as the positive meaning of metaphysics they seek to replace. Patočka writes:

> God is dead, yet the material nature, producing with lawlike necessity both humankind and its progress, is no less a fiction and it has the special weakness that it includes no mechanism that would restrain individuals in their individual effort to escape and make themselves at home in the contingent world as if no one were to come after them, having their little pleasures of the day, their pleasures of the night.[4]

The United States, perhaps more than other countries, lacks a mechanism to "restrain individuals" in their pursuit of substitutes for transcendental meaning or, even more problematically, their pursuit of means to "escape" the question of meaning altogether. The particular dilemma of the contemporary world is that, since Nietzsche and Heidegger, the destruction of metaphysics has not led to an understanding of history or of meaning.

Nietzsche's diagnosis of Europe as nihilistic "sums up all the crises of the time: the political and the social crises are rooted in a moral crisis."[5] What is lacking is an understanding of meaning in human life and its relation to historical action. This would provide, not only the possibility of a political solution, but also a means to alleviate the ethical anomie of contemporary life.

Patočka states in the *Essays* that a philosophical understanding of the human being and his interaction with the world must contain, at its core, a philosophy of history. The elemental fact of historicity means that an analysis of human activity can be successful only once the implications of that historicity have been clearly defined. The human being is a historical being, but this does not mean that all human activity is historical. Humans do not act historically insofar as they live only to put food on the table and keep from dying. It is as they create a politics in order to discuss issues of greater importance than the mere preservation of life that they epitomize historical action. Patočka's political thought, from his reconceptualization of human freedom to his understanding of the polis as an institutionalization of freedom, can be grasped only through an analysis of his philosophy of history.

Rather than attempt to solve the question of history, Patočka's work tries to understand it as a problem. Understanding its problematicity, therefore, is crucial to the incorporation of freedom into everyday activity as well as to our prospects for a recovery from the devastating political reality of the past century. As we continue to misunderstand history by seeking to solve it, we rule ourselves in a way that is not consistent, but arbitrary or "accidental." It is for this reason that Patočka points to the "chief possibility" of our civilization as the "possibility of a turn from accidental rule to the rule of those who understand what history is about."[6]

In order to arrive at a coherent sense of Patočka's political theory, we have to begin with human historicity and the specific way he understands it. From here I can proceed to the thesis, drawn from Edmund Husserl, that history in this specific sense has a particular "beginning," and that this beginning coincides with the origin of the science of politics. It is in the emergence of the Greek polis, Patočka contends, that freedom and problematicity come to be first revealed as themes of human existence. From here, the birth of politics out of freedom, I follow Patočka as he traces the progressive estrangement of both politics and philosophy from their beginnings. This discussion of history brings us not only to a new conceptualization of the basic content of politics and its roots in historical action, but also to a consideration of two further problems: the crisis of politics in the twentieth century (chapter 5), and the more fundamental problem of the foundation that underlies our self-understanding as human beings (chapter 6).

THE BASIS OF HUMAN HISTORICITY

It is important to note, as Erazim Kohák does in his philosophical biography of the thinker, that Patočka was a historian of ideas in addition to a philosopher. He wrote extensively, for example, on two of the greatest figures in Czech political and philosophical history: Jan Amos Komenský (Comenius), and T. G. Masaryk.[7] It would be a mistake, though, to conclude from this that Patočka was interested in recording the history of philosophy in any sort of objective, historicist manner. In the first place, the extensive work done on Comenius was as much a product of circumstance as the fulfillment of a genuine desire to create a historical record. Under the Czechoslovak communist regime, Patočka was repeatedly denied the right to work, teach, or publish in his chosen specialty, and was grateful to find meaningful employment and opportunity to publish as an archivist in the Masaryk Institute and then, after that was dissolved by the authorities, at the Comenius Archive of the Pedagogic Institute in Prague.

Patočka was, in all respects, a philosopher of history. His approach was distinguished by a clear and unambiguous critique of the study of history as a search for an objective order or governing natural laws. The objective order of history offered no clue to human meaning, even though human meaning occurred explicitly within the order of history. Patočka focused on history, but he was no historicist. Nor did he believe that history could usefully be studied in compartmentalized form, as, for example, the isolated study of "economic history" or the "history of philosophy." Such studies, he wrote, offered us "so little satisfaction" as to make us aware of the need "to widen our perspective."[8] History, as Patočka understands it, cannot be observed "objectively" as by a disinterested observer; the recording of events and the keeping of annals, therefore, does not constitute the writing of history.

A proper understanding of history is essential to philosophy because the human being is inherently and continually a historical creature. Historicity is a condition of his being, demonstrated in his most basic activities. One of those activities is speech—the use of language. Throughout, Patočka consistently claims that individuals are not open to the possibilities of their lives until they overcome the hold that the world of things has on them. In "Negative Platonism," it is the human ability to communicate via language that proves to be crucial to our effectively dealing with this world of things, thereby preserving the possibility of rising above that world. The central point is that, with language, we not only respond to things, we anticipate them. In doing so, we demonstrate our ability to transcend the given present.[9] Through language we can move beyond the limits of the present, making language "thus a history, not a structure given once and for all." "This historicity," Patočka continues, "of the structure of language, however, is possible only because humans are not fixed in their relation to sense data because they are 'free.'"[10] Through language we confirm our freedom in terms of objects of the senses; we show that we can create a certain "distance" from things and, in doing so, transcend the immediate necessity of their hold on us. In language we project temporally beyond the present moment and object. "Here we become aware that every assertion, and so also language as a whole, presupposes the temporal horizon intrinsic to man, a horizon of ongoing experience."[11] This is the horizon of our historicity.

It is not only language that demonstrates our historicity, however. We are also historical because, as Heidegger notes, we are interested in our own being and we reach out in seeking to form it, to give it substance. This is a historical act, for history is not simply defined by the events that take place before our eyes, but also by our engaging in those activities that are most fully human—in other words, by pursuing a heightening of our own being. Here the influence of Husserl and Heidegger on Patočka's philosophy of history demands attention even though, in the end, the Czech pursues a different course than either of his German teachers.

Although it is Husserl to whom Patočka is indebted for inspiring a focus on European history and its central axis of "the idea of rational insight and life based on it (i.e., a life in responsibility)," it is only with the help of Heidegger that he is able to work out the specifics of a philosophy of history that avoids an extreme subjectivism.[12] The influence of both Husserl and Heidegger is evident even in Patočka's earliest writings. For instance, in his very first essay on the subject of history, the 1934 piece entitled "Some Comments Concerning the Concepts of History and Historiography," a focus on an understanding of human freedom as the crucial element to our historicity betrays an early study of Heidegger—specifically, as Erazim Kohák notes, of the first division of *Being and Time*.[13] This emphasis did not characterize all of Patočka's early work on history, though, for in another article written just a year later the emphasis on Heideggerean themes is entirely absent. Instead, "Some Comments Concerning the Concept of a 'World History'" from 1935 begins by expanding on the critique of the positivistic approach to history mentioned in the earlier article. What is described in 1935 as a "naive historical positivism" that reduces history "to whatever can be objectified," is more reminiscent of Husserl's critique of the "misguided" rationalism of the European sciences in his "Vienna Lecture" than of any Heideggerean theme.[14] The political direction in which Patočka takes his reflections in this article is, as we shall see, also quite non-Heideggerean.

The different lines of thought evident in these early essays are reconciled only forty years later, in the *Heretical Essays on the Philosophy of History*. Here the relationship between history and phenomenology is explicitly dealt with, and the relative merits of the Husserlian and Heideggerean approaches directly compared. Patočka compares Husserl and Heidegger on the question of history because he is convinced that history is crucial to the pursuit of phenomenology. Although it might seem that phenomenology as Husserl first elaborated it was primarily concerned with static phenomena, Patočka notes a shift in interest in Husserl's work toward the motive, the genetic element of phenomena. This shift is evidence, he argues, for the importance of historical analysis to phenomenological philosophy.

> In the course of his intellectual career, Husserl increasingly stressed the genetic over static analysis, as well as the role of passive genesis, the genesis of all presumably merely given components of lived experience in internal time consciousness. Everything that is static points to a genesis and so to history. *Thus history is the deepest content level which phenomenology can reach.*" (emphasis added)[15]

Yet Husserl's approach to history, though it points in the right direction, cannot be considered genuinely historical. This is because it bases its understanding of "deep" phenomena on the perspective of an impartial subjectivity, a "disinterested spectator." Claiming a disinterested status, it betrays "a subjectivity that is fundamentally ahistorical in our sense of the term."[16] Heidegger, in contrast, resists the attempt to establish a disinterested perspective as the basis for an understanding of being. His analysis is therefore historical where Husserl's fails to be.

> By contrast, Heidegger's conception is historical, not only in the sense that phenomenological analysis leads to a definite genesis but most of all in rejecting the disinterested spectator as a presupposition of phenomenologizing. Instead, it focuses on an interest in being as the starting point and the condition for understanding the deep phenomenon, the phenomenon of being.[17]

We act historically in those moments when we demonstrate that we are human, that is, in those moments when we take an interest in and actively care for our humanity, our being, our soul.

Patočka considered the methodology pioneered by Heidegger to be "better suited to serve as a starting point for philosophizing about history" because it was grounded in the understanding that we are interested in our own being, and it sought to investigate the problems of freedom and responsibility that accompanied that interest.[18] In this, Heidegger's work would help to shed light on the nature of historical action while Husserl's was unable to. Patočka, then, is quite explicit in his use of Heideggerean themes in the *Heretical Essays*. He notes as much in the second of his essays, but also makes clear that the deductions he derives from his study of Heidegger are entirely his own.[19]

Despite Patočka's use of Heideggerean motifs, it would be inaccurate to conclude that Patočka of the *Heretical Essays* has become what one might call a "Heideggerean." Patočka is explicit to keep his use of Heideggerean motifs consistent with his assumption of an ethics that firmly rejects relativism and nihilism. Ethics and the need to assure concrete freedom within a political setting are of concern to Patočka throughout his career, and he finds that it is not only possible to reconcile these themes with Heideggerean philosophy, it is necessary to examine them in its light. Only in this way, he argues, can we hope to comprehend the unique situation in which the human being finds himself.

While Patočka begins from Heideggerean motifs, he proceeds to make "deductions" from them for which he alone is responsible. The general tenor of these conclusions, with their emphasis on concrete political and ethical comportment, could in fact be said to often run directly counter to the Heideggerean approach, which exhibits a distinct lack of interest in these elements of human life. In contrast to Heidegger and to many of his followers (the seminal figure of Hannah Arendt excepted), Patočka attempts to show a consonance between Heideggerean ontophenomenological motifs and the type of philosophy developed by Socrates, with its emphasis on both truth and morality and its setting, not in a secluded forest hut or a distant Academy, but directly in the center of human society—in the polis. In the analysis of Patočka's philosophy of history and politics to follow, it will be readily apparent that, even as the Czech philosopher continues to make use of Heideggerean concepts, he derives conclusions from them as to the relationship of politics and philosophy that are distinct from the arguments of contemporary Heideggerean scholarship.

A PHILOSOPHY OF HISTORY

Patočka's interest in history led him, first of all, to distinguish it from mere historiography, from the simple recording of events. Action was truly historical, he contended, when it established a continuity with the future by grounding itself, not in the instinctual desire for self-preservation, but in the characteristically human potential for self-reflection and freedom. We act as historical beings simultaneously with our reflective consideration of the possibilities open to us. The epochal moment for the Western world came with the development of philosophy. Philosophy marked a turning point in human self-understanding; it marked the development of a mode of activity that was explicitly self-reflective and skeptical of simply given knowledge. By invoking a claim to reason, philosophers gave up the surety of such knowledge in favor of a problematic, but characteristically human, approach to life. From this point onward one could speak of events relating, not merely to the desire for self-preservation, but to the possibility inherent in a being who is interested in his own being. It marked the beginning of the mode of human activity to which Patočka refers when he speaks of "historical" activity.

As I indicated in chapter 2, the influence of Husserl's *Crisis of European Sciences* on Patočka's development was inordinate, and this is nowhere more true than in the latter's philosophy of history. Although he does not follow Husserl in insisting on a subjective transcendental phenomenology, he does adopt the basic outline of history that Husserl controversially proposes in *Crisis*. Patočka's adoption of that outline, with its positing of a "prehistory" and a "history proper," is somewhat surprising; it appears, on the surface, to be superficial and counterintuitive. Looking beneath the surface, though, one finds a carefully differentiated concept of history and an argument that is cogent and well defended. History, in Patočka's account, does not refer to human activity as such, but to that activity made possible by our ontological self-awareness. History is primarily determined by the depth of the relation of the human to his own being. Patočka's philosophy of history, then, has a Husserlian framework but an ontological core. In the early chapters of the *Heretical Essays*, this framework is discussed in detail and the relevant concepts analyzed in terms of their ontological significance.

Before proceeding, some difficulties presented by Husserl's framework need to be considered. In the first place, as I explained in chapter 3, Husserl's speculative philosophy—including his philosophy of history—suffered from the lingering influence of Cartesian philosophy, resulting in not only an inappropriate subjectivism but also a misguided hope that one could methodologically transform philosophy into an "apodictic" science.[20] This latter aspect is particularly problematic, for it seems to imply that Husserl's framework for history is tied to the very dream of absolute knowledge against which the Heideggerean critique is directed. Yet Patočka makes it very clear that not only does he not follow Husserl in this pursuit, the very idea of such an apodictic certainty in philosophy is impossible. He refers directly to Husserl when he writes that:

> Philosophically it is not possible to preserve (i) the postulate of philosophy as an absolutely apodictic science, or (ii) the idea that a transcendental idealism . . . would either correspond to this idea or could guarantee to the world the meaningfulness which the struggle against a merely factological science and against a privately subjective philosophy of mere world views demands. (In particular, it cannot resolve the question of truth and of transcendence.)[21]

Philosophy searches for a meaningfulness that is neither "privately subjective" nor "merely factological," but it is impossible to achieve that meaningfulness through a philosophical search for apodicticity. Philosophy cannot lead to absolute certainty.

A second problem, which I will discuss in more detail shortly, has to do with the apparent reduction of all of human history to the European experience. This trait, in light of the increasing awareness of non-Western cultures and the content of their cultural and intellectual traditions, represents a weakness in Patočka's work that may be hard for many readers to overcome. The weakness is not debilitating, however.

The center of gravity of Patočka's philosophy of history responds to the deficiencies of Husserl's work. History is redefined, in the *Heretical Essays*, in terms of a fundamental ontology. The recording of events is not history; events are historical only insofar as we are interested in them because they have a lasting effect on us. History, Patočka writes,

> is meaningful or meaning-related only when someone cares about something, when we do not have before us sequences merely observed but rather ones which can be understood in terms of an interest in and relating to the world, of an openness for oneself and for things.[22]

Only with this addition can Patočka propose Husserl's outline of history as a starting point. The understanding gained by the ontological analysis forms the basis of Patočka's philosophy; the analysis of the relation of history to the rise of the Greek polis provides the basis for a theory of politics.

Patočka's philosophy of history incorporates two major elements: the first is the question of the origin of history and its significance for Europe, and the second is an analysis of the content of historical action and its importance for our self-understanding. The content of history is human activity in and for freedom. Historical activity incorporates the realization "that there are possibilities of living differently than by toiling for a full stomach in misery and need." It is in this sense that history as Patočka strictly defines it is tied directly to the outburst of civilization in ancient Greece: "The Greek polis, epos, tragedy, and philosophy are different aspects of the same thrust which represents a rising above decline."[23]This thesis, when applied to the social being of humans in light of contemporary, postmetaphysical theory, constitutes a wholly new approach to the question of the ground of politics.

Husserl and Eurocentrism

Apart from its Heideggerean influences, Patočka's philosophy of history is also distinguished by a further Husserlian element that bears discussion at the start, for it represents a weakness inherent to this line of thought. It is the notion, again drawn from Husserl's *Crisis* texts, that the very concept of history itself, is essentially Western. In the *Heretical Essays*, Patočka describes the Husserlian account quite explicitly:

> Edmund Husserl speaks of European history as a teleological nexus whose axis is the idea of rational insight and life based on it (i.e., responsibility). In his view, this teleological idea distinguishes European culture from all others; at the same time, the idea of a life in reason, the insight-ful life, singles out Europe from among other cultures as the essential among the contingent. Insight and reason are the "inborn" idea of humanity as such; thus the European spirit is at the same time universally human. European culture and civilization are universally valid; the others only particular, however interesting they may be.[24]

Patočka recognizes that, on its face, this seems a naive form of rationalism; nevertheless, he ascribes to its main point, that "history," as he will define it, is primarily a European phenomenon and central to the brand of phenomenological philosophy that he is pursuing.[25] The basis of this conclusion, simply stated, is that history is directly related to the emergence of philosophy, which is itself a Greek, or European, phenomenon. And it is via the "process of philosophizing" traceable to the Greeks that the world or, as Patočka puts it, the "whole of beings," is uniquely able to reveal itself, to manifest its own nature.[26]

The key elements here are first of all the claim that the European spirit, the spirit of reason, is universally human, and second, that it is only via philosophy as it developed in Europe that it can become manifest to us as a theme of our existence. As a concept, reason coherently describes the quest for understanding definitive of human existence. Further, it can be argued convincingly that the European heritage, particularly the heritage of ancient

Athens, is an unparalleled attempt to uncover the nature of this quality, an attempt that resulted in social and political institutions based, not on the model of the household, but on reason as the basis for the conduct of human affairs. Where Husserl's account runs into trouble is with the assumption that European philosophy is not only the best, that is, the most highly differentiated, account of human rationality, but it is the only account that in any way points toward the experience of reason. The philosophical thought of non-Western cultures, the argument goes, simply did not achieve a conceptualization of reason as the essential human characteristic, and so is necessarily secondary in comparison to Europe. This conclusion, however, appears to be based on a merely superficial glance at non-Western or mythical achievements and a dismissal of the content of those experiences.[27] Such a superficial glance is decidedly insufficient.

The question at hand is not one of comparing contemporary European civilization with non-European, however; Europe, too, has failed to embrace its own heritage and has lived largely under the influence of metaphysical transfigurations of reality. But in European history, at various moments, history (as Patočka defines it) has broken out and the heritage of insight and care for the soul has been reflected in human actions. The goal with respect to the non-European world must be to examine other cultures with an eye toward similar moments, albeit in different form. Following Husserl, Patočka fails to extend his search beyond the limits of the European experience. A claim of universal validity, however, as both Husserl and Patočka present it, demands at a minimum a more wide-ranging exploration.

There is, therefore, an element of reductionism in Patočka's presentation and reliance on Husserl's attempt at philosophy of history. Yet the Czech philosopher is not so naive as to ignore the implications of his reduced scope of history. He defends this scope by arguing that the insight that defines European civilization has but a single pole—the pole of philosophy.

> Commonly it is said that European culture, or whatever you call it, has two poles: the first is the Judeo-Christian tradition and the second is antiquity. In my view, as I have tried to characterize it, Europe stands on a single pole, and that is so because Europe is insight, Europe is life founded on insight.

That pole is Greek philosophy; the Judeo-Christian tradition, while fundamental to European history, had its effect only after it had been Hellenized:

> The Judaic, which is of course enormously important in the Judeo-Christian tradition, had to Hellenize itself, had first to travel through Greek thought, in order that it could become that which it is for Europe. Christian dogmas are spoken about, but

Christian dogmas nevertheless justified themselves. Christian dogmas were not merely myths. And the thought itself of the other world, the other, just world, and of the deity who is a deity of pure good, this is nowhere other than in Plato, it is there for the first time.[28]

Although this argument in outline has a certain cogency, it is insufficiently defended by historical research. The research required, no small amount, was most likely well beyond the realm of possibility given the restrictions placed on Patočka's academic freedom. This is regrettable, for such research would greatly strengthen the conclusions reached without necessarily contradicting the main thrust of the argument—that the contribution to humanity offered by Greek philosophy is indeed unique, and in no way more so than in its use as the ground on which to construct social and political institutions. It is perhaps here, in the confluence of philosophy and political freedom, that the Greek, or European, heritage is most unique and, perhaps, most universal. The promise of this historical epoch, however, remains undelivered, even (if not especially) in Europe. It is Patočka's hope that, by uncovering its roots and reexamining them through the penetrating lenses of contemporary philosophy, he can encourage or effect change, not only in the way mankind lives, but in the way it organizes itself politically.

Prehistory and the Beginning of History

Despite the attention paid to the Husserlian and Heideggerean influences in Patočka's work, Patočka's conception of history was not limited to what he learned from his two teachers. In "Some Comments Concerning the Concept of a 'World History'" from 1935, for example, Heidegger is not mentioned and his influence seems negligible; instead, Patočka's own concerns come to the fore: namely, a prominent concern for the specificity of history and its relation to the concrete world. This article introduces a concept of history as present, not in novel events or occurrences, but in actions that reflect continuity, actions of "more than individual significance in which we participate when we sense a community of interest with something that has been."[29]

The perception of continuity manifests itself in terms of perceived "primordial forces" that seem to govern our lives. In speaking of historical "forces," Patočka realizes quite well the apparent contradiction with his own dislike of historical abstraction; he notes that "we are, to be sure, expressing ourselves abstractly and we could lead the reader to an error, compromising, in a sense, the historicity of these concepts." But he makes clear that none of the "forces" of which he speaks stands outside of the stream of history or is "given prior to history, so that it would constitute, so to speak, an extrahistorical explanans of history."[30] Instead, these are historical commonalities that are actual only within specific historical formulations. Among the forces that Patočka has in mind are several that determine our political existence; with this explicit, early acknowledgment a tone is set that will determine the course of his philosophy of history and politics in contradistinction to the work of Heidegger in particular.

> Among the examples of such primordial forces let us cite the desire to govern, capable of broad variations, leading both to imperialistic expansion and to lawful affirmation of the civil society in a state. Another such force is what is often called the "spirit," that is, the conscious relationship of a human to his own world in the forms of philosophy (and science), of art, wisdom, religion. Every such force stands in the polarity of the individual-social tension, it is both a matter of the individual and of the society, though in most diverse gradations and relations.[31]

The "individual-social tension" at the heart of the concept of politics is something to which humanity is inherently subject in its very historicity. The relation of the individual to society even affects the human desire to understand oneself and one's situation in the world and cosmos. In this early article on philosophy of history, Patočka's conviction as to the relationship of politics and philosophy is evident. It is a conviction that remained with him throughout his life, and it illustrates the basis for the claim that his work is often best understood as political philosophy, as distinguished from the work of his more famous instructors.

This political emphasis is reflected in Patočka's introduction to the specifics of his philosophy of history in chapter 1 of the *Heretical Essays*, in which he offers a further critique of Heidegger's approach. Heidegger, he claims here, is deficient in lacking a viable perspective on the whole of the world in which we live, the "natural" world. His perspective is limited to a single mode of comportment within the world: the mode having to do with the thematic understanding of being. But, Patočka writes, "the 'natural' world, the world of human life, can only be comprehended as the totality of the fundamental modes of human comportment." Heidegger focuses on the "fundamental philosophical question of the meaning of being," but neglects the other modes that do not deal with it explicitly.[32] Human comportment is always a type of movement, but only one human movement is explicitly oriented to the theme of its own openness, its own manifestation. This is what Patočka elsewhere called the "movement of truth," and it is, he contended, only a part (albeit an important one) of overall human movement. Other movements or modes of comportment depict our rootedness in the world and our drive to protect and preserve that world. "Only an examination and a comprehension of the mutual relations of all these move-ments," Patočka concludes, "would provide a picture of the natural world, the *Lebenswelt*, the world of human life."[33] An understanding of human existence in its fullness, encompassing politics, requires such a picture of the "natural" world if it is to be accurate. Without it, the possibility is raised that crucial questions, questions of the political tension between the individual and society, will be set aside if one focuses, as Heidegger, solely on the thematic question of being. There is the additional risk that, instead of being ignored, politics may come to be considered a mere handmaiden to the greater question of being, opening the door to its misuse as a means to an end, a means justifiable in light of that end.

The "natural" world is not, however, the world of human history. History, rather than an "organic extension" of the "natural" world, repre-sents instead a radical disruption of it.[34] Whereas human life is composed of multiple movements, human history, with its appeal to a continuity that tran-scends the individual, specifically reflects the movement of truth. Patočka's definition of "history" is thus far from conventional. The making of history occurs when we are able to rise above mere life, that is, above a life of service to our physical needs. The degree to which we are able to differentiate between a life whose sole aim is to continue living and one open to a greater range of possibilities is one factor by which it is possible to distinguish a his-torical life from a life that is unable to transcend the "natural" world.

This is not the only means by which we can make this distinction, however. Patočka writes that we can also speak of the "natural" world "in a somewhat different sense," as the "world prior to the discovery of its prob-lematic character."[35] Referring to the world as preproblematic, Patočka is contending that the "natural" world—which I noted earlier was a world in which humans lived simply, intuitively and without self-reflection—is one of pregiven meaning. It is a world in which meaning comes simply and directly from tradition and from the gods who stand over humans and rule them. Thereby the world is reliable and meaningful for humans; it is also, however, unreflective and thus unproblematic. "The basic framework for the possibility of such natural dwelling on earth is to exist unproblemati-cally."[36] In that the ultimate goal here is merely to live, there is a sense in which such a life resembles that of animals—but only to a point. As humans, the possibility is always present to problematize life, even if that possibility is hidden and unlikely to break forth. The world described here, the preproblematic world, is also, according to Patočka, a "prehistorical" world. In it, we do not attempt to differentiate between life and meaning as it is simply given to us, and the possibilities of life and meaning available to us through reflection.

At this point in chapter 1 of the *Heretical Essays*, Patočka begins to draw on the work of Hannah Arendt, a philosopher who was instrumental in focusing his attention onto the sphere of politics. "Here," he writes, "we need to attempt to take up, phenomenologically, the analysis of 'practical, active life' carried out by Hannah Arendt and inspired by Aristotle's distinctions between theoria, praxis, and poeisis."[37] Arendt's investigations were crucial because, unlike Heidegger's, they took account of those aspects of human existence not exclusively concerned with the Heideggerean theme of unconcealment—namely, those concerned with the practical, active life. They reinforced the broad outlines of Patočka's own critique of Heidegger, and offered support for the Czech's intuitive sense of the importance of politics.

The key Arendtian distinction for Patočka was between work and action, between the household and the polis, and it helped greatly to clarify the distinctions that had already been drawn between the realm of the "natural" world and that of the Socratic realm of freedom.[38] Arendt's influence is reflected in both the phenomenology of movement and the philosophy of history developed in the *Heretical Essays*. In terms of human existence, it is work that is our inescapable fate; it is, Patočka writes, our "fundamental mode of being in the world" because, as human, as living, we are constantly exposed to an inescapable need to consume to which work is our response.[39] We work in order to keep ourselves alive. Work, therefore, reflects our bondage to life. It also presupposes a possibility of freedom, however, for as we come to resent the impositions of our work, as we perceive it as a necessary imposition upon us, we see that there are possible periods in which we need not work. "The world in which the bondage of life to itself takes place on the basis of a concealed freedom," Patočka writes, "is the world of work; its proto-cell and model is the household, the community of those who work to assure their sustenance."[40]

In concluding that work, the "fundamental" human mode of being, reflects a bondage of life to itself, Patočka is saying that insofar as work is the center of our existence we do not live historically. The civilization constructed around work, whose model is the household, is not historical—it is prehistorical. Work, Patočka argues, is "not only a nonhistorical factor but actually one working against history, intending to hold it at bay." The great civilizations of the ancient world, in their devotion to the continuance of life, were in this sense great households, and were entirely prehistorical.[41] Work, of course, does not disappear with the beginning of history; it is merely the case that historical eras are defined by their self-conscious attempt to seek something in life beyond the simple continuance of the biological functions guaranteed by work. Here the unconventionality of this philosophy of history is evident. History does not have to do with past occurrences simply, nor with their recording through writing or historiography. The relating of events and the keeping of annals may reflect a prehistorical understanding of existence if they take place within an era or civilization based on the household and geared simply toward the maintenance of life.

With the advent of Greek and Roman civilization both Patočka and Arendt recognize that the rule of the household undergoes an important change. In place of the household, a public sphere arises and offers the citizen a new possibility. This is the thesis to which Arendt points, and from which the *Heretical Essays* take their impetus: "That the house ceases to be the core of the world as such, becoming simply a private domain alongside and juxtaposed to which there arose, in Greece and Rome, a different, no less important public sphere."[42] With this development a space is opened up for free action, for political action. This is the twin beginning of philosophy and politics and, Patočka contends, also the first time that humans begin to act consciously so as to challenge, to question, and to reflect thematically on the uniqueness of their situation in the world. They begin to act historically. Patočka's goal in these essays is to demonstrate that the essence of human freedom and possibility, that is, the realization that humanity could break the chains of its bondage to the order of work and the household and begin to live freely, first took form with the development of the idea of the polis. "Starting from this thesis," he writes, "we shall, in what follows, endeavor to demonstrate that the difference is that in the intervening period [between the replacement of the civilizational model of the household with that of the polis] history in the strict sense had begun."[43]

In this way and with Arendt's help, Patočka advances his thesis as to the development of the mode of activity that deserves to be called historical. In doing so he must delimit as nonhistorical all those millennia of human experience that fall outside of the rather narrow band of the European experience. Philosophy, politics, and history, then, are specific modes of human being, not to be understood in general terms. And yet they are all human phenomena and so remain in contact with the "natural" world of human existence and the nonhistorical movements of humanity. They also represent a break from that world, however. The nonhistorical mode of life, Patočka has suggested, can be spoken of as "natural," for it is fundamentally nonreflective, nonquestioning. It accepts world and community "as something simply given, something that simply manifests itself" in the interplay of gods and mortals.[44] The break to which both Arendt and Patočka point comes about when humans decline to accept their situation as simply given, when they, in the terms of ontological phenomenology, begin to thematically explore the question of why the world and its contents manifest themselves as they do.

> To uncover what is hidden in manifestation entails questioning, it means discovering the problematic character not of this or that but of the whole as such, as well as of the life that is rigorously

integrated into it. Once, however, that question had been posed, humans set out on a long journey they had not traveled hitherto, a journey from which they might gain something but also decidedly lose a great deal. It is the journey of history.[45]

The journey of history begins with inquiry into the world as a problem.

The phrase "the beginning of history" refers to the beginning of an epoch; it is a beginning Patočka locates in ancient Athens, when a thematic approach to ontological understanding first came to light. While the phenomenological movement of truth characteristic of historical periods existed in ancient, non-Greek empires organized on the model of the household, such empires lacked the "explicitly thematic orientation characteristic of a historical epoch." Instead, these civilizations saw life as something of an "ontological metaphor" with the world of nature standing for and symbolizing the being that was its foundation.[46] With the development of philosophy and politics, a rupture took place from which, at least for European man and his descendants, there was no turning back. Life opened itself up to the possibility that labor and work were not the only opportunities available.

THE POLIS IN HISTORY

In addition to Arendt's thematization of labor, work, and action, she further contributes to Patočkan political philosophy through her political interpretation of the Heideggerean emphasis on the polis. Patočka follows Arendt in the realization that it is not only the development of philosophy that is crucial to the mode of free action, but also the institutional model of the polis. The polis was where a philosophy of freedom could concretely manifest itself; it represented the opportunity for the self-aware citizen to reach forth, to no longer merely accept but to actively risk and strive. The polis was both the means to and the symbol of a new human possibility that announced a historical era: the possibility to initiate rather than simply accept. It was also, inherently, a foundational model for democracy—an institution unthinkable on any basis other than the equality of citizens.

> This new human possibility is based on the mutual recognition of humans as free and equal, a recognition which must be continuously acted out, in which activity does not have the character of enforced toil, like labor, but rather of the manifestation of excellence, demonstrating that in which humans can be in principle equal in competition with each other. At the same time that means living fundamentally not in the mode of acceptance but of initiative and preparation, ever seeking the opportunity for action, for

the possibilities that present themselves; it means a life in active tension, one of extreme risk and unceasing upward striving in which every pause is necessarily already a weakness for which the initiative of others lies in wait.[47]

The polis, Patočka argues, was a place where people could act historically. They could live in awareness of the insights opened up by philosophy, consciously abandoning a nonhistorical culture of passive acceptance for a life in active tension. Patočka sees the rise of the polis and of politics as an attempt to incarnate freedom into human life. It is a turning point in the course of human development for it offers, for the first time, a concrete setting in which to act freely and self-reflectively, to act historically. For these reasons the rise of the polis is connected to what Patočka unabashedly calls "the very beginning of history in the proper sense of the word."[48]

Patočka recognizes that, with his thesis, he is dangerously close to engaging in the very speculative historiography that he has from the start condemned. Yet he is clear to note that the rise of the polis was a gradual process that can be neither localized—traced to a particular few individuals—nor attributed to an ideal dedication to human welfare. It was the result of a society taking advantage of its possibilities. The Czech philosopher does not want his reflections to be "understood as an idealization of the Greek polis, as if it arose from the spirit of selfless devotion to 'the common good.'"[49] It was a human event, not a divine one.

This does not imply, though, that the polis was simply another form of ancient community, ethically indistinguishable from others. In both *Plato and Europe* and *Europe and the Post-European Age*, Patočka points to a "moral insight," symbolized by the injunction to care for the soul and specific to the Greek polis. He does not claim, however, that this took the form of a suprahistorical event of some kind, as, for example, an instance of revelation. The origin of the polis and its moral insight was a historical event in the sense that, just as human history reflects the moral relations inherent in periods of growth and decline, so "moral insight is nothing other than the sedimentation and codification of this experience."[50] The polis, entailing the recognition of its citizens as free and equal, gave concrete form to this sedimentation of moral experience.

The emergence of the polis, then, was a human event of epochal significance. In it is incarnated the spirit of the Western world, a spirit which, Patočka maintains in following Husserl, has a universal significance. It is the spirit of freedom and possibility:

Here, in very specific conflicts on a modest territory and with minimal material means is born not only the Western world and its spirit but, perhaps, world history as such. The Western spirit and world history are bound together in their origins: it is the spirit of free meaning bestowal, it is the shaking of life as simply accepted with all its certainties and at the same time the origin of new possibilities of life in that shaken situation, that is, of philosophy. Since, however, philosophy and the spirit of the polis are closely linked so that the spirit of the polis survives ultimately always in the form of philosophy, this particular event, the emergence of the polis, has a universal significance.[51]

Jan Patočka's philosophy of history is a philosophy of Western history, a philosophy of history as human activity that follows the model laid down in ancient Greece via the concurrent development of philosophy, reason, and politics. The claim of universal significance is vast, yet Patočka makes a concerted attempt to defend himself against a charge of historical idealism. Despite this, it is arguable that he overreaches in proclaiming the Greek polis to be the origin of "world history as such." Even if we accept the very specific and exclusive redefinition of the term "history," Patočka's account still lacks the comparative investigation of non-Western experience minimally necessary for his thesis to be accepted without objection.

The hereticism of these essays is hard to miss, for they abrogate the conventional understanding in its entirety and replace it with an understanding of history as activity that concretely reflects the insight of philosophy. These are essays about philosophy and about the origin of a particular conceptualization of the role of politics. Yet this conceptualization, a Western one, does concern a matter applicable to all humans: the matter of freedom. For this reason and despite Patočka's overly narrow definition of history, the content of these essays remains profoundly significant for human beings and their political institutions. It remains to follow the thread of these reflections to their conclusion, and from there, to judge both their coherence and their relevance more fully.

TWO ELEMENTS OF HISTORICAL LIFE: FREEDOM AND PROBLEMATICITY

As we delineate a picture of the realm of politics as the site of philosophical action, we increasingly come into contact with two concepts that form the basis for Patočka's conclusions: the concepts of freedom and problematicity. Action on the Socratic model is action grounded in freedom and a recognition of problematicity. The two concepts are related and interdependent.

Freedom

The concept of freedom, we will recall, is central to the nonmetaphysical stance of Patočka's negative Platonism.[52] There, freedom is defined in terms of our ability to transcend the realm of objectivity. This transcendence, however, is not transcendence toward any thing, like a transcendent Idea or Being, but transcendence over and away from those things or objects that exert a hold on us. In the *Heretical Essays*, Patočka expands on and clarifies this, noting that transcendence, not intentionality, is the "original trait" of a life that differentiates itself from those things that have no concern for their own being, things that "do not exist for their own sake nor have any 'for the sake of'—or have only a glimpse of it, as animals might."[53] Transcendence is a human element, differentiating us from things and animals.

In transcending the material and the objective, we do not move away from the world, but toward it. The transcendence of humans is always toward, not the things of the world, but the world as a whole. The foundation of that transcendence is our freedom. Here again, in grounding this human attribute in freedom and not in reason, Patočka must recognize a debt to Heidegger: "transcendence towards the world, however, is originally not given by the activity of thought and reason, as it was for Kant; its foundation, rather, is freedom." And it is Heidegger who is recognized as the philosopher of freedom for it is he who first views history not as a series of independent events but as, in Patočka's words, a "responsible realization" of our humanity.[54] Our responsibility is to be fully human, and to do so requires that we examine our lives, that we pose the question of our own being. In posing questions in this way, we act with both responsibility and freedom, for questioning after being is predicated on that transcendence of the objective realm definitive of freedom.

The act of self-examination, of questioning, brings us face to face with the realization that the world is not as simple and unproblematic as we may have thought it to be. Questioning, by its very nature, tests the certainty of what may have once been taken for granted. In Patočka's terms, it "shakes" our presuppositions and causes us to live in increasing uncertainty. Dealing with this uncertainty, however, accepting its inevitability, is an inherent part of responsibility. Responsibility, therefore, and here Patočka is extending Heidegger's analysis, "presupposes not only an understanding for being but also a shaking of what at first and for the most part is taken for being in naive everydayness, a collapse of its apparent meaning to which we are led in the explicit posing of the question of being."[55]

At this point Patočka takes the analysis in a new direction, a direction that Heidegger did not pursue. Although freedom and historicity remain the fundamental concepts, they are set into a social context. Patočka's understanding of our being, unlike Heidegger's, has a decidedly practical element to it: it concerns our social existence and our concrete attempts to order it. This analysis, then, does not repeat Heidegger's, which we shall see as we trace its movement toward, not a consideration of the polis simply, but a consideration of the polis as a model for a politics of freedom and equality.

Freedom is indispensable to the quest to understand our situation in the world and to live in truth. Yet it also requires of us tremendous risk. Freedom requires both that we distance ourselves from the objects of the world and recognize that, in doing so, we open ourselves up to the risk of error and problematicity:

> Freedom thus means risk; it means the continual possibility of error and it means the necessity for deciding; it means the hardness of contradiction, the need to decide about it as if we were sovereign, and at the same time the impossibility of sovereignty; it means thus anxiety before (the apparent) void into which man is set by his limiting position.[56]

The possibility of error, the hardness of contradiction, the necessity of decision—all are requirements of freedom and help to distinguish a responsible life from a life ruled by myth and a hierarchy of simple, given meaning. These elements form a necessary backdrop to a life of freedom, and therefore to those forms of democratic organization that attempt to incarnate that freedom into the institutions of government.

An objection may be raised that this definition of freedom makes it an elitist, existentialist adventure available and relevant to only a certain few individuals. These individuals, in declaring their freedom, would raise themselves above the common needs and restrictions of mankind, becoming free of traditional authority. In this case, freedom would be something not universal but limited; it would be of little importance to the mass of humans subject to a daily struggle for subsistence. Yet this impression is counter to Patočka's intentions and would represent a misreading of his analysis. He explains that freedom, though experienced to different degrees by different people and perhaps understood thematically only by a few, is yet profoundly relevant to all. "The experience of freedom, it is true, is less common than passive experience, but freedom, or, better, the possibility of freedom, is something relevant to humans as such." "We can also say," he continues, "that every human has some experience of freedom," even if he does not encounter it in the context of an overall understanding.[57] But particular humans experience a great deal more freedom than others, perhaps even to the extent that those others may be unaware of the very possibility of a free life. But does this make freedom a relative privilege for the few? Patočka argues emphatically that it does not. The possibility of freedom, he says, is available to all; it is, therefore, the ground for our humanity as well as our dignity.

> Freedom is not an aristocratic privilege, rather, it is relevant and valid for all; without it human would not be human. Human dignity stems from it also, even when humans are not aware of it, not

from the putative fact that "Man" is the most powerful among the animals.[58]

Our humanity results, not from being the most capable animal, but from differing essentially from animal life. The foundation of that difference is the possibility of freedom, which itself is contingent on the human possibility of comprehending our place in the world and understanding the ground of our freedom, understanding our being as human.

Patočka's conception of freedom does not reduce to a form of existentialist individualism. It is developed as a specifically social—and political—concept, presupposing a responsibility not only to oneself but to society. Though the responsibility of "[d]eciding about one's life, about its meaning and its depth, rests in our hands, in the hands of every individual,"[59] and he cannot deliver himself of it, this responsibility does not play itself out in isolation. Its source is in the self but its purpose is not to be self-serving. "Complete freedom means life out of one's self, in truth about one's self, but not only for one's self alone." The responsibility that accompanies freedom extends necessarily from the individual to society. "The free man then realizes this relation of his own actions to society as a necessarily assumed relation and experiences it as a feeling of responsibility."[60]

Problematicity

The theme of problematicity is taken up most directly in a text based on apartment lectures from the 1970s. Entitled "The Spiritual Person and the Intellectual" and intended to comment on and accompany the *Heretical Essays*, this text refers directly to the problems introduced in the *Essays* and helps us to read them in the context of Patočka's lifelong philosophical and ethical concerns. Whereas the *Essays*, particularly the last, resort to a use of metaphor and symbol that can confuse or put off the first-time reader, "The Spiritual Person and the Intellectual" reminds us of the basic Socratism of the themes under discussion. Here we return to what Patočka maintains is a Socratic notion of philosophy as recognition of the problematicity of life. The Socratic individual does not live to avoid the problematic. To the contrary, he lays himself open to all of the experiences—including the problematic—that we are naturally heir to.

The experience of problematicity is a typically human experience. We are all confronted, at some point in our lives, with situations in which our simple beliefs, our self-evident understandings, are shattered. "Those experiences, which show us that this whole way of seeing the world as self-evident and assumed is something that disappoints, something open to negative outcomes, these experiences are rare; they are rare but, in the end, everyone encounters them in some way or another."[61] It is not the encounter with such experience, of course, that is crucial; it is our response to the encounter that marks the decisive movement.

The experiences to which Patočka refers are variable, from those moments when we come to realize that the people around us in whom we believed are themselves flawed and live in contradiction, to more devastating tribulations associated with disaster, death and political upheaval. What these experiences have in common is that they force us to face the reality that our life is not ruled by logic and order, as we originally thought it to be.

> All of them show at once that life, which appeared so obvious, is in reality somehow problematic, that something doesn't correspond, that something is not in order. Our original attitude is that it is in order, that all of these small unpleasantries, disagreements and incongruences have no significance and that it is possible to get over them.[62]

In this essay, Patočka is reflecting on the individual capable of facing up to this contingency, to this problematicity in life. The ability or courage shown in the willingness to resist reductive thinking is the same quality first noticed by Plato when he sought to distinguish the virtuosity of a Socrates from that very different, technical virtuosity of the Sophists. It is, Patočka argues, not a question of one's occupation, but a spiritual quality. Thus he refers to the Socratic individual as a "spiritual person," knowing full well that such phrases do not resonate with the modern ear.[63]

The Socratic way of life, properly understood, is one that accepts reality as it appears, unadulterated and in all its uncertainty. This means a way of life that does not hide from negative experiences, but relegates itself to their inevitability; the spiritual person "lays himself open to these very things and his life consists in being in this way exposed."[64] This way of life is free and self-reflective. The price of this freedom is high, however. The spiritual person must relinquish the safety of the solid ground under his feet. He or she must accept the responsibility to "live in no way on solid ground but on something that moves; to live without an anchor."[65] This is life, not as a fulfillment of a plan, but as a journey or a quest; it is a life of unceasing movement seeking understanding.

The court of final appeal, in this account, is neither a supreme being nor an objective science or methodology; it is one's own fragile humanity and reason. Accepting this, however, humanity does not emerge to find itself lost at sea without either anchor or rudder. Life is not futile or aimless, it is supported by the knowledge that self-understanding, expressed through philosophy, is itself a foundation that lends support and stability. Philosophy problematizes in order to dispel the illusion of a secure foundation for one that reflects human reality; the foundation it uncovers must itself be recognized ever again as problematic. In philosophy it cannot be otherwise.

> Essentially, all of philosophy is nothing other than the development of this problematicity, in the way that great thinkers have grasped and expressed it. The battle to extract out of this problematicity something that emerges from it; to find a solid shore, but to again problematize that which emerges as that shore.[66]

Freedom and problematicity relate not only to politics, but to philosophy itself. Living in truth, living not as a sophistic intellectual but as a spiritual person, requires the openness to reality that philosophy—epitomized by the Socratic perspective—attempts to capture.

The Greek experience is of such importance to Patočka because it represents, not only the emergence of philosophy, but also the simultaneous emergence of politics. In the rise of political life on the model of the polis, in the rise of a public space where citizens can debate the conditions of their existence within a framework of equality, the same uncertainty, problematicity, and uprootedness define the conditions of existence. Political life is not a passive, accepting life, it is life characterized by a reaching forth, a "life unsheltered." "Such life," Patočka writes, "does not seek to escape its contingency, but neither does it yield to it passively."[67] Political life on the model of the polis demands initiative of its citizens. It demands that they abandon a life of acceptance for one of outreach. In moving to the model of the polis the old myths on which the household-based society was held together are let go. With the movement to a polis, as Patočka puts it, "nothing of the earlier life of acceptance remains in peace; all the pillars of the community, traditions, and myths, are equally shaken, as are all the answers that once preceded questions."[68]

The life of freedom in the polis, the life envisioned in Socratic philosophy and described again by Hannah Arendt as the life of action, is one in which metaphysical anchors are untied. We uproot ourselves from the soil of myth and tradition, meaning not that we simply reject it, for much in myth and tradition is reflective of truth, but that we abandon it as a crutch to which we turn for simple answers when life presents us with difficult problems. In this way we confront our life; we assume responsibility for it. Patočka writes of political life as "life in an urgent time." "This constant vigilance," he continues, "is at the same time a permanent uprootedness, lack of foundation." It is a life that is confronted by its own precariousness and finitude. Only in facing it can a truly free life unfold.[69] The recognition of problematicity is, at the same time, a rejection of all such systems, gods, and methods that would "save" us, that would deliver us from problematicity. To assume freedom and recognize problematicity is to act as a human being. "Without aspiring to the superhuman, [life] becomes freely human."[70]

The concepts of freedom and problematicity and their relation to history were introduced, in this discussion, in terms of their relation to Heidegger. Yet Patočka has applied these concepts not only to the way in which we reflect on our own being thematically (as in Heidegger), but also to the way in which we "carry out" our being. Our "carrying out" of being, our "comportment," is defined as "our practical dealing with the practical things of our surrounding world." Patočka considers it not only the most visible component of our being, but also the best point of entry for a penetration to its depths.[71] Our relations to things and to other beings in our practical dealings with them reveal our relation to the whole, which is determinative of our being. Heidegger is a model for Patočka only to a certain point. Whereas Patočka pursues the questions of freedom and problematicity through an analysis and understanding of our comportment in the realm of politics, along Socratic lines, Heidegger takes a course that leads him, not in the direction of politics (excepting his ill-fated adventures with National Socialism), but explicitly away from it.[72]

PHILOSOPHY OF HISTORY AND POLITICS

Philosophy and politics are inseparable, Patočka concludes in the *Heretical Essays*; the care of the one implies and necessitates the care of the other. This thesis, and its rigorous explication, make Patočka a political philosopher in the truest sense of the term.[73] To demonstrate the truth of this claim the links between what Patočka defines as philosophy and what he understands as authentic politics need to be examined. Two points are relevant. First, Patočka contends that the historical emergence of politics occupies a special position in relation to philosophy—it is more closely connected to philosophy than either religion or art, for example. And second, he argues that it is the simultaneous and interdependent rise of politics and philosophy that is, in the end, responsible for the very emergence of the possibility of history itself.

The relation of politics to philosophy occupies as central a role in Patočka's philosophy as it did in Plato's. Although politics becomes the subject of explicit analysis only in his later work, it is present as an embryonic theme throughout his career. Even the earliest essays contain evidence of its centrality. In a 1933 essay on political Platonism, for instance, Patočka writes that, while the philosopher is never exactly a politician, "his activity in the world is based on the philosopher possessing a political idea."[74] The philosopher must be active, and this activity cannot be understood as exclusive of the issues related to the organization of society.

Even when Patočka chooses the symbolism of "caring for the soul" to represent his primary philosophical concerns, the centrality of the political is never neglected. As I noted in chapter 3, care for the soul as a philosophical symbol represents the insight derived from Greek experience and embedded in the European consciousness as its spiritual principle. What has not yet been noted is the way in which care for the soul has a particular, tripartite structure that takes special account of politics. In *Europe and the Post-European Age*, which is a more concise discussion of the themes of *Plato and Europe*, Patočka bases his chapter divisions on the three elements that make up this structure: care for the soul as an expression of an ontological arrangement, care for the soul as care for the polis, and care for the soul as self-understanding and self-control. It is the second of these perspectives that concerns us at the moment.[75] Care for the soul as care for the polis restates the notion at the center of Plato's *Republic*: that the order of the city naturally reflects the order of the individual soul.[76] Caring for the soul thus requires that one act with constant reference to the political—that one care for the polis.

Patočka's most explicit discussion of the connection between politics and philosophy takes place in the notes he appended to his *Heretical Essays*. Here he directly addresses the special status of politics in relation to other fields. Patočka begins these notes with a series of rhetorical questions about his attribution of such preeminent importance to the development of philosophy and politics in the ancient Greek period, questions he proceeds to answer in his own defense. After first questioning the status given to philosophy over poetry and art, he asks:

> Is it not as unfair as inconsistent to attribute a special importance to politics in relation to philosophy, to declare philosophy and politics in nearly the same breath to be the founders of history strictly speaking when in terms of collective social influence we might be far more justified in attributing that role to religion, which, as in the case of Israel, clearly had the decisive word in the formation of the bearers of history, such as nations?[77]

He responds to his own question by reaffirming his answer: No. Politics and philosophy together constitute the foundation of history; they represent a mode of being that is of greater importance to human history than religion. How is this so? Politics, in its proper form the epitome of human social being, presents us with the most direct means to express the freedom and the active striving that represent the highest level of human movement, the movement in which the variety of possibilities of human qua human are examined and pursued. The original point of politics is freedom, and freedom is the greatest of our possibilities.

Politics, then, as conceptualized and epitomized in Socratic philosophy, occupies a higher position in relation to philosophy than either religion or art, for original politics has as its purpose the transmission of philosophical insight to humanity, humanity as a whole and in its most fundamental mode—the mode of its social being. Politics presents us with the possibility to strive for and live a free life. It directly connects the spiritual life to praxis, while religion and art must be largely content with symbolizing that spirituality.

> The reason for this special position of politics is that political life in its original and primordial form is nothing other than active freedom itself (from freedom, for freedom). The goal of striving here is not life for the sake of life (whatever life it may be) but only life for freedom and in it, and it is understood, that is, actively grasped, that such a life is possible. That, however brings this original politics into a wholly different proximity to philosophy than that of religion and art, however great their importance in spiritual life. If then spiritual life is the fundamental upheaval (shaking of immediate certainties and meaning), then religion senses that upheaval, poetry and art in general depict and imagine it, politics turns it into the practice of life itself, while in philosophy it is grasped in understanding, conceptually.[78]

While philosophy has as its goal the understanding of our being, politics, as Patočka is defining it, "turns it into the practice of life itself." This conceptualization, strongly influenced by Hannah Arendt, attempts to define politics in distinct contrast to those minimalist contemporary understandings that see it as merely a means to the organization of labor or allocation of resources.[79] Politics reflects our essential humanity, embodied in the ultimate human possibility of freedom. For this reason, it can never be an arbitrary exercise. Patočka's understanding of politics, like his understanding of history, is a highly specific one. Politics as the Greeks understood it, he argues, is meaningful insofar as its purpose is to allow for freedom. In this sense, therefore, politics demands recognition of equality. The model for such a "community of equals," and for the explicit recognition of freedom as a theme, is the Greek polis.

> We have sought to show that the invention of politics does not simply coincide with the organization of work on a foundation of religion and power. That is the source of empires, but not of politics which is possible only with the conception of bestowing meaning on life out of freedom and for it, and that, as Hegel said, cannot be brought about by a solitary one (a ruler, the pharaoh) being "conscious of freedom." Humans can be that only in a

community of equals. For that reason, the beginning of history in the strict sense is the polis.[80]

The reference to politics as the organization of work on a basis of religion or power is of course a reference to Karl Marx, who erred in this contention as well as in his argument that human history was governed by an abstract dialectical structure of relationships. The notes to the *Heretical Essays* make this point clearly. Politics is far more significant than modern political theory generally makes it out to be.

It is not only Marxism with which Patočka takes issue, it is any philosophy grounded in abstraction over the genuine experience of phenomena. Politics goes astray when the abstract replaces the concrete and the experiential as its foundation. Patočka's position is clear: "We need to philosophize on the basis of phenomena and not of hypothetical constructs out of principles." This means we need above all to remain faithful to experience. "What," he continues, "does phenomenon mean? Phenomenon is what we see, what is present in our experience. . . . Thus the question of human social being is also in the first place a phenomenological question."[81] This reliance on the themes of phenomenology, above all, attests to the conviction that it is experience that must guide theory, and never the reverse. For this reason a study of history, the terrain of human experience, is inherent to philosophy. And the study of history in these pages leads to the conclusion that the history can be defined neither in terms of a general recording of events and facts, nor in terms of abstract, hypothetical constructs, but must refer specifically to those concrete human activities geared toward a thematic understanding or expression of our social being.

History, as we have seen, first became possible on a broad scale with the common emergence of philosophy and politics. The importance of this historical event consists in its setting in motion an earthquake of sorts. The rise of politics in the Greek world had the effect of "shaking" the foundations of earlier civilizational models. The new foundation offered by politics was one that demanded responsibility but offered manifold possibilities, albeit merely human ones. Patočka emphatically concludes his discussion of politics and history by laying out the link between history, politics, and human possibility: "History," he writes, "arises from the shaking of the naive and absolute meaning in the virtually simultaneous and mutually interdependent rise of politics and philosophy. Fundamentally, history is the unfolding of embryonic possibilities present in this shaking."[82]

The rise of philosophy and politics, conditioned on the understanding that true meaning is never as simple as an objective fact, opens up the possibility of freedom. A free existence, again, distances itself from metaphysical constructs as well as from the most basic instinct of the natural world, the mere will to live. Humanity has the possibility to be ruled neither by a "system"—of gods or of dialectical forces—nor by the bondage to life itself characteristic of the "natural" world. Patočka tries to impart a conception of history grounded in the recognition of this possibility. The rise of philosophy and politics first bring it into the center of human life—via the creation of a setting for these pursuits in the Greek polis. This perspective is reflected, and adequately summarized, in a passage from an article about the politics and philosophy of the Czech president T. G. Masaryk that I will cite in full:

> This curious fact [that philosophy, precisely defined, exists only in societies arising from out of Greek thought], it seems to me, depends exclusively on the historical nature of philosophy. Philosophy, thinking, by its emergence *creates* history, that unique impact on the overall activity of mankind. Only by means of politics and philosophy, those two closely related expressions of freedom, did man become historical in the real sense of the word, i.e. living not just naturally, simply using what was available, what could simply be affirmed, but by what always, though unseen, accompanies human life, seemingly as *marginalia*, but what in truth is the precondition of all human life and behavior. History arises when people in a certain insignificant region of the earth cease to live for life and begin to live in order to conquer, for themselves and those who share their will, the space for their recognition, the space for freedom. That is politics in its original definition: life from freedom and for freedom. But freedom is equivalent to a space for thought, i.e. the realization that freedom is not a thing among things, that free existence stands on the border between what exists and what cannot be called existing, since it frees man from the dependence on things in order that he might perceive them and place himself outside of them, understand them and his own position among them.[83]

In making freedom and politics central to both philosophy and history, Patočka presents us with a philosophy of history that is "heretical," and also the basis for a theory of politics.

The notion of politics that Patočka envisions, I should add in conclusion, is not one that ignores questions of political order. Although he does not pursue political theory in the sense of a blueprint for political organization, Patočka's philosophy is directed toward the more practical side of politics in a way that Heidegger's, for example, is not. While one may argue that the Heideggerean conception of the polis is not political, no such claim can be made for Patočka. Richard Rorty, for example, has noted that, while Heidegger was uninterested in the difference between democracy and totalitarianism, Patočka was clearly concerned with the "connection between philosophy and the ideally free and happy community." This was a connection, Rorty continued, that "repelled Heidegger."[84] Not so Patočka: "Care for the soul," the Czech philosopher concluded, "is possible obviously only in a well-ordered community."[85]

It is the model of the well-ordered polis, then, a community of equals held together by philosophical insight, that responds directly to philosophy as care for the soul. Jan Patočka's life and career did not play out in such a community, however. He began his studies amidst the experience of a crisis in contemporary thought and pursued his career through a succession of devastating political upheavals and periods of totalitarian repression. He saw, in the world of the twentieth century, a predominance of extreme views. Patočka sought a recovery of principles exemplified for him in a particular institutional model and a particular mode of being. These were principles from which European politics and philosophy had become, by the twentieth century, thoroughly alienated.

EUROPE, SCIENCE, AND METAPHYSICS

In the previous chapter's discussion of metaphysics and "Negative Platonism," I referred to the influence that metaphysical thinking had had on the conquest of nature via the progressive development of science and technology. The movement from classical to Enlightenment thinking was not, of course, a rapid or direct step. Between the two lies a vast stretch of time during which both scientific and philosophical thought were subsumed within the dominant perspective of European Christianity. A significant portion of Patočka's philosophy of history is dedicated to tracing a continuity in European thought embedded in a basically metaphysical framework. The positing of an absolute and objective Idea was an event, he charges, that affected not only the development of Christianity but also the development of science and, in its wake, led to a scientific or objectivistic understanding of politics. Patočka outlined this argument first in the 1950s with "Negative Platonism," but then again in greater detail in the 1970s with the third of his Heretical Essays: it is this latter text that contains the details of his thesis and the profound effect that it had on his understanding of contemporary politics and its shortcomings.

Light and Darkness

In chapter 3 of the *Heretical Essays*, Patočka characterizes both the positive potential of genuine philosophy as well as its decline into metaphysics via a metaphorical description of events that reverses the traditional understanding of the symbols "light" and "darkness." Greek philosophy had offered a new vision of eternity in the concept of *phüsis*, the eternal and imperishable genesis and perishing of all that there is. Implicit in this concept of nature and the cosmos was mystery, portrayed via an image of a darkness out of which the light of the dawn of the cosmos and its order is born. There is contained, in this image of a dark night, a sense of the transcendent mystery of human reality which is positive, for out of it order and meaning are created. Yet philosophy, like democracy in Athens, was undermined by the human desire for solidity, for the certain meaning of objective foundations. The metaphor of darkness, of risk and mystery, was overtaken by a desire for light.

> However, just as the life of the free polis was granted but a short time to unfold in its free daring, fearlessly aiming for the unknown, so also philosophy, aware of its bond with the problem of the polis and sensing in the germ already its perils and perishing, was led by a striving for a definitive and new bestowal of meaning to see in that darkness only *a lack of light*, the night as a waning of the day (emphasis mine).[86]

The transition Patočka describes leads away from a philosophy that responds to being, and toward one that prefers the objective absolute to an uncertain mystery. With the certainty of an absolute, all is brought into the light, while the symbol of darkness, of a tentative mystery, is reduced to a negative counterpart. The latter symbol, which is prominent in the sixth *Heretical Essay* and contributes to its controversial tone, is considerably clearer when seen in this context, for it is evident that Patočka uses it to symbolize the element of problematicity inherent in the free polis and the care for the soul.[87] This uncertainty, this darkness, is the origin of light; to ignore its generative properties and attempt to negate it as one reaches for clarity is, in Patočka's imagery, akin to denying important aspects of one's humanity.

Christianity and Metaphysics

The rise of Christianity in the Roman Empire was an event of world-historic proportions, and one not unrelated to the changes in philosophy and the decline of the free polis that it followed. In Patočka's analysis, there is continuity between the formulation that set that change into motion—the Platonic Idea as an "other" world—and the Christian conception of God. This means that the development of Christianity from out of Judaism was contingent on the inheritance of a Greek formulation. As he puts it, "[d]ivine transcendence, whose conceptual foundations undoubtedly do not lie in Israel's treasury of ideas, is an inheritance of the 'true world' formulated once by Plato and transformed theologically by Aristotle."[88] The Christian conception of the human relationship to a divine and transcendent God is described, in what is unfortunately a somewhat superficial account given in broad strokes, by Patočka as a response to the perception that even metaphysical philosophy could not deliver the certainty it promised. Though it had sought to do so with metaphysics, philosophy could not provide humans with clearly intelligible and positive meaning. In faith, however, in "God's word addressed to humans and the response to this word," positive meaning was guaranteed and along with it a means to face human misery without utter resignation.[89]

Christianity, while it did not allow man to understand God in perfect clarity, offered the security of a reciprocal relationship in faith, a new community to replace the loss of the polis. That community, grounded in a metaphysical relationship rather than in freedom, nevertheless offered a genuine meaningfulness and sense of equality.

> Thus the question of meaning is resolved positively by dismissing philosophy and by countering scepticism with the word from an otherwise inaccessible "true" world. On this basis there grows a new community and a new way of coming to cognitive terms with the totality of what-there-is. It is a new community, which, to be sure, is no longer simply the work of humans but in which humans do participate freely. It is not only a community of humans with each other, a mutual recognition in which they guarantee each other a spiritual perpetuation in the memory of glory. It is, rather, a community of humans with God who is their eternal memory and the perception of their essential spiritual being. It is a community in which, for all its hierarchy, all humans are equal before the face of the ultimate "true" reality; in which they are thus true fellow participants in a meaningfulness which they did not create but which they are called to bring about.[90]

Christianity offered a positive meaningfulness and a community that could withstand the tribulations of human life in the world, even the difficulties of life in despotic political regimes in which equality was denied. Equality was an integral part of the human compact with God, guaranteed on a higher level.

The rise of Christianity provided a foundation for human life and understanding, and with it the security of solid ground under one's feet. This existential security also had an additional effect: it removed a barrier to intellectual inquisitiveness. The foundation provided by Christianity left man free to pursue "all speculative daring" without fear of a fall into meaninglessness.

Here, then, we need to grasp the new place and significance which metaphysics assumes in the complex of Christian faith and doctrine. . . . The significance of metaphysical thought and metaphysical inquiry becomes that, within the framework provided by faith and guaranteed thereby, it is possible to some extent to come to understand what faith offers. Rational cognition thus reaches transcendent goals without fear of going astray, while on the other hand we can devote ourselves to all speculative daring without being led to the regions of scepticism where meaninglessness lurks. Reason as the natural organ for the understanding of truth loses its place of pride in life, but we might claim that this loss is at the same time a gain: for it gains firm foundation, certainty, and with it daring.[91]

The "speculative daring," without fear of skepticism, to which Patočka refers is exemplified in the progressive scientific quest for knowledge and control of nature.

Science and Metaphysics

The development of science, it was noted earlier, was a process also contingent on the ascendency of metaphysics over a philosophy of freedom. In the analysis of Patočka and others, it was a specific characteristic of the Christian assumption of metaphysics that humans were set above nature in such a way that it, in effect, became theirs to rule and control. One of those cited as a source for this line of reasoning is Karl Löwith. Löwith, Patočka notes, pointed out a connection between the Christian view of nature and the modern crisis of meaning epitomized by nihilism.[92] It is a connection on which Patočka builds in his own analysis of science and the foundation of meaning in the modern world.

According to [Löwith], another Christian source of nihilism is the relation to nature as a reservoir of objects given to humans to rule and care for. The idea which first meant care for things entrusted to humans turned in the modern age into a doctrine of domination and exploitation of the treasury of nature with no regard not only for nature itself but for future humankind as well.

More important, however, is that for the Christians nature need not be that concrete reality within which they are submerged and to which they belong as to one of the fundamental loci of the epiphany of its mystery but rather, at least since the age of nominalism, an object of judgment and speculation. Nature is not given and evident but rather distant and alien, to be formed by the means of our psyche. The locus of meaning and being is God in God's relation to the human soul: nature is the locus of cold, abstract reflection. Thus with regard to nature modern humanity builds not on antiquity, but rather on the Christian mode of regarding it with a cool distance and distrust.[93]

The view of nature as something to be examined, controlled and exploited, when combined with the "speculative daring" with which human beings are imbued when they have a secure foundation of meaning, was instrumental in the development and progressive advancement of natural science. Nature, no longer something autonomous with which we interacted, began to be considered a formal object, an object of natural science investigation.

Christianity, then, positively influenced the development of the very thing that would challenge its supremacy in the world. The scientific worldview would not only overthrow Christianity on the European stage, it would dethrone it with an appeal to a new, severely restricted viewpoint, a refusal to consider evidence not subject to scientific explication. The success of mathematical natural science

> becomes the source of a new, soberly audacious view of the whole of reality which recognizes no beings other than those at which we arrive by such mathematical reconstruction of the world of the senses in which we naturally move. Thus, with the help of the Christian conception of meaningfulness and nurtured by Christianity, a new conception of reality grew in the womb of the Western European society.[94]

This new conception of reality, unlike that which it gradually replaced, did not look for a meaningfulness of the whole. In fact, it became inevitable that the success of the sciences would increasingly make irrelevant the very notion of a nonscientific source of meaning.

The transition from a theocentrism to a scientific anthropocentrism does not mean that Western man has rid himself of the longing for truth or meaning. This longing persists in the anthropocentric age and manifests itself in movements that offer, on a secular or scientific level, the same certainty of meaning once offered by Christianity.

> European humanity has become so accustomed to this Christian conception of the meaning of history and of the universe that it cannot let go of some of its substantive traits even where fundamental Christian concepts such as God the creator, savior, and judge have ceased to be significant for it, and that it continues to seek meaning in a secularized Christian conception in which humans or humanity step into God's place.[95]

In these "secularized" formulations of metaphysics meaning and ultimate clarity is provided, based either on the infallibility of method as in the natural sciences and positivism, or more perniciously, as when the formulations concern supposed social or historical forces, on the promise of a redemptive end in a political movement or a philosophy of history that explains itself in terms of logical sequences. It is possible, particularly with the latter type of formulation, that whole societies may be drawn into an anthropocentric metaphysical scheme. Most such schemes, like Comte's "Cult of Humanity," will not be successful, but there is also the possibility that societies may "by force and defiance seek to enforce meaning where ex datis there can be none, as in the case of Marxism. Not Marxism as a teaching, as a critical social science, but as the 'sacred' doctrine of new, restructured, and aggressive societies, exploiting the corroding scepticism of the old."[96] In addition to Comte and Marx, Patočka points to Hegel and Sartre for the metaphysical nature of their philosophical programs. Nietzsche, though often praised for his diagnosis of the problem, also reflects the fallacy of the anthropocentric solution to the absence of positive meaning. In fact, Patočka writes, the phenomenon of the "secularized Christian conception" is actually "an unwitting example of the Nietzschean contradiction embodied in the prescription that if there is no meaning, we need to create it 'by imposing an order on the portion of the world within our reach.'"[97] The solutions of these thinkers are not merely speculative philosophical solutions, they are also political solutions, solutions that embody the secularization of the metaphysical longing for certain meaning and direction.

In the modern scientific perspective, which now dominates even the social sciences, the human is often considered as little more than "an organism maintaining a metabolic exchange with its context and reproducing itself."[98] This is the case, not only in Marxism, but also, perhaps, in certain forms of liberalism. In these cases, Patočka notes ironically, it is as if man has reverted to a situation characteristic of prehistory, a situation of bondage of human life to itself.

> Thus it seems as if the whole movement of history, after all the drive for absolute meaning in politics, in philosophies of a metaphysical cast, in religion that probed as deeply as Christianity, ended up where it began—with the bondage of life to its self-consumption and with work as the basic means of its perpetuation.[99]

But in fact, this comparison does not do justice to the age of prehistory. It may seem as if the nihilism of modernity has something in common with the period prior to philosophy, "[y]et it is not so," Patočka contends. "Prehistoricity is not characterized by a deprivation of meaning, it is not nihilistic like our times. Prehistorical meaning may be modest, but it is not relativistic."[100] A pervasive meaninglessness is not a characteristic of

civilization founded on the model of the household; it is rather a consequence of the human desire to replace human meaning, problematic
meaning, with a certain truth. When certain truth turns out not to be
compatible with scientific inquiry and skepticism, the result is a descent
into nihilism.

A Recovery

This question of meaning is a problem for the contemporary world, and
nowhere more so than in the realm of politics. The lack of a center of
meaning, in the wake of the decline of metaphysics, is not merely a sociological problem (though Patočka notes that the whole discipline of sociology basically grew up out of the perceived need to understand the
pathologies specific to modern man), it is a political problem. Politics turns
the subject matter of philosophy into the practice of life itself; in the postmetaphysical world, the practice of life has taken its lead from the void of
meaning left by the decline of metaphysics.

The human need for meaning has not evaporated in the scientific era.
To the contrary, insofar as traditional forms of meaning are no longer available or convincing, then the search for meaningful substitutes is increasingly prevalent. Patočka's analysis of the modern world implies that
metaphysics has been replaced in the realm of politics by two alternatives,
neither of which is satisfactory. As a first alternative, man may seek to
replace lost meaning with a messianic philosophical system or political
movement that promises a substitute, on the level of the secular, for a lost
sense of metaphysical meaning and certainty. Otherwise, he may embrace a
form of liberalism that manages to evade the temptation by basing itself in a
scientific materialism, thus avoiding the question of meaning altogether. In
the fifth "heretical" essay, Patočka deals with the question of the "decadence" or "decline" of the contemporary world, by which he means not its
failure in the realm of morality, but its loss of contact with "the innermost
nerve of its functioning," the self-awareness that comes with an understanding of history and the care for the soul. The alternatives open to
"postmetaphysical" man, he concludes, encourage this decline, for they resolutely avoid, after the decline of metaphysics, a genuine and open
approach to the question of meaning.

Patočka's philosophy of history and politics is a concrete response to a
difficult situation. Its focus is the rediscovery of history in the active pursuit of freedom, the epitome of which was the historical founding of the
polis as a site grounded in the rejection of given meaning and the acceptance of the problematicity of merely human meaning. This philosophy of

history and politics is a response to the twin philosophical and political problems of the contemporary world: the problem of scientific nihilism on the one hand and objective versions of metaphysics on the other. He is not the first to suggest a solution to this perceived crisis, but his approach is unique in finding, in European history, a conception of freedom and a view of the soul that accepts the meaningfulness of the whole within which humans exist.

> Dostoyevski proposes Byzantine Christianity, Nietzsche an eternal return of the same as the solution to the crisis. Yet the very foundation of Christianity, the rediscovery of eternity, presupposes a repetition of something which once was real at the very beginning of the European era: the soul as that within us which is related to that unperishing and imperishable component of the whole which makes possible truth and in truth the being not of a superman but of an authentically human being.[101]

Patočka's philosophy of history and his analysis of the polis aim at such a "repetition" of a classical insight. This is not a repetition in any common sense, however, for it is an option to us only now, after contemporary thought has renewed the possibility of our access to it.

In order to concretely consider the feasibility of a politics integrated with an understanding of history, Patočka must first examine in greater detail the condition of the contemporary age that makes his work an imperative. He must also describe the content of that politics and defend its problematic conception of meaning. In the following chapter, I take up the question of Patočka's critique of politics in the twentieth century, and outline the philosophical politics he envisions as our only authentic alternative. I conclude by examining the role and form of the ethics that emerges from this philosophy of history and the soul.

5

Politics and Ethics in the
Twentieth Century

In the last two *Heretical Essays in the Philosophy of History*, Patočka
turns from developing a philosophy of history to applying its principles
in the contemporary world. Here we have a clear expression of the political
side of his philosophy. Although Jan Patočka became known as a dissident
in Czechoslovakia in the 1970s, his political philosophy cannot accurately
be characterized as "dissident" philosophy. Its focus is not resistance and
its relevance is not limited to periods of ideological repression. The ground
of Patočka's political dissidence is a form of political morality and commitment to truth. Politics must be subservient, he argues in Charter 77, to
something that transcends it and holds it accountable. While this may
resemble a straightforward metaphysics of morals, the resemblance is
deceiving. This type of foundation for politics is just what Patočka wants to
avoid. His philosophical outlook, as we have seen in the preceding chapters, is based on an understanding of historicity and problematicity that
explicitly denies the possibility of an objectivized metaphysics. And yet
there is an unambiguous moral element to the political philosophy of Jan
Patočka, an element that is the product of, not in conflict with, his ontological philosophy of history.

In this chapter I examine Patočka's political texts, including the final
and most radical of the *Heretical Essays*, with the aim of illuminating their
political and ethical implications. Patočka believes that an understanding of
human ontology and historicity, as he has developed the concepts, will lead
the individual to a mode of comportment that is inherently truthful and
ethical. This behavior on the part of dedicated individuals, by extension,
provides the greatest possibility for the genuine improvement of, not only
political society, but Western civilization as a whole.

The texts in question, the final two *Heretical Essays* as well as essays
on the spiritual foundation of political activity and the appearance of a
modern "supercivilization," reveal not only Patočka's understanding of
political ethics but also his personal relationship to the tumultuous political

scene in Central Europe during the twentieth century. These texts will also lead to an examination of his experience with communism and his decision to act as a dissident, culminating in his involvement with Charter 77.

PATOČKA AND POLITICS

Governance in the contemporary world, Patočka argues, has the character of an "accidental rule" [1]—accidental because it is rule infused neither by an understanding of humanity nor of history. This lack of understanding manifests itself in the politics of totalitarian movements, but also in the more conventional politics of the scientific age, where the individual is reduced to a mere role and conceived of as a "force" rather than a human being. "The question," Patočka writes, "is whether historical humans are still willing to embrace history." [2]

Embracing history means understanding human historicity. Modern civilization fails to embrace history inasmuch as it treats it as a puzzle to be decoded, a problem to be solved. It is precisely in seeking to grasp history, to foresee its conclusion and thereby end its fatal uncertainty and contingency, that we abandon it and lose sight of own historicity. "Modern civilization," Patočka writes, "suffers not only from its own flaws and myopia but also from the failure to resolve the entire problem of history. Yet the problem of history may not be resolved, *it must be preserved as a problem.* [emphasis mine]"[3] An age that reduces understanding to a mathematical equation cannot hope to understand history as a problem not subject to a solution. The recognition of history—of human life as problematic, and of the human being as historical—is precisely what contemporary, technological civilization denies.

In the last two *Heretical Essays*, Patočka takes up the question of the twentieth century. His aim, after diagnosing the character of the century, is to consider the variety of responses available to the individual. The hope for a simple solution has already been rejected—it is contrary to our very historicity. Accepting this, however, is a difficult prospect requiring considerable struggle and fortitude. Again following Plato and Socrates rather than Heidegger or Husserl, Patočka locates hope not in history or in society, but in the individual, the "spiritual person" who is able to recognize and accept problematicity. Only through such people does the possibility exist for a "*metanoesis,*" a "turn" of the civilization as a whole.[4]

Though he requires that such individuals act politically, Patočka is not suggesting a system of rule on the order of Plato's *Republic.* It is not a question of placing them in the position of guardians or rulers. In contemporary society they already occupy positions of importance: they may be engineers or artists, writers or clerics, perhaps even political leaders. The question is not one of their becoming politicians, but of their acting politically—their acting publicly and in mutual recognition so as to lead society toward the understanding of history presupposed by the existence of a historical civilization.

The question of Patočka's political writings is not an easy one; very little has been written on the subject, with some analysts concluding that the Czech philosopher has little to say about political philosophy.[5] Yet Patočka expressed himself politically on many occasions and consistently made explicit the underlying relevance of his philosophy to politics. The relevant essays appear, not merely in his dissident phase, but throughout his career. In order to grasp Patočka as a "political" philosopher, then, I will examine these texts as a group.

Europe and Existentialism in Patočka's Early Work

The course of Patočka's career was profoundly influenced, as I have noted, by the events of his time.[6] The first of many decisive turns of history for Patočka and all Czechs occurred when the glory of the first independent Czechoslovak Republic under Masaryk was confronted with the rise of Adolf Hitler and National Socialism, followed shortly thereafter by the betrayal of the West at Munich and the Nazi occupation of the Sudetenland. Like Husserl in his *Crisis* lectures, Patočka expressed his critique of this approaching storm in terms of resistance to an attack on the philosophical spirit of Europe. The young Czech was greatly inspired by the elder philosopher's rejection of this "irrationalism" and call for a rebirth of Europe "through a heroism of reason."[7] Unlike Husserl, though, Patočka saw something in the *Existenzphilosophie* of Jaspers and Heidegger that did not conflict with his search for the rational spirit of Western thought. In many of his texts of the thirties, these influences combine to produce a philosophical approach that, while recognizable as that of a young man—characterized by a sense of philosophy as heroic resistance and a rejection of all naive "*leaning on* an absolute power" for support[8]— nevertheless projects a basic continuity with his more mature work.

Characteristic of these texts, for example, is a strong critique of religion and an exhortation of a life in "amplitude" over a life in "balance."[9] He also takes issue, significantly, with T. G. Masaryk's condemnation of what he called "titanism." Titanism, as Masaryk saw it, was equivalent to Dostoyevsky's understanding of "nihilism as a deification of man, enthroning man in place of God as the highest lawgiver." While "Dostoyevsky speaks of nihilism, Masaryk speaks of titanism."[10] Though no nihilist, Patočka is not inclined toward Masaryk's reading. He criticizes Masaryk's oversimplification of the problem into one of subjectivism versus objectivism, of modern subjectivism versus the idea of an objective reason in God. For the young Patočka, Masaryk's formulation is overdetermined. It implies that "man's striving to give meaning to his life" is tantamount to Titanism, and that the man who does so, who "gives up the moral crutch of an external command" and denies his dependence on "salvation from without," inevitably finds himself in a "blind alley."[11] Patočka rejects the deterministic nature of this conclusion. In fact, he argues, the subjective "titanic" approach may actually uncover the "germ of a solution" in its rejection of an absolute and objective foundation in God.[12] The alternatives are not as clear-cut as Masaryk's dichotomy between a nihilistic subjectivism and a moral objectivism would suggest. Above all, Patočka wants to examine human existence by looking at human beings and our world, not by focusing on a transcendental being who picks us up when we stumble. For Patočka it is the *world* as a whole and our relation to it that transcends us and forms the context for our striving. Thus he issues an apology of sorts, contra Masaryk, for the philosophical "titan" willing to reject facile objectivism.

There is a dangerous element to this quasi-existential posture, of course. It could be argued that Patočka comes close to titanism in the nihilistic sense to which Dostoyevsky refers. Such a conclusion, though, would be premature. The curious mix in these early texts of "existentialist passion with utmost scholarly rigor," as Erazim Kohák described it,[13] manifests instead a tension between a youthful, existentialist urge to reject traditional philosophy and a Husserlian urge to renew European reason. Although Patočka's early writings are distinctly characterized by this heroic conception of philosophy, they are not essentially existentialist, and certainly not nihilistic, texts.[14] While Patočka recognized and appreciated in existentialism its critique of traditional thought and its diagnosis of crisis, his own prescriptions called for a reflective renewal, rather than a rejection, of the spirit of European philosophy and politics.

Patočka rejects neither "European culture" nor the Nietzschean critique of that culture. He wants to learn from Nietzsche and his theme of titanic resistance to the gods. Patočka's idea of philosophy demanded quasi-titanic courage, a willingness to forego an absolute foundation for our ethical and social being. Yet he never seeks to follow Nietzsche into, and then out the other side of, a fundamental nihilism. Never does he succumb to the danger of preaching redemption from the standpoint of a God, a position suited to Nietzsche's *Übermensch*. In 1934, the young Patočka characterized the key difference in his own approach to philosophy:

As Christianity by consecration, as Buddha by dissolution into the universal, as socialism by the vision of a future society, so

Nietzsche wants to redeem life through the Superman. Could philosophy ultimately mean that there is no salvation in life?[15]

Patočka argues that life cannot be saved, but by this he means that it has no recourse to a savior, neither to an absolute being nor to a system that will bring progressive perfection. The lack of a savior does not mean an ultimate nihilism, however. As Husserl contended, Western civilization need not be abandoned; it must merely be understood once again in relation to its nucleus in the ancient Greek concept of reason—the nucleus of the concepts of philosophy and politics, democracy and the polis.

The degree to which Patočka defends the essential spirit of European philosophy, even in his early years, is evident in a 1939 article entitled "European Culture" and aimed against the rise of National Socialism. Here the universalist spirit that defines European civilization is defended against the romanticism at the core of National Socialism. That nationalistic romanticism, Patočka saw, represented a serious threat to the principle of democratic governance associated with Western politics since the Enlightenment: that free people could govern themselves with voluntary self-discipline. The rise of National Socialism showed, in fact, that this principle *"in and of itself"* was not enough to overcome international tension.[16] The Enlightenment did not equate with the idea, the spirit, of Europe; it reflected some aspects of that spirit, but obscured others. In this brief text, Patočka refers only superficially to a "contemplative aspect" of European civilization, represented by Greek philosophy. Yet he states clearly that the best hope for overcoming the international tendencies toward political dissolution leads through this aspect. "If some kind of cure for the ills of European civilization is to come about," Patočka writes, "a way must be found back to the idea that is a correlative to the contemplative, and to recapturing the inner life. The Enlightenment must be revitalized on its true, purified foundations."[17] The argument of this essay does not compare to Patočka's more mature work, but it does illustrate that, beneath the verbiage about a heroic "life in amplitude," Patočka remained dedicated to constructing, not dissolving, the bonds of European civilization.

Patočka's early conception of philosophy, though at times overdetermined in favor of a youthful heroism, nevertheless prefigures his understanding of history as the relinquishing of an absolute ground under our feet and over our heads. In the years following World War II and the liberation of the country, Patočka returned to the university and focused his energies on filling a desperate need for lectures in the basics of Western philosophy. His work from this period consists primarily of these collected lectures on the Greeks. His work on Socrates, Plato, and Aristotle was meant to be accompanied and complemented by his essay on "negative

Platonism," with its notion of freedom as a rejection of objectified, metaphysical constructions.

"Supercivilization" and the Question of Socialism

The period of the 1950s saw Patočka attempt to engage and understand the historical epoch in which he was living. With the end of the Second World War, it was clear that the form of European civilization had been drastically altered. Empires had been dismantled and faith in traditional models had given way to a competition for supremacy among various forms of rationalist, universal systems. Patočka responded with a thematic consideration of the very question of contemporary civilization; he sought to understand whether the modern variety represented just another civilization among civilizations, or whether it was something fundamentally different, a form of "supercivilization." This question meant that he would have to take up specifically the two dominant versions of modern civilization, the socialist versus the liberal democratic.

It was in this period that Patočka wrote one of his most explicitly political essays, concluding in it that the current civilizational epoch was one unlike any other—it was an epoch of rational "super-civilization." This article—an unfinished piece entitled "Supercivilization and Its Inner Conflict"—is a fascinating example of his political thought, containing some of Patočka's most explicit analysis of the theory behind contemporary political organization. In it, Patočka attempts to illuminate the core of contemporary civilization, paying particular attention to the conflicting possibilities it offers. It is a consideration of the very concept of modern civilization undertaken, as Ivan Blecha notes, from within one version of it.[18] Patočka contended, in summary, that the idea of modern civilization, characterized by its commitment to universalism and faith in a "heightened rationalism," was of a different order than in civilizations of the past. This "supercivilizational" order manifested itself in the superiority of the sciences and the reduction of philosophy to a question of method.[19] The bulk of the article, though, is not a description of the supercivilization, but an analysis of the ongoing conflict among different versions of it. Patočka not only offers an insightful look at what he calls "*radical* supercivilization," which is the embryo of totalitarianism, but he contrasts it with similar analyses of the alter ego of modern totalitarianism, the liberal democratic order that is but a more *moderate* version of supercivilization.

Modern supercivilization, he argues, is distinguished by these " moderate" and "radical" forms. While the former is consciously self-limiting, concerned with questions of means rather than goals, the latter, the " radical" supercivilization, seeks a form analogous to the idea of a "universal church." [20] It is radical supercivilization, Patočka contends, that is geared toward the totalizing of life by means of rationalism; it seeks a new center, "from which it is possible to gradually control all layers all the way to the periphery." [21]

Patočka finds numerous examples of radical supercivilization in recent history; he cites, for example, the Cult of Reason and the French Revolution, Comte, Marx and Engels, and also the British utilitarians Bentham and James Mill. Characteristically present in these movements is not only a rationalistic universalism, but also a sense that they can provide the means to life's fulfillment. Historicity loses its force in these movements, for they lay claim to the whole of time:

> Supercivilizational radicalism also reconstructs the ancient concept of *kairos*, the entirety of time, of course no longer in the form of religion, but of religious-political salvation; a "time for" action, for a great, decisive work, a "day" of freedom and definitive accounting, the decision of which is given specifically to that delegated, so to speak characteristically chosen, committee of elected theocrats.[22]

In this experience there is also a quasi-mystical component of radicalism, manifesting itself in the stress on collectivism, on the totalizing character of the experience. Radical supercivilization favors explosive, revolutionary changes in society; in this sense it has more in common with " the irrational side of man over the reasoning." Despite this, radicalism often has an acute sense of moral issues and an ability to appeal to them heroically, making it particularly attractive to "young individuals and nations," to the civilization "*in statu nascendi.*" [23]

Patočka's analysis of modern radicalism is insightful, but it forms only a part of his achievement in this article. What is particularly significant, I think, and what differentiates this analysis of modernity from others, is its analysis not simply of the radical but also of the moderate. In contrast to radicalism, moderate civilization conserves the spirit of "rational criticism and construction" by retaining a sense of distance from it, that is, by making use of it, but without giving it a dogmatic character, without making it the" exclusive principle" of all life.[24] "Supercivilizational moderatism is protector to its own rational principle," Patočka writes, "precisely because in moderate society there is a great variety of interests, among which reason can function as a balancing authority." [25]

The moderate form of the rational supercivilization has as its function the formation of political societies that respond to its essence. In contrast to radical forms, it seeks to ensure that rule does not issue from the arbitrary will of particular people or decrees, but instead respects human freedom.[26] Moderate civilization, however, is not immune to the faults of radicalism; it is always in danger, Patočka writes, of slipping into the irresponsibility that characterizes radical forms. Yet in its moderate version, modern civilization is able to resist the descent into radicalism; its conservation of the spirit of reason protects it from the dangers of dogmatic ideology: "Unlike its opponent it is not so easily subject to the danger of phrases and hysteria." [27]

The primary values of the universal supercivilization are centered in freedom and in the individual. While the historical roots of these values trace to ancient Greek and Judaic civilizations,[28] the emergence of the supercivilization is more directly connected to the appeal to individual freedom characteristic of early liberalism. It is important to note, however, that Patočka does not connect individual freedom to economic forms of liberalism, but to the emergence of liberal thought in religion; it was with the Protestant movement in the sixteenth to eighteenth centuries that the notion of "religious self-determination of the individual before God" began to determine our view of freedom. The "modern principle of freedom," he continues, "does not stand or fall with economic liberalism."[29] An economic, or "atomistic," liberalism, in fact, is not an exemplary but a degenerate form of moderatism, and may impel people toward radicalism rather than protect them from it. Thus the crisis of moderate civilization, the question of its ability to resist radical influence and preserve its moral essence, is simultaneously a crisis of liberalism. It is a question of whether liberalism will proceed along atomistic or positivistic bases, or will recover a more essential view of the human being. "The crisis of liberalism is the crisis of moderate civilization, but liberalism and moderatism are not the same," Patočka concludes.[30] While the concept of the supercivilization has at its core the question of the individual, this question is not adequately reflected in the atomistic tendencies of liberal individualism.

The principle of the supercivilization stresses the individual, not by defining him as an atom, but by allowing him to distinguish himself in an altogether new way. While other societies have distinguished between the levels of the human and the divine, they have nonetheless presented them as reciprocally interpenetrating on the same level. The modern supercivilization, in contrast, has for the first time made possible a distinction between these levels, a distinction "between that which is in the power of man, a finite being, that which is the region of his positive and subject knowledge and his rationality . . . and that which is beyond him." Two levels are distinguished with the understanding that human life extends to both, that the level of the objective is penetrated by something that it is not possible to simply judge, that is not at our disposition.[31] In this conceptualization, the human individual is understood as distinct from the divine, the transcendental, but not as indifferent to it. At this level humans are not indifferent to others, as they are on the level of radical individualism.

It is the atomistic form of liberalism that has dominated in the modern world. The result, Patočka alleges, has been a degree of crisis in the very concept of the modern, rational civilization, leading to an increased temptation toward radicalism. Thus Patočka appears as a critic of liberalism, with the goal not of destroying it, but of rescuing it from its own tendency toward decline. Liberalism needs reform in order to set individualism back on its proper foundation.[32] The goal is a political theory that responds to the individual as a responsible human being, not as an indifferent atom. Explicitly excluded, here, is the notion that a certain technique of societal organization, an institutional engineering, is enough to correct for the manifestations of crisis in modern life. To the contrary, the greater the degree to which liberal society is schematized, is reduced to an exportable set of institutions, the greater is the inclination toward the systematization of life itself, and so to a strengthening of general decline.[33]

"Supercivilization and Its Inner Conflict" thus presents the universal, rational civilization as potentially positive, but makes it clear that, in practice, it has more often than not manifested itself in a degraded form. The twentieth century has seen a battle for supremacy between such forms, the battle of radical Marxist-Leninist or National Socialist forms of collectivism versus the offspring of moderate supercivilization represented by atomist and positivist forms of liberalism. For Patočka, working on the level of political philosophy, the challenge was always the same: to explore thematically the roots of political phenomena and ideology, and to uncover a path by which European civilization could recover and renew its understanding of and commitment to human freedom. Rather than contesting a particular regime—including, for a time, his own—he explored below the surface, for it is only at the elemental level of the relationship of politics to the human being, the level of philosophy, that truly effective change can take place.

One way in which Patočka's commitment to the exploration of possibilities may have manifested itself was in his relationship to his own regime—the Czechoslovak socialist government. In the decades after the war Patočka led the life of a decidedly nonpolitical philosopher. While it was clear that he rejected the communist power-holders in Czechoslovakia—he declined a request to sign with the Party even though it meant the end of his career—he otherwise refrained from political critique, even when the Stalinist excesses of the regime were at their worst. Patočka's relationship to socialism and the politics of the fifties and sixties may reflect the fact, as Ivan Blecha concludes in his study of the thinker, that he was "caught off guard by the developments of the time."[34]

By remaining resolutely apolitical and by working in obscurity, "buried away" in archives, Patočka was able to retain his personal integrity without the necessity of direct political confrontation. He seems to have chosen to neither throw himself "at all cost into a foolish confrontation with power," nor to give up his principles.[35] Yet Patočka's relation to communist politics was not simply a matter of avoiding confrontation. He also expressed a degree of uncertainty about the political situation, which would occasionally manifest itself, as his former students attest, in an apologetic attitude toward the communists. He is reported to have said, for example, that "somewhere there must be a reason why their present lie at one time gained so much power not only over people, but even in people. Apparently it has its original, truthful core."[36]

This stance, or lack of one, disappointed those students who sought a more unequivocal judgment. One of them, the future Rector of Charles University Radim Palouš, has gone so far as to attribute to Patočka a weakness for the "gnostic infection" that had decimated the university authorities. Palouš is referring, here, to the concept elaborated by Eric Voegelin to describe the immanentization of transcendent reality into an anthropocentric *hubris*, typical of totalitarian communist ideology.[37] Palouš argues, in fairly explicit terms, that Patočka, though he never let himself be "seduced" by the advantages of joining the communists—he remained "a persecuted intellectual"—nevertheless reflected a "mistaken inclination" toward his persecutors by refusing to discount the potential for "some positive social trend" in their ideology.[38]

Palouš' conclusion, it should be noted, is among the more uncompromising of the reactions of Czech intellectuals to this phenomenon. Perhaps more representative is the analysis of Ivan Blecha, who concludes that Patočka was "uncertain" about the situation and attempted, before condemning the situation outright, "first to understand the age from within."[39] Even Radim Palouš makes clear that, in the end, it is impossible genuinely to fault Patočka. He recognizes that the philosopher, after all, "never bowed to idols" and, despite that "he himself 'suffered under Pontius Pilate,'" he "refused to allow himself an incomprehension out of *ressentiment.*"[40] Palouš, in fact, comes to a conclusion similar to Blecha's: that Patočka consistently sought—perhaps too much so—to understand fully the phenomena around him before issuing judgment. Patočka's attitude, one might conclude, is representative of the perspective symbolized by the Prague Spring of 1968, that brief period that former dissidents often remember with even greater fondness than they do the events of 1989. In the Prague Spring, Czechs sought to dismantle, not the institutions of the communist government or its purported ideal of social justice, but the ideological lies and untruths on which it rested. The goal was to rid the government of its ideological, "gnostic" essence and to introduce freedom in the form of a socialism "with a human face." Czech society was full of the hope—naive, as it turned out—of positively affecting political developments without resort to warfare. This was a hope, it seems, that Patočka also harbored.

Charter 77 and Individual Dissent

Hope for positive reform peaked in the Spring of 1968, and was cruelly crushed in the Autumn of 1968. The Soviet-led invasion of Czechoslovakia brought an end to the Dubček reforms and a beginning to what came to be known as the period of "normalization."[41] Czech students and intellectuals were particularly devastated by the invasion. Once again banned from the university, this became the defining period for the development of Patočka's political thought. Not only was it the period of both the *Plato and Europe* lectures and the *Heretical Essays in the Philosophy of History*, it also marked the Czech philosopher's explicit incursion into the realm of political action as a spokesman and author of Charter 77. Patočka reacted against his banishment—a "premature" retirement—by simply continuing to work. He began to lead underground, "apartment" seminars for interested students willing to risk their careers for the sake of truth and their studies. There is a palpable sense in his lectures from this period of the philosopher responding to the direct needs of his students, each of whom was seeking a reason to continue to hope in the wake of the crushing Soviet invasion. It is the individual, the "spiritual person," to whom Patočka turns in his consideration of history and politics in these lectures. In hoping to effect change, to bring about an open and moderate form of civilization, structural reforms were insufficient. The locus of change had to be in the soul of the individual.

Despite risking persecution by holding illegal seminars in private apartments, Patočka remained basically apolitical even into the early 1970s. In 1976, however, a dissident movement that included many of his students began to coalesce around the fate of an obscure rock group, the "Plastic People of the Universe," who were persecuted for lyrics unbecoming to the socialist state. The trial of the "Plastic People," who played a style of music that Patočka considered unlistenable, nevertheless was to lead the now elderly philosopher into a role with which he was unfamiliar—that of dissident protester.

Under the leadership of Václav Havel and Jiří Hájek, a document was proposed that would do no more and no less than call to general attention that the trial of the "Plastic People" meant that the Czechoslovak Socialist Republic was failing to adhere to the Helsinkii Agreement on human rights to which it was a signatory and which therefore had the force of law in Czechoslovakia. Though it took some persuasion, Havel and others were able to convince the scholar to take on the role of cospokesperson for the

Charter. He accepted this role despite the clear understanding that he would be subject to persecution, and in the name of a style of music that he could not stand. In 1977, at age sixty-nine, Patočka began to speak and write as the philosophical and moral voice of Charter 77. The Charter was, for all intents and purposes, a moral protest in the name of truth.

Patočka's participation in Charter 77 not only lent the protest—it was a protest, not a political or human rights "movement"—the respectability it sought, it also gave it its first and greatest martyr. The lengthy interrogations to which Patočka was subject after his inevitable arrest were too much for him, and he suffered a stroke and died several days later. Patočka's premature death resulted from his standing up and telling the state what it did not want to hear, that is, the truth. His death in this way suggests an analogy to the fate of Socrates that is both so obvious as to seem cliché, yet so fitting as to demand recognition.

The analogy to Socrates is not out of place, for Patočka lent to the Charter the sense that it was led by a figure committed to truth. His activity on behalf of the Charter was most certainly driven by this commitment. Charter 77 was a reflection of Patočka's philosophical perspective in many ways. It is important to note that it was not a political movement organized around or representing a competing ideology; it did not advocate the overthrow of the government or any particular action beyond the act of speaking the truth. And the truth it advocated was contained in the contention that politics was not a matter of technical control but of moral sentiment—that this morality was binding on government because it preceded it. "Humans do not invent morality arbitrarily, to suit their needs, wishes, inclinations, and aspirations. Quite the contrary, it is morality that defines what being human means."[42]

Charter 77 did not represent an attack on government; it sought to the contrary to "strengthen [its] legality."[43] The Charter did so by standing for the simple principle of the equality of citizens before the law. It did not seek to enumerate individual rights that would stand above history and insulate the individual from that state; rather, it argued that government must respond to the same conviction that governs the individual: unconditional "sovereignty of moral sentiment" over states and individuals.[44] Charter 77's hope for politics was that citizens could learn to act as free and responsible persons, and that government would recognize this orientation by respecting the moral dimension of political life.

Although his involvement in Charter 77 was a natural outgrowth of his political philosophy, Patočka did not use his position as spokesman to try to bring the complexities of his work to a wider audience. To the contrary, he kept his message simple. When speaking of the source of the "moral sentiment" to which he referred, Patočka in fact alluded to the obligation to oneself associated with Kant. He spoke of the driving force of the Charter as a "commandment that is higher than any political privileges and obligation and which is indeed their genuine and only firm foundation."[45] It appears, from this language, that Patočka's interest lay in discovering an unconditional, ahistorical ground for both politics and ethics. This assumption could not be further from the truth.

One might argue that the language of Patočka's texts as Charter spokesman had what Leo Strauss would call an exoteric element to them.[46] They were intended as pamphlets for public consumption. These documents posited a moral sentiment without the underlying phenomenological and historical analysis that made transparent the way in which morality is not a product of an ahistorical categorical imperative or other metaphysical framework. What appears to be an adoption of a metaphysics of human rights is not one. I discuss the source of this morality in chapter 6, but in order to determine the precise relation between Patočka's political thinking—including his involvement in Charter 77—and his philosophy, I must first examine the concluding chapters of the *Heretical Essays*.

The focal point of Charter 77 was the individual, and the context of communist Czechoslovakia of the 1970s demanded that the individual be prepared to sacrifice. Any action in resistance to the ideology of the regime carried with it the certainty of punishment, it amounted to a premeditated sacrifice. It is to these individuals that Patočka is speaking in the last of the *Heretical Essays*, showing them that their resistance, their sacrifice, in fact draws on the very principle of rational civilization. When the powers that be have co-opted the symbols of "light" and of "day" and have turned them to ideological purpose, the truthful must have recourse to different symbols.

THE *HERETICAL ESSAYS* AND THE TWENTIETH CENTURY

With the last two of the *Heretical Essays in the Philosophy of History*, Patočka takes up the issue of the contemporary world and its relation to the problem of history. He does so first with an analysis of the fundamental character of the modern age (essay five), and then an application of that analysis to the major political events of the century (essay six). Though he often relies on a Heideggerean idiom in these essays, a close reading shows the consistency of his position. At the heart of our contemporary civilization lies the question of the individual and the thematic understanding of his or her historical being. Here as elsewhere in his body of work, self-understanding is symbolically achieved through care for the soul.

The subject of the fifth essay is framed as a question, and it again draws on the Heideggerean analysis of the character of technology. In what he calls a "sketch of the rise of the modern age and of its fundamental metaphysical character,"[47] Patočka asks the question: "Is Technological Civilization Decadent?" His question is not a moral but an ontological one. Having argued that the truly human life is inherently historical, meaning grounded in freedom and acted out in relation to being, Patočka now seeks to explore the degree to which modern, technological society denies this as a possibility. To answer this question, he writes, the first thing we need is a "criterion, a standard by which we could judge something decadent or positive."[48] The criterion sought, the notion of "decadence" or "decline," should be relative, not to the question of value judgments—it should not be an abstract value or a moral concept—but instead to human life in its basic functioning. A life is positive when it functions according to its possibilities as human; it is decadent when it loses contact with those possibilities, "when it loses its grasp on the innermost nerve of its functioning."[49] A society, a civilization, is considered decadent to the degree that it encourages such a life.

The thesis of the essay holds that the technological age, by virtue of a general reduction of meaning to that which is quantifiable, has increasingly eliminated the manifold of possibilities by which humans relate to themselves, to their own being, and to responsibility. This technological age, Patočka contends, is a time unlike any other, with science and technology having "swept away—definitively, it now seems—humankind's other, older attempts to shape, even to produce their lives."[50] And despite objections,[51] the progress toward greater and greater production of force and mastery of nature continues to proceed optimistically.

Patočka makes the historical argument that the spirit of modern, scientific rationalism is not a modern phenomenon. Most recent developments, he says, can be traced backward to certain practical tendencies of Christian theology, which themselves trace to the influence of Platonism. The bulk of the chapter is made up of Patočka's outline of the transition from the foundations of authentic historical activity in, for example, epic and dramatic poetry (tragedy), through Plato, neo-Platonism, Christianity, the Reformation, and the rise of modern capitalism and science. He sketches a line that is semicontinuous, purporting to show, not the uniqueness of the modern age, but its continuity with the dominance of metaphysics over European life.

Drawing on Heidegger's analysis of inauthenticity, the description of man relating not to his own humanity but only to the things around him,[52] modern individualism is depicted as a facade over an age that actually encourages the individual to identify himself with a "role." Man's freedom is merely the freedom to choose a particular role. Our civilization thus ignores the genuine problem of the individual, "the problem of the human person." Taking this problem seriously requires that humans not "be identified with any role they may assume in the world."[53] The individualism of Western liberalism offers no serious response to this problem; in fact, encouraged by technological progress, it increasingly reduces the individual to the status of a physical force. It is for this reason that Patočka concludes provocatively that the problem cannot be reduced to the level of the political regime, for no contemporary regime-type bases itself precisely on the individual freedom to which he is pointing: "The real question concerning the individual," he writes, "is not at issue between liberalism and socialism, between democracy and totalitarianism, which for all their profound differences equally overlook all that is neither objective nor a role."[54]

The problem of modern, technological civilization, then, is that it lays ontological questions to one side, it dismisses the Socratic injunction to examine one's self and one's life. Here a fully human life becomes "more difficult because the matrix of its possibilities does not include the relation of humans to themselves and so also to the world as a whole and to its fundamental mystery."[55] The modern individual, in accepting the "role" offered to him by technological civilization, effectively gives up his own self. He becomes disinterested in his own being as a problem and a question, and so gives up his humanity. "Being ceased to be a problem," Patočka writes, "once all that is was laid out before us as obvious in its quantifiable meaninglessness."[56] With the loss of the problem of being, the self is also lost. While modern civilization increasingly enables people to live longer and healthier lives, it does not respond to the principal human need, which is "not only to live but to live in a humanly authentic way."[57] To compensate, the technological world increasingly offers not only longer life, but also means for humans to avoid themselves through the pursuit of the superficial. Patočka's fifth essay offers extensive analysis of the way in which the "orgiastic" increasingly overtakes human responsibility.[58]

The analysis, while decidedly pessimistic, is not despairing. Returning to his original question, Patočka concludes that technological civilization cannot simply be labeled "decadent." This for two reasons: first, it has become evident that the character of the modern age is not entirely of its own making, but the bequest of earlier ages. Second and more important, and here Patočka returns to the point made in his 1950s analysis of moderate "supercivilization," despite the restriction in the scope of certain human possibilities wrought by this age, "it is also true that this civilization makes possible more than any previous human constellation: a life without violence and with far-reaching equality of opportunity." So even though this goal may yet elude us in actuality, it remains within our potential and brings with it an even more significant possibility. The "chief possibility" that emerges with our civilization and its potential is that of a "turn" away from the "accidental rule" of those whose aim is to enforce a preconceived meaning, and toward the rule of those "who understand what history is all about."[59] In other words, the technological achievement of this civilization, though it supplies increased opportunities for humans to avoid the responsibility of understanding history, also presents, and perhaps for the first time, the possibility that those who understand the nature of human historicity and freedom will be able to rule. If we are able to free ourselves from the "struggle with external want" on a global or civilizational basis, then humans may be afforded this possibility. Rule can transfer from those whose aim is nothing other than to preserve life to those who understand that history is not a problem to be solved but one that "must be preserved as a problem."[60]

While the overall analysis, Patočka admits, stems from insight developed by Heidegger, the application of that insight has an original, political quality. The most serious consequences of the modern estrangement from the question of being become manifest, not in individual psychoses or sociological maladies, but primarily in our political existence. From the perspective of states, the quantification of being has meant that humans can be perceived as little more than forces to be manipulated. Force itself becomes a metaphysical entity, a foundation through which geopolitical activity is realized. "The next and last chapter of our essay about history," Patočka adds, "will seek to show how this is reflected in contemporary historical events and the alternatives they present."[61] The politics of the twentieth century, exemplified by the First World War, show that a world transformed into a laboratory of accumulated forces is a world subject to the release of those forces in uncontrolled warfare.

"Wars of the Twentieth Century and the Twentieth Century as War"

It is the last of Patočka's *Essays* that may appear to readers as the most striking and "heretical." "Wars of the Twentieth Century and the Twentieth Century as War" is an examination of the politics and philosophy of warfare from the perspective outlined in the previous chapter—the Heideggerean analysis of the distancing from being that causes people to relate to themselves and to others as if they were roles or physical forces. This relation, Patočka argues, is connected characteristically and causally to the devastating warfare, both hot and cold, of the twentieth century. It is important to note that this essay, more so than the earlier parts of the *Heretical Essays*, is a text whose clear context is the struggle of Czechoslovak dissidents against the communist regime. While the bulk of the *Essays* constructs and elaborates a philosophy of history and human historicity, the final essay draws on specific aspects of that philosophy and applies them to twentieth-century politics. The result is a striking text that, while not particularly representative of either the tone or content of Patočka's overall philosophy, extends and applies that philosophy without betraying it.

"Wars of the Twentieth Century" is the essay to which analysts point when they wish to argue that Patočka may not be the consistent defender of European reason that he has appeared to be.[62] The reason, quite simply, is what appears to be the essay's evocation of war, conflict, and darkness over the values of peace and "the day." These are the passages that even Paul Ricoeur, an admirer of Patočka, has called "strange," and "frankly shocking" in their discussion of the "darkness and the demonic at the very heart of the most rational projects of the promotion of peace."[63] I have argued in this study, however, that even the most disconcerting of Patočka's metaphors and analyses do not imply an outlook that differs, in any fundamental way, from that presented in *Plato and Europe* or his other works organized around the concepts of a "life in truth" and "care for the soul." In examining these controversial themes and metaphors we shall see that, despite a difference in tone and idiom—the text arguably overextends its application of Heideggerean themes to political reality and presents it in an oversimplified and foreboding light—the essay's conclusions fit into overall scheme of Patočka's philosophy. It remains the figure and philosophy of Socrates, extended somewhat with an appeal to the pre-Socratic, Heraclitian theme of conflict, or *polemos*, to which Patočka looks as a model for philosophical and political activity in the polis.

"Wars of the Twentieth Century" begins with an examination of the character of the First World War, a war that Patočka calls "the decisive event" of the century, determining "its entire character."[64] This war was revolutionary, and thus attempts to explain it based on conventional ideas fail to reveal its character. Underlying the war was a new ideology, a growing Nietzschean conviction that the traditional faith on which Europe saw itself resting had imploded:

> The shared idea in the background of the first world war was the slowly germinating conviction that there is nothing such as a factual, objective meaning of the world and of things, and that it is up to strength and power to create such meaning within the realm accessible to humans.[65]

One answer to this perceived lack of meaning was in science and, in this regard and despite appearances to the contrary, it was post-Bismarckian Germany that was the most revolutionary. Insofar as the democratic states clung to the imperial idea, "their claims to democracy begin to appear as components in their defense of the global status quo."[66] Germany, though, was leading a revolution toward the enforcement of "the reality of the new technoscientific age." It was creating and enforcing this idea in its pursuit of the organization and accumulation of energy and the creative power of its working masses.[67] This was the idea that force was the dominant and necessary feature of the modern age.

Germany, of course, was not the only country moving in this direction, but its progress was the most revolutionary, the movement of countries like France being somewhat "humanized by their desire for individual life."[68] The end of the war brought the defeat of Germany, but not of its revolutionary aim; that aim was ably taken over by Russia, which succeeded where Germany had failed. The Soviet Union was able to mobilize its society behind a form of rule based in pseudo-scientific rationalism. The First World War, Patočka continues, was decisive because it demonstrated that the transformation of the world along techno-scientific lines—into a laboratory of forces—can proceed only with the help of war, i.e., "acute confrontation," because such confrontation is the most effective means of releasing the inevitable buildup of forces.

World War I, then, represented "a definitive breakthrough of the conception of being that was born in the sixteenth century with the rise of mechanical natural science."[69] War, it is important to note, has been defined here as "acute confrontation," for it is not merely military combat between nations to which Patočka is referring, but the process of confronting and sweeping away all that stands in the way of the transformation or revolution in progress. War, the "acute confrontation" with all of the "conventions" that inhibit the release of force, is the means by which the rule of force actualizes itself. "In this process humans as well as individual peoples serve merely as tools."[70]

What Patočka is attempting to describe in these pages is a picture of the twentieth century primarily drawn from his experience with communist totalitarian rule. The Russian Revolution and the resulting decades of Soviet rule epitomize this picture, for they represent the clearest example of the political incarnation of the "new technoscientific age." The power of organization and the manipulation of individuals become the guiding principles of this rule, which they effect by means of continuing warfare.

After the end of the world wars, warfare does not come to an end. What ceases are the brief, violent conflicts, but warfare against the conventions of society that resist transformation persists. The new war is "a war that establishes itself as permanent by 'peaceful' means."[71] It is the "war against war," the war to establish a permanent peace, and it progresses by informing people weary of violence and death that the highest of all values is life itself. Only when convinced of the overriding value of mere life are people willing to play the roles demanded of them in order to preserve it. What Patočka is describing is a new rule of ideology; it is important to note, however, that it is not limited to authoritarian or totalitarian systems, but is present in any movement in which the goal of peace and mere life is given an eschatological significance.

The ideology of Soviet communism was one that promised both lasting peace and a new life, though it demanded both the body and the soul of the individual in return. This ideology, of course, was originally considered the most enlightened and progressive of political movements. It epitomized, in this sense, what Patočka calls the "forces of the day." The forces of the day are the forces of eternal progress; they seek a perfect peace and condemn conflict and contingency as barriers to that goal. At their most elemental level these forces are not unique to the twentieth century; they can be described in eschatological terms as movements aiming toward a "solution" to human problematicity: a final peace, an end of history, and so on. From their perspective, "life, especially historical life," appears as a continuum within which individuals function as the bearers of a general movement which alone matters.[72]

In violent wars fought on behalf of ideology, these are the banners under which we fight and die. In the second half of the twentieth century, however, the rule of force and technology has been enforced primarily by peaceful means. Warfare transmutes itself into "acute" confrontation with the "conventions" of the past, "those muting factors represented . . . by respect for tradition, for former ways of comprehending being which now appear as outworn superstitions and a means of manipulating others."[73] The modern understanding of the individual as merely a role or a force merges in this century with an eschatology of peace, of a "better tomorrow." The pursuit of this dream by means of a nonviolent war against pretechnological ways of comprehending being, however, combines with the hot wars of the first half of the century to define the century as one, not of peace, but of war.

All of this represented, as Patočka and the Czechoslovak dissidents knew very well, a battle against the individual. It was one of Patočka's great achievements (and partly his purpose) in this essay to reveal a means by which embattled individuals could come to realize the significance of their resistance. Patočka did this through analysis of the concept of sacrifice. With this analysis he both justifies continued dissidence and offers solace to those whose personal sacrifice is overwhelming. The analysis draws on the writings of two witnesses to the horrors of the First World War: the Frenchman Teilhard de Chardin and the German Ernst Jünger.[74] The particular sacrificial experience analyzed is that of the front line soldier. The phenomenon of the front line, which is "absurdity *par excellence*" in its murderous brutality, is such that it has the potential to effect a fundamental transformation of human existence. Despite its horror, perhaps because of its horror, Patočka controversially contends that "in the depths of that experience there is something deeply and mysteriously positive."[75]

In most cases, he points out, the forces that have brought the soldier to the front are the "forces of the day," those quasi-eschatological visions of a final peace, victory, and freedom that accompany and justify warfare. Drawing on Teilhard de Chardin and Jünger, Patočka argues that the experience of the front is such that these visions lose their power over the soldier. He is, in the horror and absurdity of his situation, freed absolutely from the hold of the abstract idea or ideology. "The front-line experience . . . is an *absolute* one. Here, as Teilhard shows, the participants are assaulted by *an absolute freedom*, freedom from *all* the interests of peace, of life, of the day."[76] On the front line, visions of the day have no power over the individual. He instead realizes that these visions do not depict reality, they project a false image of it. Thus, the experience of the front justifies a reversal of the prevailing metaphors. The symbols of peace and the day do not adequately portray human reality; instead, it is the symbol of the night that responds to the mystery and problematicity that is our being. It is with this in mind that Patočka maintains that "[t]he grandiose, profound experience of the front with its line of fire consists in its evocation of the night in all its urgency and undeniability."[77]

The front line soldier offers Patočka a clear analogy to the fate of the dissident in a communist state. He describes the situation in which war has been continued by "peaceful means." "Currently war," he says, "has assumed the form of that half peace wherein opponents mobilize and count on the demobilization of the other."[78] This is the strategy of the rule of ideology in peacetime—it is to produce a state of "demoralization" in its opponents by appealing "to the will to live and to have." The rule of force is accepted as the price one must pay to live well. While a return to a front line in rejection of this state is something difficult to actively desire, Patočka argues that there are situations in which it can mean an "immense liberation from precisely such servitude" as under communism.[79]

Thus the notion of being on the front line becomes, for Patočka and his dissident students, the symbol for their resistance to the ideology of untruth in communist Czechoslovakia. "The front line is the resistance to such 'demoralizing,' terrorizing, and deceptive motifs of the day. It is the revelation of their real nature, it is a protest paid for in blood which does not flow but rots in jails, in obscurity, in life plans and possibilities wasted."[80] Here the reference to the dissident is explicit, for it is he who rots in jails in obscurity, sacrificing life plans and possibilities for the sake of the truth. Indeed, the analogy can be extended further to the philosopher himself who, as Socrates testifies, inevitably comes into conflict with the city. In this activity, despite its requirement of sacrifice, one attains the freedom that one seeks. The front line is a site of potential freedom: "It is to comprehend that here is where the true drama is being acted out; freedom does not begin only 'afterwards,' after the struggle is concluded, but rather has its place precisely within it—that is the salient point, the highest peak from which we can gain a perspective on the battlefield."[81]

The narrow focus of this essay notwithstanding, Patočka's philosophy continues to aim at a resuscitation of contemporary Western civilization broadly speaking. In this regard, the point of the essay is not the presentation of a solution but the asking of a question. Patočka recognizes that, despite the devastating wars of the century and the many front-line soldiers who have returned from war to help reorganize their societies, the effect of their experiences on society has remained essentially "nil." Thus the question: "How can the 'front-line experience' acquire the form which would make it a factor of history?"[82] The failure of this experience to become a factor of history makes it clear that this is not a question with a ready answer. Yet it is a crucial question, for it reflects on the potential influence of philosophy on history and politics; philosophy, like the clarity gained on the frontline, is born when one shakes oneself loose from the hold of naive, undifferentiated, and unreflective thought.

Two points are stressed in Patočka's account. First, the core of a solution, to the extent one can be said to be possible, lies in the fostering of understanding—of history, of freedom, of the essence of philosophy that demands that one forego the surety of simply given knowledge and ideology. Patočka's second point is more concrete. The experience described by Teilhard and Jünger does not transfer to society because it is an individual experience. What is needed, both in the case of dissidence in Czechoslovakia in the seventies and in terms of an approach to political action in the modern age generally, is something more than individual experience. What is needed is a concerted effort by those who have shaken loose of the hold of ideology, what Patočka calls a "solidarity of the shaken." "The means by which this state is overcome," he writes, "is the *solidarity of the shaken*, the solidarity of those who are capable of understanding what life and death are all about, and so what history is about."[83]

The goal, then, is twofold. It is first and foremost the general goal of philosophy as Patočka sees it: to "shake" human beings into an awareness of their own historical nature, their own possibilities for freedom via the assumption of a self-reflective stance and the rejection of ideology. In the specific context of the problems of the twentieth century, this translates to a more specific action—the attempt to make those capable of understanding willing to accept the sacrifice that is required. In other words, the goal is:

> To shake the everydayness of the fact-crunchers and routine minds, to make them aware that their place is on the side of *the front* and not on the side of even the most pleasing slogans of the day which in reality call to war, whether they invoke the nation, the state, classless society, world unity, or whatever other appeals, discreditable and discredited by the factual ruthlessness of the Force, there may be.[84]

Accompanying this is a second goal, one which Patočka himself helped to realize with his sponsorship of Charter 77. This is the goal of concerted action, of solidarity. In the context of a communist state in the late twentieth century, it took just such a solidarity to call the world's attention to the fate of free thought in Central Europe in 1977.

When both goals are combined, the effect on political society can be profound. The effect, however, will not be an explicitly political one, for the "solidarity of the shaken" is not conceived of as a political movement or party. It is not a coordinated scheme to wrest power from those who hold it and replace it with a new, positive scheme.

> It will not offer positive programs but will speak, like Socrates' *daimonion*, in warnings and prohibitions. It can and must create a spiritual authority, become a spiritual power that could drive the warring world to some restraint, rendering some acts and measures impossible.[85]

The action of Charter 77, which proposed no political "program" and was not a political "movement," epitomized the goal of Patočka's "Wars of the Twentieth Century and the Twentieth Century as War." It was a protest with the simple goal of speaking the truth, always the greatest threat to a corrupt government. Though Charter 77 did not result in the fall of the communist regime in 1977, the spiritual authority that it represented and created, led by Václav Havel and other students of Patočka, was singularly influential in leading the "Velvet Revolution" of a decade later.

In the concluding paragraph of "Wars of the Twentieth Century," Patočka appeals to another symbol, one that arguably runs counter to the tenor of his Platonic writings—he appeals to the Heraclitian symbol of *polemos*, or conflict.[86] Once again, his inspiration is Heidegger and his goal to show that the ground of human reality cannot be reflected in a simple, metaphysical structure.[87] Heraclitus' depiction of being as *polemos* is appropriate, it is argued, for it reflects the same vision noted independently by both Teilhard and Jünger in their analyses of the front-line experience— a vision of unity attained in the midst of conflict. Nevertheless, Patočka's appeal to this symbol appears somewhat inapposite for several reasons. First, the symbol of *polemos*, often translated as "war," seems to contradict the tenor of the essay, which condemns the phenomenon of war in the twentieth century. A second and related problem has to do with the appeal to Heidegger, for the use of the concept of *polemos* in Heidegger's *An Introduction to Metaphysics* is associated, by virtue of both the timing of the original lecture and its language, with the German philosopher's involvement with National Socialism. Based on Patočka's invocation of *polemos*, therefore, it would be conceivable to read this essay as a glorification of war; but this would be a misinterpretation.[88]

It is, in the end, the theme of *polemos*, as well as that of the "night," which stand out in this essay, tending to obscure its connection to Charter

77 and the activities of Czechoslovak dissidents and human rights activists. These symbols, then, must be examined in terms of the themes they are meant to reflect. Otherwise, it is understandable that the effect of this essay on the reader will continue to be primarily one of the "shock" referred to by Ricoeur.

In the case of *polemos*, the first point concerns its translation into English. The intent of the symbol as Patočka uses it is to refer, not to "war" in the sense of a militarized struggle, but to "conflict." In conflict, we have a parallel to the phenomenon that is at the very root of philosophy, the shaking of naive faith in simply given knowledge that is the first step toward an attitude of self-reflection. *Polemos* cannot be understood to symbolize the wars that have characterized this century for, as Patočka went to great lengths to clarify, these wars represented, not a struggle to free the world of metaphysical, ideological thought, but a campaign to enforce such thought and make it permanent through the rule of force.

In regard to the second point, it is again the case that, despite the inspiration that Patočka derived directly from Heidegger, there is a significant difference between the two philosophers in the way the symbols are used. When Heidegger refers to Heraclitus' use of the concept of *polemos*, he speaks of it as the conflict inherent in the process of history as "world-building."[89] His stress is on the "creators" in the nation, who must struggle to open up a world. The use of the Heraclitian symbolism in this manner, coming as it did in the mid-1930s, carries with it an association of German romanticism, a sense of longing for a movement such as that described infamously in Heidegger's Rectoral address at Heidelberg: "The Self-Assertion of the German University." The association is unavoidable and it is difficult to read Heidegger's invocation of polemos and "world-building" in this text without thinking of his involvement with National Socialism. In Patočka's case, the dominant association is precisely opposite. What is sought is a concept of politics that above all else resists the lure of a resolution to the problems of history.

For Patočka, *polemos* is a symbol that neatly expresses the essential commonality of politics and philosophy. To be genuine, politics must be free, meaning it must struggle with the addiction to mere life and simply given wisdom that characterize pre-historical civilizations in which freedom is not an explicit theme. Philosophy, too, is a struggle. Patočka's understanding is made clear when he argues that it is only through this struggle that one sees into the nature of things—"*to phronein.* Thus *phronesis*, understanding, by the very nature of things, cannot but be at once common and conflicted."[90] The spirit of conflict and the struggle for excellence (*areté*) among equals within the boundaries of a city is essential not only to the operation of the polis, but also to the very insight that is practical wisdom. "Thus *polemos* is at the same time that which constitutes the *polis* and the primordial insight that makes philosophy possible."[91] As a symbol it is not appropriate to the warfare that regularly raged unchecked in this century. Rather than a force that dissipates, it is one that can serve as a foundation for unity and wisdom.

Despite this clarification, it was, and is, entirely possible that one could misread this discussion as an evocation of an extreme standpoint—of a Nietzschean, or a postmodern, rejection of a moral center to the *polis*. Conflict can, of course, be extended to extremes, and so it was, Patočka told his students, "[f]or precisely this reason that the moral side of conflict is important, as Socrates represented it."[92] Even though the concept is pre-Socratic it is nonetheless emblematic of Socrates and his dialectical interrogation of reality. It was only with the gradual movement toward systematized metaphysics that human struggle was deemphasized. It was never the case that Patočka sought to elevate *polemos* into the kind of extreme symbol that could be used as a rallying cry for resistance and revolution. The concept was intended to reflect reality, not to take on the characteristics of a metaphysical guidepost that stood above reality. Patočka in fact warned his students against just this sort of misunderstanding, saying in the same series of seminars that "I did not speak about conflict as about some kind of universal guide, to assume something like this is precisely what we must guard against."[93] The vision of Heraclitus is a relevant parallel, then, in the sense that it is only through an understanding of life as problematic, as characterized by a lasting struggle rather than an everlasting peace, that humans can hope to experience freedom.

Though *polemos* is perhaps the dominant metaphor emerging from "Wars of the Twentieth Century," also disturbing is the way in which Patočka subordinates the values of "peace" and the "day" to that of "darkness." This reversal of metaphors is certainly counter to the conventions of the Western tradition; in Christian and Enlightenment symbolism, for example, the symbols of light and peace are used to illustrate the highest goods.[94] Yet Patočka's symbolism is not intended to reflect an extreme attitude toward political reality. Instead, the evocation of "darkness" over "light" or "day" is meant to reintroduce the notion of mystery, of uncertainty and problematicity, which is an inevitable component of human existence. Darkness, it is noted, is the basic condition out of which light or knowledge first arises. It was with the progressive development of metaphysics, Patočka claims, that darkness came to be viewed as merely an absence of light, that problematicity came to be seen as a condition to be rejected, to be overcome.

In his lecture on "The Spiritual Person and the Intellectual," from the same period as the *Heretical Essays*, Patočka introduces the idea that the "light of dawn" does not emerge from a void, it emerges from darkness. Knowledge emerges from uncertainty, not in the sense that uncertainty is simply the absence of knowledge, but that it is a necessary precondition of the appearance of knowledge that we struggle with uncertainty and problematicity and accept them as unavoidable. He writes:

> Doesn't this suggest that there belongs to the nature of reality— when we take it as a whole, namely, as a reality that shows itself, that is revealed—something that is itself problematic, that is in itself a question, that is *darkness*. This does not mean darkness which is perhaps only our subjective ignorance, our subjective lack of knowledge, but rather something that is a precondition for a thing to appear in the world at all.[95]

The symbol of darkness used to such effect in "Wars of the Twentieth Century" and elsewhere, then, is a metaphor for the analysis of human problematicity. It is, in addition, a constant reminder that we are finite, that our life is precarious and our politics an urgent attempt to maintain order in the absence of a permanent and stable foundation on which we could rest.[96] The concepts of problematicity and finitude are crucial to a unifying theme of Patočka's philosophy, the acceptance of responsibility via the conscious rejection of metaphysical symbolizations of an absolute reality. Patočka's outline of an ontological understanding of historicity in the *Essays* is grounded in this theme.

This analysis of the twentieth century and its wars is a profoundly personal text. It bears the distinct imprint of resistance, of a call to the enlightened to draw on unexpected sources in their search for a reason—and the strength—to continue in their struggle. It is, in large part, a dissident text, by which I mean that the political circumstances surrounding it directly relate to the language of the essay, particularly the dark, poetic imagery that it favors. Patočka's argument is directed toward his fellow dissidents. He argues that, given the modern condition in which man and society are often held captive by a politics of force and a mechanical understanding of human being (exemplified by Czechoslovak communism in the seventies), the required posture is one of resistance, sacrifice, and a hope derived, not from the corrupted symbolisms of the regime, but from the more mysterious regions of human reality. Thus the symbols of the regime are unmasked as hypocritical, and the notion that one can draw strength and experience freedom in the depths of repression and uncertainty is stressed. Yet precisely what made this work effective in its time weakens it when the experience to which it refers fades from memory. In this sense, because it clearly refers most directly to the experience of Czechoslovak dissidents in the 1970s, its relevance, at least of the use of provocative imagery, is diminished with the passing of the dissident experience.

Although one could draw a parallel between the experience of the front-line and confrontation between Socrates and the Athenian Senate, the imagery Patočka chooses makes this a difficult proposition to accept. Nevertheless, several factors do favor a more Platonic reading. First, despite the imagery, the concepts with which the essay concludes are Platonic: first is the symbol of the *"metanoia,"* or "conversion," experienced by the philosopher, and second is the symbol of the Socratic *daimonion.*[97] The former, a "turn" toward understanding characteristic of Plato's liberated cave dweller, is the most for which the individual may hope, and the latter the closest he will come to an actual guidepost for political action.

Second, the importance of these elements is supported by an accompanying text that belongs to the body of work on the philosophy of history. "The Spiritual Person and the Intellectual," a transcript of an apartment lecture delivered shortly after the writing and distribution of the *Heretical Essays*, is explicitly relevant to the conclusions of the *Essays*. This text, as yet unpublished in English, offers both complement and contrast. Its subject is the "spiritual person," meaning the person indicated in "Wars of the Twentieth Century" as capable of conversion, or *metanoia.*[98] "The Spiritual Person and the Intellectual" is a distinctly different treatment of the same theme central to "Wars of the Twentieth Century": that meaning must be sought, not in slogans and promises and ideologies, but in the very fact of our freedom and our ability to recognize and come to terms with the problematicity of historical existence and the impenetrability of being.

THE SPIRITUAL PERSON AND THE POLIS

The "spiritual person," like the front-line soldier, is also a "shaken" individual. Though it is Socrates who exemplifies the "spiritual" attitude, this is not an essay about philosophers. Instead, Patočka describes the way in which the term *intellectual* properly describes, not the *sophist* who of course may also call himself an intellectual, but the person who truly understands the human situation. This "spiritual" perspective is not restricted to a few elite philosophers, though. The "solidarity of the shaken" is not comparable to the fellowship of guardians in Plato's *Republic*. Spiritual individuals are not expected to band together as a political party, as a concentration of power, they should merely draw from their solidarity the strength to assume a leading and public position in their chosen fields.

This theme, the role of the spiritual person in the city, is the backdrop of this essay. In the sense that Patočka imparts to the term, spirituality has all the characteristics of the Socratic mode of life. The primary concept, discussed in the previous chapter, is "problematicity." The spiritual person— or the philosopher—does not simply recognize problematicity, he or she is impelled by a commitment to freedom (for others as much as for himself) to impart this wisdom to the city, and in doing so to contradict and condemn its naïveté and shake its very foundations. The purpose of the philosopher is to awaken the city to a new possibility, a new ground; this is done by problematizing knowledge, not by simplifying it.

> Socrates and Plato were problematizers of life, they were people who did not accept reality as it is given, but saw it via a shaking— but the consequence of this shaking for them was precisely the *possibility* of some kind of particular, *other* life, another direction of life, something like a *new ground* on which it is now possible to measure what is and what is not.[99]

As a philosopher, Socrates cannot be silent about this "other life." He thereby assumes a crucial yet bothersome role in the city; by his activity and his questioning he problematizes the traditional foundations of the polis.

Patočka's reference to the possibility uncovered by Socrates and Plato as a "new ground," brings our attention to the question of the degree to which this philosophy can provide a foundation on which to base a political society. The challenge to metaphysical foundationalism is associated with philosophy since Nietzsche. Patočka believes that this challenge, a nonmetaphysical view of reality, is already a characteristic of Socrates and his dialectical interrogation of reality. Socrates, in a sense, bridges the ancient and the new. Despite involvement through Plato in the development of metaphysics, Socrates' activity in the city is concordant with the critique of contemporary, antimetaphysical theory.

> And because Socrates stands solidly, this man who, under the reign of the tyrants, at the risk of his own life, maintains his opinion that it is worse to do injustice than to suffer it, and because this man on the other hand continually repudiates with his way of speaking those who presume to have knowledge of the good, meaning that he shakes the prevailing certainty upon which the polis lives, and at the same time he himself does not say what the good is, but only appeals to people to do a bit of hard thinking, to reflect as he does, in order to seek, in order that they *responsibly* examine every one of their thoughts,—this means not accepting mere opinion as if it were insight, as if it were the insight to live based on the authentic examination of that which is here, which is present—therefore Socrates is at the same time a man both ancient and new, both merging in one.[100]

This is the Socrates that epitomizes the spiritual person. His goal is not to create a new myth for the city, but to shake it loose from the grasp of all mythologizing. Nietzsche and Heidegger are wrong in failing to pursue what they may grudgingly recognize—that the essence of Socrates is not a facile pursuit of metaphysics, but a challenge to the polis to stand free of all forms of simply given knowledge and to think responsibly.

As discussed in chapter 5, Patočka understands philosophy as interdependent with politics. With "The Spiritual Person and the Intellectual," he takes this theme a step further, discussing the consequences of this interdependence for the individual and for the city. Drawing on Plato, Patočka notes three choices open to the philosopher. First is the path of Socrates: "to show people how things are in reality," though this means conflict with the city and the likelihood that one may lose one's life. Second is the path that Plato chooses—"withdrawal from the public," withdrawal from conflict with the city in the hope of creating a "community of spiritual people" where the philosopher may live and not die. Beyond these choices, Patočka writes, "the third possibility is to become a sophist. There are no others."[101]

Although one could argue, particularly in light of Patočka's history of noninvolvement with politics up until 1977, that the second option of an Academy detached from the polis is a just one, by this late stage in his career Patočka had resolutely come to the conclusion that the only choice was the first one, despite the sacrifice involved. The second option, in fact, was something of a false one to the degree that its goal was to separate philosophy from society. This, Patočka argued in *Plato and Europe*, could not be done. "The true person, the philosophical man, cannot be a philosopher only for himself, rather he must exist in society . . . in society with others, because in the end no one wrenches himself loose from this situation."[102] The goal for the philosopher, implicitly, was to make this society truthful, one in which the philosopher could actually live.

Society does not easily take advantage of its possibilities. The role of the philosopher, or of the spiritual person, is not only to explore those possibilities but also to prod society in their direction. This is, Patočka rightly contends, a political task. While spiritual activity does not evoke politics in the modern sense of the term, it is nonetheless political activity.

> The spiritual person is obviously not a politician in the usual sense of the word, he isn't political in the common sense of the word: he doesn't take sides in the disputes that rule this world—but yet he is political in a different way, obviously, and he cannot not be, for the non-self-evident nature of reality is exactly that which he hurls in the face of society and of that which he finds around him.[103]

It is partly for the sake of society that the philosopher is concerned with declaring the "nonevident" nature of reality. Yet society does not appreciate being shown a vision of reality that contradicts the one on which it rests. Rather than embrace it, the holders of power will fight against it, thus the inevitable conflict between the philosopher and the city described by

Plato. Patočka's addition to this theme, in his later work, consists of an analysis of the political responsibility inherent in the spiritual standpoint. The spiritual person's political activity is inevitable; he must stand before the "positive powers," and "the person of spirit must, of course, advocate his position."[104]

Sacrifice and Responsibility

For all its surface idealism, this responsibility—as Central European dissidents knew well—demanded of the individual a very real sacrifice. It is to Patočka's credit that he appends to his late philosophy an analysis of this phenomenon, the meaning of sacrifice itself in relation to a life in truth. Although I noted above that the proper choice for the philosopher was engagement with the city *"despite"* the sacrifice involved, there is a clear theme in Patočka's later work to the effect that a true sacrifice, even of one's own life, provides a benefit to the spiritual person from an ontological standpoint, a benefit that can outweigh the suffering. The spiritual person is rewarded not despite his or her sacrifice, but through it.

Patočka writes most specifically on this theme in his Varna Lecture from 1973, appending a discussion of sacrifice—which is "mythicoreligious" in origin—to a consideration of Husserl and Heidegger on the question of technicization and technology.[105] The notion of sacrifice implies an understanding that cannot exist in a purely rational or technological view of the world. It demands a recognition that some things are higher, of a different order, than others: "A sacrifice for something or for someone presupposes the idea of a difference of order between human being and the being of things, and within the sphere of the human in turn possibilities of intensification or of failing of being."[106] In the technological age, as I have noted, the individual (and so the individual as victim) is reduced to a role, the question of being reduced to a mathematical equation. But an examination of sacrifice "points to an entirely different understanding of being than the one exclusively attested by the technological age."[107] Living in the truth requires a willingness to sacrifice some of the security offered by these equations and calculations. "The paradoxical conception here," he concludes, "is that man gains by a voluntary loss."[108] Through a comprehension of sacrifice, a person may recover his being even as he loses all else.

When formulating his idea of sacrifice, Patočka refers to the example of two Russian thinkers: Alexander Solzhenitsyn and Andrei Sakharov. Their example exemplifies the meaning of the concept in two ways. First, their willingness to sacrifice helps us understand the content of "freedom" as an ontological, not a physical condition. Freedom is not defined here negatively, as in the absence of restrictions upon movement or the avoidance of jail and other threats to a comfortable and safe life.[109] To the contrary, freedom can be gained even as we voluntarily relinquish certain aspects of it. It can be gained through action that is self-revealing, action that makes us aware that we are not, and need not be, beholden to mere life.

Solzhenitsyn and Sakharov were also important in a very different sense, though, one that relates directly to the notion of the "solidarity of the shaken." These two Russian thinkers, in many respects, could not have been more different. While Solzhenitsyn was a religious man, concerned with continuity, nation, and tradition, Sakharov "exemplifie[d] an entirely post-metaphysical modernity." He was, in Patočka's words, a "hypermodern man."[110] In the difference between these two men, in that, despite their differences, they would speak and act in a sort of concert to oppose communist oppression, lies the essential force of the "solidarity of the shaken."[111]

The common element with Solzhenitsyn and Sakharov, as with the vision in Teilhard de Chardin of enemy soldiers in the front-line trenches coming to feel a greater solidarity with each other than with the politicians in the rear, was a sense of the truth of their own humanity that outweighed any material advantage or dogmatic slogan that could be offered to them. Basing one's action on this sense defines what Patočka means when he speaks of *responsibility*. Responsibility is not a moral value. It has no abstract content. Nor is it an Aristotelian virtue, responding to a sense of proportion or moderation. Instead, it describes the manner of living in which one acts in response to one's own being, as well as to the world perceived as a whole. The sense Patočka gives to responsibility implies something akin to the Socratic *daimonion*, not offering positive programs but "speaking in warnings and prohibitions." It is a "spiritual authority,"[112] but one that originates from our own sense of being, not from a being external to us. As we respond to our being, as we are interested in it, we are captivated by our responsibility and cannot be indifferent to it. In the opposite situation, when we try for whatever reason to escape from or forget ourselves or our humanity, then we abdicate our responsibility. The responsible attitude is one in which we are exposed; sacrifice, as in the case of Solzhenitsyn and Sakharov, can be a responsible act.[113]

There is also, in Patočka's concept of responsibility, an element that makes it not only an individual event but a communal one. Responsibility and the possibility that it may entail sacrifice, as we have seen, mean linking one's life to freedom. Yet, consequent to Patočka's stress on our social nature, there is the added factor that freedom is not simply an individual matter, it relates not only to the individual, but also to others. It is in this sense that Patočka describes the being of humans, as opposed to mere consciousness, as "something capable of accepting responsibility and respecting responsibility, that is, the freedom, of others."[114] We inherently relate to others because our being is never an isolated, enclosed entity. It is in the world, of nature, of objects, of other beings. Our work, including the work that is our striving for freedom, is never pursued for oneself alone. As Patočka put it in another context: "Responsibility means: it is not only for me, it is also for the other and it has to be for the other, I don't work for myself, I am not free in relation to myself alone, rather I am free in relation to all, I am free for the society which supports me."[115]

Responsibility makes sacrifice no longer an individual event, but something undertaken for all. There is a parallel to be made to the Christian conception of sacrifice, and Patočka is not unwilling to make it. In his discussion of sacrifice in his Varna Lecture from 1973 he notes that "Christianity . . . placed at the center a radical sacrifice in the sense of the interpretation suggested above and rested its cause on the maturity of the human being." He continued, "perhaps it is in this sense that we need to seek the fully ripened form of demythologized Christianity."[116] This last comment is somewhat startling considering his otherwise unambiguous rejection of dogma, religious or otherwise. Christianity in its dogmatic forms, Patočka consistently argued, presents a metaphysical foundation for the morality it proposes. Yet many of its themes, like that of sacrifice, undeniably reflect human experience. A demythologized Christianity, then, might be one that continued to press its themes and symbolisms yet was delivered of a dogmatic reliance on an absolute being that is given and concrete. Patočka does seek a ground for ethical activity—but he seeks it in phenomenological philosophy rather than in dogmatic theology.

ETHICS AND MORALITY

As a philosopher, Socrates did not have simple "positive moral teachings" to give to people, and it is this model that Patočka follows. Yet at the moment when he achieves his greatest international renown, as spokesman for Charter 77, Patočka introduces a formulation that seems to contradict his "problematic" interpretation of reality. He writes of an unconditional morality, higher than and binding on both the individual and the state. At least one analyst, Aviezer Tucker, has stressed this language in concluding that Patočka's philosophy leads to a positive formulation of certain universal human rights. Yet this is a conclusion that runs counter to the Czech philosopher's denial of all metaphysical and suprahistorical formulations.[117] The question to be asked, then, is whether the appeal to morality of the Charter does not contradict the critique of metaphysics. Can Patočka, in other words, make a coherent appeal to a transcendental political ethics without abandoning his earlier conclusions?

Patočka's work, in line with the Czech tradition that produced T. G. Masaryk, has a clear and unambiguous respect for ethics and morality, particularly in the practice of politics. This is strongly reinforced by his reliance on Platonic language, something Heidegger purposefully avoided. The high point of Patočka's appeal to morality, most certainly, came with his participation in Charter 77. It is from this period that Patočka makes the following statement:

> No society, no matter how well-equipped it may be technologically, can function without a moral foundation, without convictions that do not depend on convenience, circumstances, or expected advantage. Yet the point of morality is to assure not the functioning of a society but the humanity of humans. Humans do not invent morality arbitrarily, to suit their needs, wishes, inclinations, and aspirations. Quite the contrary, it is morality that defines what being human means.[118]

Morality is not only crucial to human society, it is actually definitive of our being. We do not invent morality, it invents us.

But how can we be defined by morality if it does not exist a priori, over and above us? While most can agree that, no matter what its source, a moral order should not be arbitrary, simply suiting our "needs, wishes, inclinations, and aspirations," the question of a "moral foundation" that defines us is more difficult. The language of the texts written in defense of Charter 77, more so than in any other example from his corpus, seems to imply a metaphysics of morality. States, he wrote, are subject to "something unconditional that is higher than they are, something that is binding even on them, sacred, inviolable."[119]

What Patočka describes as a "binding" force, however, is not intended to invoke a metaphysical constant. Instead it is described as a "moral sentiment." That which is binding on states is not something to which one can point as to an object. It is neither relative to an individual or a group of individuals, nor does it originate outside of humanity. The source of the morality to which Patočka points is the being of humans itself. Patočka wishes to show that, if we delve into the question of the possibilities presented by our being, particularly the possibility of enhancing it, and if we take account of the world as a whole, and not as a collection of particulars, then we will arrive without the help of metaphysics at the conviction described above—the moral content of a life in truth. "*Charta 77*" [sic], he states, "is an outgrowth of this conviction."[120]

This interpretation of Charter 77 is contested, however, by the claim that Patočka's ethics, in the end, revert to a Kantian formulation. It is a claim supported by the author's own oblique reference. He writes that Charter 77 "does, however, remind us explicitly that, already a hundred and eighty years ago, precise conceptual analysis made it clear that all moral obligations are rooted in what we might call a person's obligation to himself."[121] The reference is clear: Patočka associates the moral obligation proposed by the Charter with Kantian analysis. Are we to understand, then, that the ground for our behavior is a categorical imperative? Is the Kantian analysis the nonmetaphysical formulation we are searching for?

The answer to these questions is "no," although the way in which Patočka describes the moral aspect of Charter 77 does indeed bear comparison to the categorical imperative. In fact, Patočka was asked by a student about this very point during one of his "Four Seminars on the Problem of Europe," and his response is revealing. Patočka says that he considers Kant's thought to be an attempt to get at the root of the problem, to formulate the essential "difference" referred to above—the difference between being and beings, in Heidegger's language. But there is a problem in that Kant's formulation is "decidedly nonhistorical, it is valid for every person in every circumstance the same."[122] It takes the form of a universal formula that stands above humanity and history. In this it is certainly easier to explain, to appeal to, but it fails to adequately respond to what Patočka sees as our historical nature.

In the examples of Solzhenitsyn and Sakharov cited above, Patočka contends that the meaning of their sacrifices is tied to their particular situations. In their circumstances they were able to increase their freedom and enhance their humanity (or being) through their actions. Their appeal was not to a universal formula or set of abstract rights, but to a moral sentiment tied to the fact of their humanity, that they could perceive truth and live truthfully and that such a life would make them more, not less, human. As Patočka described it with particular reference to Kant, the action of the Russians "does not have to do with some universal formula like the categorical imperative, but about something, that only in a concrete historical situation has force and validity."[123] In his philosophical writings and seminars, the connection of human freedom and human action to history is clear and unambiguous. But in his public proclamations in support of Charter 77, which were intended to be as brief and easily accessible as possible, the historical aspect is not explicit. Instead, it is the concept of the moral sentiment that is stressed. By stressing it, Patočka ran the risk of being misinterpreted in a Kantian light. Yet in the context of his philosophical work there can be no confusion. His thought is inherently historical; it does not reduce to a universal formula but stands on the basis of the fact of human historicity.

Thus we end up with an ethics based in a "moral sentiment" that is both transcendental—in the sense of transcending the particularities of our will or desires—and historical. The realm of this moral sentiment, this insight, does not exist for us *in concreto*. It is there not as a present reality, but only insofar as we respond to it in a historical situation. Patočka attempts to explain this point, the question of human morality, in a consideration of the meaning of the term *intelligence*:

> If, then, intelligence in the sense of free reflection is always bound to a moral posture, to choosing between right and wrong, with which is connected loss or gain of the authentic, spiritual "I," then by virtue of it's final assumption it is still only a realm into which we penetrate via "moral attitude, . . . " Of the realm into which we grow via moral insight, it's possible to truly say that it is "not of this world," because this realm does not make itself out, does not determine itself as given and present, but rather opens itself such that we hear a certain claim and we respond to it.[124]

We hear and respond in particular situations, and in doing so we move in truth; we appeal to a realm that exists insofar as we act to enhance and fulfill our possibilities as human beings.

The Nihilist and the Humanist

In addition to his critique of Kantian ethics, Patočka attempts to clearly distinguish his own interpretation from two other possibilities open to modern man. The spiritual person, in rejecting metaphysics, is tempted by but must ultimately resist the pull of both nihilism and humanism. In "The Spiritual Person and the Intellectual," Patočka notes that the individual who lives through and accepts problematicity is ultimately subject to a cruel fate. There is a cruelty in the seemingly endless skepticism to which he must subject the world, for it leads, almost inevitably, to an all-encompassing doubt, a negation of all meaning. The spiritual person is tempted to resign himself to "the thought that life and the world are not only problematic, but that meaning as an answer to this question not only is not found, but that it *cannot* be found, that the ultimate result is *nihil*—a self-negation, a self-denial."[125] He is tempted to resign himself, in other words, to nihilism.

Yet nihilism is not a solution nor is it the only recourse in a world where all other idols have been broken. In the concept of problematicity all is not negative and lacking unity. A unified life is possible on a skeptical basis, on a basis of problematicity: "In the spiritual life it is consequently possible to find unity precisely *without a solid ground*, and it is possible without dogma to overcome this complete negativity, negative skepticism, negative nihilism."[126] The spiritual life does not rest on a "solid ground," it admits to no dogma, but its interrogation of reality does not make life subjective or nihilistic. To the contrary, the questioning attitude of philosophy "is something that rests upon the deepest foundations of our life."[127] Unity is possible without a unifying doctrine.

This does not exhaust Patočka's analysis of nihilism. He also responds to Nietzsche, whose diagnosis of the death of metaphysics was followed by a search for a creative means of replacing it. In chapter 3 of the *Heretical Essays*, Patočka takes up the challenge of those who would embrace a certain nihilism in the wake of a loss of faith in absolute meaning. This was Nietzsche's solution, to accept the death of absolute meaningfulness, but to put in its place a creative will to power that itself can acquire relative meaning. But as Patočka conceives of the relationship between life and meaning, this must be an impossible attempt:

> In its practical unfolding, life cannot rest on a relative meaning which itself rests on meaninglessness, since no relative meaning can ever render the meaningless meaningful but, rather, is always itself dragged into meaninglessness by it. An authentic life in utter nihilism, with the knowledge of the meaninglessness of the whole, is impossible, becoming possible only at the cost of illusions.[128]

While Nietzsche's diagnosis of the crisis of meaning is acute, his prescription for the active creation of meaning through will to power is unworkable. One could persist in an attempt of this sort only by deluding oneself and others, by creating the illusion of a meaningful life. Nihilism, then, takes on the form of a dogmatic solution that is just as illusory as what it hoped to replace: "the theses of a nihilism so conceived, however, are no less dogmatic than the theses of a naive unbroken faith in meaning!"[129] Nietzsche, in his headstrong confrontation with the loss of meaning, ends up not with a liberating freedom but with another form of uncritical dogma.

Nietzsche's embrace of nihilism has not been the only option open to people in the postmetaphysical age. Accompanying the very crisis of faith to which the will to power is a reaction has been a tremendous rise in human scientific knowledge. This advance in human knowledge, in fact, is a primary cause of the decline in traditional metaphysics. As humans solve many of the great mysteries of humanity by scientific means, we see a transference of faith from superhuman sources of rationality to mundane sources. Faith is placed in humans themselves and in their ability to continually progress toward a better and more knowledgeable future. I am speaking, rather broadly, of the perspective referred to as humanism. In Patočka's analysis, modern anthropocentric humanism is discarded, for reasons that parallel the rejection of nihilism, as a *solution* to the question of meaning.

In two essays dealing with the topic of humanism, Patočka speaks of it in two forms. The first is a humanism characterized by a general faith in man and progress that Patočka terms "harmonism" and associates with some of the works of Masaryk. This general humanistic attitude "forms the background of the great majority of moral and social thought of modern humanity," he wrote in an undated essay from the end of the 1930s entitled "The Harmonism of Modern Humanists."[130] In his "Negative Platonism" of a decade or so later, Patočka is even more specific in pointing to an integral humanism with ties to positivism and the conviction that the scientific conquest of nature will replace the need for theology. In both cases, Patočka's position is clear: modern humanism bears the same characteristic markings as the metaphysics it claims to be doing away with. It is an elevation of human beings and their rational abilities to a status formerly reserved for the divine.

In the earlier article, Patočka discusses humanism in terms of "harmonism," the particularly modern conception of mankind based on the conviction that internally, man is a harmonious figure with limitless potential for progress. As he puts it: "Man in the faith of harmonism is in his essence a happy figure, whose nature is meant for unlimited growth."[131] Patočka's critique of this posture is straightforward. Far from comprehending humanity in its essence, this view reflects a transference of faith from traditional sources to an anthropocentric conception of rationality. The result is a simplified and distorted picture of the human being. "The man of harmonism is a closed, ready being, simple and entirely transparent."[132] Though it was never finished, the point of the essay is clear: a harmonistic ethics, an approach to moral problems based on this simplified notion of humanity, is insufficient and unable to respond to the complexity of the being of humans.

In the more polished "Negative Platonism," we will recall that Patočka conducts an analysis of the metaphysical roots of modern scientific rationalism and concludes that, far from overcoming the metaphysical desire for a complete understanding of the whole, modern humanism has actually taken over the aspiration in new form. This is surprising, on the face of it, for humanism generally defines itself in opposition to abstract metaphysics. Yet in two modern perspectives that both lead to humanism, in positivism and dialectical humanism or Hegelianism, "metaphysics is said to be an abstract formulation of theological ideas which will vanish under the light of successful human conquest of nature, of the resolution of social problems, and of a reordering of human society."[133] Though these approaches certainly differ in other ways, each results in a humanism reflecting this conviction.

The very factors meant to an eclipse metaphysics, the scientific "conquest of nature" and the "resolution of social problems," reflect metaphysical goals. Though they set themselves up in opposition to tradition, they carry on its search for a solution to history. As Patočka puts it, "In spite of all its resistance to tradition and to the form that metaphysics assumed within the church, within the traditional state, and in their schools, modern humanism continues to operate within the matrix set down by this tradition, precisely as a militant opposition to it."[134] Modern humanism mirrors the goals of metaphysics in its faith in the ability of rational rule to encapsulate itself into a system that can solve the problems of humanity. But rather than God, humanity is now at the center. While its positivistic side restricted itself to the empirical and the objective, trying to develop a "calculus of utility and well-being," it was another version, that of Hegel and dialectical humanism, that truly represented the high point of modern, metaphysical thought. With this systematization of man and history, culminating in Marx, it

> became entirely evident that, in a full working out of the spirit of
> metaphysics that means man, as historical and as social, placing
> himself in the position once reserved for the gods and for God,
> myth, dogma, and theology were reabsorbed into history and
> flowed into a philosophy that discarded its time-honored name of
> a simple love of wisdom in order to become a scientific system.[135]

The humanist dream of devising a rational system perfect enough to respond to all contingencies and illuminate all mysteries is itself the victim of the metaphysical desire for the fullness of knowledge unavailable to Socrates. Like nihilism, it limits the way in which we are permitted to view ethics and meaning. While the Nietzschean nihilist would limit any search for ethics and meaning to that which can be created by the force of will, the anthropocentric humanist would restrict the factors contributing to personal understanding to that which can be grasped wholly through reason and its systematic methodologies.

Though one could take issue with Patočka's characterization of the broad category of humanism as reductive or oversimplified, the point would remain the same: in his search to comprehend the ground of human reality, neither a nihilistic nor an anthropocentric humanist perspective is sufficient. The rejection of nihilism and humanism as means to understand human reality, and so human ethics, brings us back to our earlier question: If we must discard not only traditional metaphysics but also humanist and nihilistic-romanticist reactions to it, can it be said that there is any foundation for ethics at all?

The Foundation of Ethics

"Ethics are not built upon metaphysics"; this is the contention that grounds not only Patočka's political thought, but also his concepts of "care for the soul" and "life in truth."[136] And yet, without doubt, some form of nonrelativistic ethical thought is elemental to his philosophy.

Patočka's ethics have their source in our understanding of our own being. It is our being and the character of our relationship to it that largely determine our lives. Understood properly, the being of humans is something quite distinctive from the simple existence of things, creatures, objects. Human being, as we have seen, is most open to its possibilities insofar as it relates, not simply to the contents of the world but to the world as a whole. In Patočka's analysis of those relations, he stresses movement as the primary concept.

Conceived of phenomenologically, human movement was shown to have a hierarchical structure. Certain movement, such as that directed toward freedom (i.e., historical movement), was instrumental in opening up human possibility; it aimed for more than the simple preservation of life. This movement acted to heighten our being, and so could be classified as a higher type of human movement. It was a "movement of truth," he explained further, and was exemplified in particular human activities like the philosophical interrogation of reality, or the phenomenon of authentic sacrifice.

To illuminate the point, let's return for a moment to the discussion of sacrifice. With a meaningful sacrifice, the presence of a hierarchical structure of being is revealed. Meaningful sacrifice, Patočka maintains, shows that "there exists something like a difference, a hierarchy, a fundamental dividing line. Otherwise all so-called values are subjective and relative."[137] This is the dividing line that distinguishes the being of humans from mere being; it is not a relative difference, but a fundamental one. It is what Heidegger describes, Patočka writes, as the difference between being and beings.[138]

In Patočka's reading, this difference determines the way in which we live. It is, he says, "a difference which *is*, which manifests itself in two basic manners of being: namely, in the manner of being of things, which are indifferent to the fact that they exist, and in the manner of being of man, in whom it is not like this."[139] The key point is the latter, that this difference manifests itself in human behavior, in a "manner of being." It is a hierarchical difference that precludes a relativity of values, but still does not exist in such a form that it can be translated into a universal ladder of values. It is a difference that manifests itself, not independently or objectively, but in the course of our historical actions. It manifests itself in a "manner of being" which is precisely the "moral attitude" described in the Charter 77 texts. Only having established this connection can Patočka proceed to speak of nonrelative human ethics in the context of a critique of metaphysics.

Despite the focus on movement and our way of being, we are still left to deal with what seems to be a metaphysical teleology: Patočka argues that care for the soul means movement of the soul in the direction of good. Yet as I have already shown, this classical formulation hides a content that specifically denies metaphysics. Care for the soul in its ontological and phenomenological sense is a "theory of motion," and the movement of the soul toward the good is not a movement toward an immovable object.[140]Instead, both the soul and the good have to be understood in terms of their relation to each other and to our being. The soul is effectively a summation of the relationship of the individual to being; it is a story of growth and decline. It "is that which defines itself in the direction of its being and that which consequently directs itself either towards legitimate growth, towards a growth of being, or on the contrary towards decline and a loss of being: the soul is an indicator of the main arteries of being."[141]

In indicating these "arteries of being," these human possibilities, the soul also indicates what we call good and evil. Indeed, the soul could not exist without good and evil, for without "arteries of being" how could an indicator of those arteries exist. Good is demarcated by the action of the soul, but the soul itself is dependent on the existence of good. Here, it seems, is a case of circular logic. Its resolution requires an emphasis on motion and possibility. We can say there is good not insofar as humans merely *exist*, but only insofar as they live humanly, meaning in the possibility of the intensification of their own being. Patočka attempted to express this formulation in a passage from *Europe and the Post-European Age* which, though cited earlier, bears repeating:

> The soul is that which has a sense of good and evil. The soul can exist only when good exists, for its basic motion is motion in the direction of good, but on the other hand even good itself has meaning as the goal and vanishing point of everything only when there exists motion. Only insofar as there exists something that can heighten its being by motion towards the good is good operative, meaning it *is*. The soul thus not only enables a conception of the overall hierarchy of being in the sense of good, i.e., a teleological conception, but it is at the same time a justification of good, it gives an answer to the question (which even Nietzsche expressly asked), why choose good and not evil, why truth and not (the possibly more practical) seeming.[142]

So we can, in the end, only speak of the "good" as a foundation for ethics in a very particular sense. Good is not an independent entity, nor is it relative to our will, conventions, desires, and so forth. It relates, instead, to our very humanity, the movement that is our soul. The operative concept, the crucial factor, is our understanding of being. Being is something that we can describe in hierarchical terms, as in the classical description of good, but it is not an objective *telos*.

It is by virtue of the ontological character of our humanity that we are able to speak of ethics at all. Ethics have their source in this humanity and in our relation to the world as a whole. Though we cannot speak of ethics as ahistorical values, we need not revert to the relativistic conviction that ethics are created by human will, or are the arbitrary product of a historical period. The contemporary dilemma, in many respects, is one of being caught between two unsatisfactory visions of reality. It is a choice between a metaphysical foundation for morals or an anthropocentric humanism that, in the end, must result in an ethical relativism. Jan Patočka's work is directed toward an exposition of the false nature of this dichotomy. This is the heart of his ethical thought; what I have presented thus far, however, does not resolve this problem so much as introduce it as a problem and indicate the direction in which Patočka moves.

Patočka's political philosophy concludes in an exposition of the relation of the individual to society. In his case this took the form of dissent. Yet dissent is not, in and of itself, a political value. It is simply the way in which Patočka's commitment to politics manifested itself in the given situation. Jan Patočka's dissent was a form of historical action, a manifestation of the mode of living that his philosophy seeks to describe concretely. Using the Platonic symbolisms of "caring for the soul" and "living in truth" Patočka points his thought in the direction of a ground for politics in freedom and problematicity, and a ground for the political individual in a commitment to an ethics that, if understood in relation to the limits of human existence, must be recognized as nonmetaphysical.

Patočka's analysis of the political reality of the contemporary world demonstrates the degree to which politics in the West has abandoned this ground. The means to recovering a politics of freedom which respects the possibility inherent in the human being can be found, if we take this work as a guide, in a reexamination of classical themes and symbols through the lenses of contemporary critique. "Care for the soul" as "care for the polis" can be retrieved as a guiding principle of contemporary, universal supercivilization only insofar as it can be grasped as a premetaphysical philosophy. This quest forms the core of Patočka's political thought.

The discussion of ethics in this chapter points to a larger, more fundamental problem that has still not been fully resolved. In the conclusion to this study I examine Patočka's attempt to resolve the problem of metaphysics by getting to its source. If we accept that there is an unconditional moral sentiment, then we must admit to an ultimate source for that phenomenon. The question of a source is the question of foundations, and it is the animating question of much of contemporary political theory if not all of postmodernism.

6

Conclusion

Foundations and Philosophy, Politics and Postmodernism

Postmodernism, taking its lead from Nietzsche and Heidegger, presents a challenge to political theory with the contention that metaphysical foundationalism is a facile and impermissible ground for understanding. The effect of this critique on politics is particularly acute, for it implies that no consistent ground for ethics or political responsibility can be said to exist. The result is a postmodern dilemma, an inability to conceptualize an ethics that transcends the particular moment. Yet Patočka, despite his allegiance to the Heideggerean critique of metaphysics, proposes just such an ethics. He posits a "moral attitude" that is neither ahistorically absolute nor entirely relative. It is not governed by a metaphysical reality nor is it subject to human will or whim. Patočka's understanding of ethics stems from a fundamental ontology and a phenomenological relationship of the human to the world as a whole. Patočka stakes out, with his discussion of the ethical content of our interest in our own being (caring for the soul), a space in-between the two poles of the debate over foundationalism. He argues that the dilemma of a choice between postmodern relativism and metaphysical absolutism is a false one. Contemporary critique is compatible with a classical concern for ethics.

With contemporary philosophy, the question of foundations becomes an explicit theme—it is dealt with as a philosophical problem in its own right.[1] Postmodern theory makes this problem particularly acute because it challenges, not only traditional conceptions of meaning, but also the very notion that a foundation for political and social thought is necessary or even possible. Patočka's thought has as its central axis the attempt to demarcate a ground for a politics that represents a morally consistent alternative to either of the two poles of the foundationalist issue. He makes a claim for a ground that is nonfoundational, a morality without metaphysics. Yet is this a tenable position? Can the existence of such a ground be defended philosophically? An answer to these questions demands an

161

exploration of the concept of the foundation in Patočka's work, and a search for the ultimate source for the meaning that he sees as unconditional in human life. Patočka centers his "foundationalism" in the intuitive human experience of reality as something meaningful in a nonrelative sense. But by abandoning an objective, transcendental source for meaning, it also becomes something problematic; a new mode of meaning is uncovered that, without succumbing to relativism, must understand itself as conditional on the relationship of the individual to the world and to his own being.

As political philosophy, Patočka's contention is that we can and must speak of ethics, but only within a framework characterized, not by a concrete foundation, but by problematicity. Political life, he states at one point, is "a permanent uprootedness, lack of foundation."[2] Interestingly, Patočka borrows an English phrase to describe the limits of the political realm: politics does not properly permit hope for what he terms the "happy end."[3] Instead, politics is a historical endeavor that should take its lead from the principles found in the early Greek polis. It should allow for, and not seek to end, free and conflictual interaction.

It is not accurate, though, to refer to Patočka as genuinely antifoundationalist—as does, for example, Richard Rorty.[4] Unlike the contemporary antifoundationalist, Patočka recognizes a basic characteristic of the philosophical quest: "[p]hilosophy searches for founding."[5] Although the "spiritual person" must forego metaphysical certainty, he or she is not reduced to indecision and immobility. Philosophy properly searches for founding, but it is true philosophy only insofar as it understands the character of what it hopes to find.

In *Europe and the Post-European Age*, Patočka characterizes the promise of philosophy with his description of the fundamental breakthrough that occurred in the ancient world. Pointing to presocratic thinkers such as Heraclitus as well as to Socrates, Patočka depicts the opening up of a new perspective. This breakthrough does not consist in an answering of questions, however; instead, it further complicates things. With Heraclitus and others, a "deepening" of the horizon of the world takes place. A new situation is introduced in which a searching lostness regarding questions of good and evil shifts from being our "fate" to our "*mission*" in life. The world speaks to us differently; we are no longer philosophically naive. "It is no longer an undamaged world . . . , but an ambiguous world."[6] Naive and comforting mythical demarcations between gods and people disintegrate; the cosmos is deepened and for the first time revealed in its all-encompassing depth. Now, Patočka notes, one must recognize oneself as a question— "Who am I?"—and must learn to expect that an answer will come only from within.[7]

It is this insight into the ambiguity of the human condition that characterizes the limits of any foundation to which we may aspire. We have true access only to immediate reality, never to the whole of reality that it presupposes. The concept of the "whole" of reality plays a key role in Patočka's phenomenological philosophy. Yet as an experiential horizon, the whole does not exist concretely. It is not an entity on which we can ground our activity. Nonetheless, it is our ontological directedness toward this "whole" that defines our humanity. The whole is itself no foundation, but rather a "presupposition" of our founding activity, of our search for understanding. Without a sense of a whole we would be frozen in nihilism, unable to move. Patočka explains his position in a passage from *Europe and the Post-European Age* that deserves to be quoted in full:

> Man stands with one leg in immediate reality, in givenness, but that givenness fully lays open the content of its reality only at the point when it is not taken as what it passes itself off to be, but when we are able to gain support and foundation together and in terms of the whole. The universe revealed in this way is an actual foundation, and only this foundation founds in the true sense of the word. . . . If we stood on both feet in reality, on the ultimate soil of the all-encompassing whole, we would never be exposed to wandering, to vain hopeless groping in circles; then our path would be consistent and clear, continually meaningful, never recurring. This we cannot guarantee nor achieve. But we can procure immediacy with a question mark and attempt to bring our path, our steps, from one immediacy to another, from one experience to the next, from one thought to another, in such a way that they will be unified and will not be destructive of each other. Then it also forms a sort of ground upon which it is possible to move. The final foundation, in view of which we experience and we think, that is, we *are* in a human way, thus forms the presupposition for our concrete assigning of reasons, for the action of founding. Philosophy searches for founding.[8]

In our activity, we move from immediacy to immediacy, from one interaction with the immediate world to another. If we can act in such a way that we do not live only for those immediacies, but in search of a fuller understanding of the whole that all immediate phenomena presuppose, then we evoke a certain consistency and unity that serves as a "sort of ground upon which it is possible to move."

This "consistency," as Patočka has argued, is not characteristic of modern Western civilization. The universal civilization that developed out of the roots of Europe suffers from confusion, a misplaced sense of security, with regard to its foundations. The age in which we live is "post-European," not simply because of the end of European hegemony, but because it is a post-metaphysical age. Traditional metaphysics has been abandoned in favor of science and rationality. But as Patočka concludes in his essay on the "Supercivilization," this process was less an abandonment of metaphysics than a "negation" of it. The ascendancy of scientific rationalism led to a negative metaphysics that attempted to reproduce reality by nonmetaphysical, that is, scientific, means. But instead of overcoming metaphysics, it merely succeeded in repeating its mistakes in rationalistic form. Following Husserl, Patočka takes issue with the use of science as a substitute for metaphysics, as a new foundation. His approach is not to discredit science, but to argue for the necessity of understanding its limitations.

> The process of the passage from metaphysical forms of thought and life to nonmetaphysical cannot be capped by attempts that are negatively metaphysical, consequently impoverishing man in regard to the possibility of possibilities; its consummation can only be a *division* of these possibilities, a measurement of their autonomy. New society cannot be founded on illusions; nor can it be founded on the illusion that we have a direct access to reality and that (at least in its basic characteristics) we understand the whole. Negative metaphysics rested mainly on the metaphysicalizing of science; the de-metaphysicalizing of science does not mean the de-realization of science, the claim that it doesn't capture reality (of objects), but merely that it doesn't capture it as a whole and directly, but rather merely partially and schematically.[9]

The problem of modern society, then, is that it has sought a new foundation to replace that which has been discredited. This is the state of the "postmetaphysical" age.

In his writings on the philosophy of history, Patočka argues that historical action is "free" insofar as it rejects the goals and ends inherent in metaphysics as well as in its scientific offspring. In giving up certain forms of metaphysics, modernity did not cease to search for the irrefutable. Indicative of this end, as Patočka puts it in the fifth *Heretical Essay*, are our consistent yet vain attempts to treat history as a problem to be solved. "Modern civilization suffers not only from its own flaws and myopia but also from the failure to resolve the entire problem of history. *Yet the problem of history may not be resolved, it must be preserved as a problem*" (emphasis mine).[10] The key to the positive possibilities of modern, rational civilization, Patočka insists, is an understanding of history that recognizes first that it is "insoluble," and second that this situation is not cause for despair. To the contrary, history must be preserved as problematic, for only that understanding is conducive to our freedom. Philosophy and politics properly search for foundations, but in order for either to succeed the problematic nature of those foundations must be recognized.

Patočka expresses his vision of the ground on which political society can form in a text accompanying the Czech edition of *Europe and the Post-European Age*. In "The Pattern of History," the foundation of political society is tied, not to the preservation of life—which is characteristic of early liberal society—but to the preservation of freedom as a possibility that takes precedence over the simple preserving of life. It is Patočka's concept of history that captures this dynamic:

> This means, however, that history is and will be only insofar as there are people who do not want to merely "live," but are truly willing, in their detachment from mere life, to lay down and preserve societal foundations of mutual respect. What is founded in this way is not a safe securing of life, but freedom, i.e., possibilities which exceed the level of mere life. These possibilities are in essence of two forms, namely the responsible care for the other and an expressed relation to being, i.e., truth. In these relations man is neither dependent nor a consumer, but in the essential sense a builder, founder, expander, preserver of society—of course, as has already been said, never without exposure to danger. This building is the building of a world which is founded in the non-visible region, but it must be made into a visible and lasting form in order to bear human life and to offer to man the possibility to be historical henceforth and always anew.[11]

A concrete and "visible" society is required, yet it must remain grounded in the nonvisible region. This is the region from which the ultimate source of human meaning is drawn. It is Patočka's challenge to describe this dynamic without recourse to the foundationalism he is determined to avoid.

THE PROBLEM OF MEANING

In the *Heretical Essays in the Philosophy of History* the concept of a foundation for historical action is subsumed under the question of meaningfulness. "Does History have a Meaning?" is the title of the third essay; in it, he seeks to inquire to what degree history, in the specific, ontological way in which it is defined, is dependent on a foundation in meaning. The postmodern perspective grounded in the Heideggerean critique of metaphysics, of course, is clear in its rejection of a transcendent meaning of history. But does this mean, Patočka wishes to ascertain, that history can make no claim to meaning at all? Contrary to what one would expect from an antifoundationalist, Patočka concludes that history is dependent on meaning. As he puts it in response to the solution offered by Nietzschean nihilism: "An authentic life in utter nihilism, with the knowledge of the meaninglessness of the whole, is impossible, becoming possible only at the cost of illusions."[12] But the meaningfulness that characterizes the historical (or philosophical) human being is of a distinctly different character than the accepted, positive meaning of prehistorical societies. The essential characteristic of history remains the rejection, or the "shaking," of naïveté. Yet this shaking is not a rejection of all meaning; its counterpart is the positive formulation of the freer, more demanding meaningfulness epitomized by political life.

Patočka's analysis of the source of meaning in this chapter makes his work explicitly relevant to the contemporary problem of foundationalism in political theory. Insofar as a society is grounded in a given and unshakable meaning, as in "prehistoric" civilization, a positive, concrete foundation is presupposed. The shaking of meaning in Patočka's philosophy of history is consistent with a critique of that foundationalism—yet Patočka is no simple antifoundationalist. He argues coherently that meaning is essential to human life, not least to political life. A meaningful ground on which we can move and progress is possible, but it depends on the self-understanding and transcendence available to us through a philosophical approach informed by contemporary ontology and phenomenology. His philosophy moves in-between the Husserlian search for a foundation in a pure phenomenological approach to reason, and the (early) Heideggerean approach of avoiding any foundational temptation entirely.

Patočka wishes to illuminate a "soil" on which it is possible not only to move but also to live in community, to construct a viable politics. What do his investigations reveal? He first concludes, as I have already noted, that the meaning on which human history properly unfolds is problematic meaning. To understand meaning as problematic, to accept even the possibility of a total absence of meaning, is to begin to understand humanity in terms of our actual experience of it. Thus Patočka writes that meaning lies in the "seeking which flows from its absence," and that this dynamic first appears in the Greek world as a "new project of life" instituted by Socrates.[13] As Patočka explains it, Socrates struggled not with a lack of meaning, but with the problematicity of meaning (based partly on the possibility of its absence). It is precisely via our grasp of this problematicity, entailing the realization that meaning is not simply there but can be won or lost, that we are able to experience meaningfulness in its genuine, human sense.

Patočka is unwilling to conceive of meaning as something autonomous, as independent of being. To do so, he argues, would be tantamount to abandoning the question of meaning's source: "To have recourse to a metaphysics means to treat meaning as something ready-made and to give up for good the question of its origin (not in a temporal-empirical but in a structural-philosophical sense)."[14] It is precisely the "origin" of meaning that we are interested in, however, for this points us in the direction of the foundation that philosophy seeks.

Rather than searching for a static source of meaning, Patočka asks us to think about meaning nonobjectively—in relation to being. Things, and the values we attach to them, attain their meaning only in terms of our understanding of them.[15] It is not the things themselves to which we must look for the origin of meaning, it is to our *sense* for them. The basic determinant of this sense for things, he continues, is our "openness" to the world, our willingness and ability to understand things in relation, not to other things, but to the world as a whole. The source of meaning, then, to the degree it can be located at all, is in our self-conscious movement through life.

> Things have no meaning for *themselves*, rather, their meaning requires that someone "have a sense" for them: thus meaning is not originally lodged in what is [beings, things] but in that openness, in that understanding for them; an understanding, though, which is a process, a movement which is no different from the movement at the core of our life.[16]

In this way, the source of meaning is in us; it is we who bestow meaning on things via our relationship to them.

To leave the discussion of meaning at this point would be a mistake, for Patočka wants to demonstrate that what he is describing is something quite other than the idea that we create meaning and that it is in our power to do so. Meaning is not relative to our subjective desires, or, as he puts it, "the bestowal of meaning on things is not a function of our will and whim."[17] Even as beings possessed of understanding, we have no power to keep things from appearing meaningless in certain situations, just as we are unable to prevent other things from appearing meaningful. The same beings, in fact, can "manifest themselves now as meaningful, now as meaningless, signifying nothing." And what does that mean, he concludes, "if not the *problematic nature* of all meaningfulness?"[18] Meaning is problematic because it is never guaranteed; attempting to make it so, to absolutize it, contradicts its very nature. The significance of the problematicity of meaning, then, is that it "warns us that we should not yield to the inclination to absolutize particular ways of understanding meaning."[19]

Yet to be discussed in Patočka's analysis is the source of that openness for things and for the world that has been denoted as the origin of meaningful relations. As I said earlier, Patočka finds the source of meaning to be located in the activity of searching for meaning, best expressed in the Socratic approach to life. But what is the initiating factor for the Socratic mode of being? It is, he argues, the experience of the loss of meaning.[20] It is when our faith in the world is shaken that we are forced to abandon objective, simply given conceptions of meaning. Once we understand that the meaning we once took for granted is in fact tentative, we can return to it only with a much greater degree of awareness. It will "no longer be for us simply a fact given directly in its integrity; rather, it will be a meaning we have thought through, seeking reasons and accepting responsibility for it."[21] The result is that something new emerges via our experience of loss of meaning.

> It means that there emerges a new relation, a new mode of relating to what is meaningful; that meaning can arise only in an activity which stems from a searching lack of meaning, as the vanishing point of being problematic, as an indirect epiphany. If we are not mistaken, then this discovering of meaning in the seeking which flows from its absence, as a new project of life, is the meaning of Socrates's existence. The constant shaking of the naive sense of meaningfulness is itself a new mode of meaning, a discovery of its continuity with the mysteriousness of being and what-is [beings] as a whole.[22]

A new mode of meaning—a human mode—arises as we act to shake ourselves free of the given. Whereas meaning grounded in a naive metaphysics relieves us of the responsibility of acting so as to ensure meaning—given meaning is there no matter how we act—Socrates' existence demonstrates the consistency and meaningfulness of an attitude that refuses foundations.

This discussion of the source of meaning reflects the heart of Patočka's philosophizing. He seeks an understanding of reality that allows for a coherent ethics and politics, that gives us a *soil* on which we can move, but not at the cost of positing a "solid ground" or explicit foundation. Yet is it clear that his approach to meaning and to foundationalism is entirely non-metaphysical? Even in the passage just cited, Patočka refers not only to the "new mode of meaning" that defines the Socratic life, he also refers to the continuity that this new mode of meaning has with the "mysteriousness" of being and beings as a whole. In doing so, in speaking of an appreciation for "beings as a whole" or the "world as a whole" as inherent to the openness that invites meaningfulness, one is forced to ask whether a new foundation is tacitly being created—one simply further removed and more shrouded in mystery than other, more explicitly metaphysical foundations.

The critique to which Patočka's work is most susceptible, in the end, is not that his work falls too heavily on the side of Heidegger or antifoundationalism. Though some have made this suggestion, the clarity and urgency of Patočka's commitment to ethics and to transcendence refutes it. Instead, it is the contrary critique that is the most penetrating, the argument that, despite protestations to the contrary, Patočka verges on a form of metaphysics to a degree sufficient to undermine his intentions. The implications of this critique are troubling. If Patočka is shown to be just another meta-physician then credence is lent to the conclusion that it is simply impossible to speak of a coherent political morality without falling into a metaphysical trap. If this is the case, then we are reduced to speaking about ethics in an entirely relative manner, we must reject the type of general principle evoked by Patočka in both Charter 77 and in his use of Platonic symbolism. The relevant question, therefore, given the argument that the meaningfulness of which we are speaking is not relative, is whether there exists a source for this meaning that is equivalent to a foundation. This question is taken up and advanced insightfully way by one of Patočka's own students, the Czech scholar Ivan Chvatík.

In an essay on "The Heresy of Jan Patočka in Reflections on the Crisis of Europe," Chvatík contends that Patočka does, in the end, allow himself to rest on a metaphysical foundation. What Chvatík points to is not religious imagery but the philosopher's use of the symbol of a "vanishing point" of meaningfulness. This symbol, he attests, amounts to the positing of a quasi-concrete source of meaning, and thus a basic foundationalism.[23] Chvatík argues that, despite Patočka's denial that he is searching for an objective source of "absolute meaning," he nevertheless engages in such a search, merely cloaking his goal in "mystery" and "darkness." For Chvatík, the symbol of the "vanishing point"—a translation of the unusual Czech formulation "*uběnžý bod*"—is evidence of Patočka's positive Platonism. Although the philosopher has meticulously developed an ontology rather than a metaphysics as the basis for his thought, Chvatík holds a Heideggerean line: "Meaning may not be identified with being."[24] It is not permissible to derive from the reality of our being any but relative meaningfulness arising in a concrete situation.

Patočka would dispute this point, however. When he speaks of the concept of "good" having meaning "as the goal and vanishing point of everything," he adds that this is only true insofar as there exists "motion." The motion to which he refers is human activity in the form of an exploration of oneself and of reality. It is by our acceptance of a mode of living as self-examination that a consistency is revealed. It is not being itself that is the source of meaning but our search for being. As Patočka describes it: "Actually we are dealing only with the uncovering of meaning that can never be explained as a thing, which cannot be mastered, delimited, grasped positively, and dominated, but which is present only in the *seeking* of being."[25]

Though it is difficult to counter effectively a consistent skepticism such as Chvatík's, there are two points in Patočka's favor. First, there is a compelling logic to his argument. It is neither being itself, conceived (incorrectly) as a constant entity, nor even our constituting of being that is the source of meaning, it is rather the responsibility of the search that we accept as we come to realize that meaning is uncertain or even wholly absent in a certain situation. Accepting this responsibility, which is not equivalent to being but merely a possibility inherent in our being, is a problematic proposition which, at bottom, has no metaphysical anchor or ballast. The mysterious vanishing point is not a point, but it *is* a possibility that is consistently ours and independent of relative particularities. By putting the source of meaning firmly in the center of the motive process, rather than in any certainty of result to which we can point prior to beginning our quest, Patočka comes as close, I think, as is possible to a solution to the question of the foundation of meaning with which it is possible to live.

The second point in support of Patočka and in contrast to Chvatík's Heideggerean skepticism is contained in the argument that merely relative meaningfulness cannot provide the stability needed for human life to unfold. Relative meaning, it has been argued, cannot stand by itself on a base of total meaninglessness. A fundamental meaninglessness of the whole would not permit relative meaning to exist independently—it would drag such meaning into its wake, making life impossible. "In its practical unfolding, life cannot rest on a relative meaning which itself rests on meaninglessness, since no relative meaning can ever render the meaningless meaningful but, rather, is always itself dragged into meaninglessness by it."[26] Humans, he concludes, "cannot live in the certitude of meaninglessness."[27]

The dogmatic belief in meaninglessness, in addition, is itself a truth and a certitude that contradicts the tenor of its own rejection of absolute meaning. The experiential truth is that we are never certain of meaning or of meaninglessness, but we *can* experience a consistency that transcends the particular when we accept a foundation that is not like any other foundation—a foundation of possibility that understands that the core of human reality is a "mystery" that will never be fully unraveled.

> And, ultimately, is there not at the very core of reality itself something like the mysterious and the mystery? . . . Is not the infinite depth of reality possible only because we cannot see its bottom, and is not just that a challenge and an opportunity for humans in their reach for meaning which is more than the flowering and perishing of the lily of the field in the eyes of the gods?[28]

The Patočkan shaking of naive meaning, therefore, winds its way in-between the poles of a concrete, metaphysical meaning on one hand and an utter meaninglessness or nihilism on the other. The appeal to mystery or a "vanishing point" is not dismissible as a positive Platonism obscured by smoke. It is patently closer to experiential reality than either of the two alternatives which it opposes.

Patočka's conclusion is thus ironic; we have access to the absolute perspective we seek only insofar as we abandon hope in a given and objective absolute. The only consistent foundation we have available is not independent of us. "Thus the shaking of naive meaning is the genesis of a perspective on an absolute meaning to which, however, humans are not marginal, on condition that humans are prepared to give up the hope of a directly given meaning and to accept meaning as a way."[29] This is, Patočka maintains, an approach to meaning that is both more demanding and freer than its dogmatically certain alternatives. It also provides, he argues further, evidence of the inherent connection between philosophy and politics.

MEANING, POLITICS, AND CONFLICT

The debate over foundationalism in theories of politics and ethics can be summed up with a simple question: whether "meaning" is entirely and inherently situational, or, to the contrary, whether there exists a means of persuasively analyzing meaning in human life in such a way that it can be shown to have a source that is not relative. Only in the latter case could we speak of meaning, and thus of values and ethics, in a way that transcends the particularities of a specific historical situation. And political thought, or political science, inherently requires us to think not solely in terms of particularities, but in terms of general principles. It is for this reason that Chvatík concludes that Patočka's thought "cannot be a guideline for political action and cannot found a political science," and it is for the very same reason that I disagree with him. It is certainly true that Patočka's thought is not suitable as a straightforward guideline for political activity; it is not the type of political thought to which one can look for specific help in establishing a constitutional order. Yet this does not mean that it cannot be used in establishing a founding set of principles that will act as a guide for a science of political order. At the very foundation of any political order must be an understanding of human meaning and its limitations. Politics, inasmuch as it is tied to the contingencies of historical reality, must ground itself not in the grand plans of a society modeled on supposed knowledge of the absolute, but in a persuasive depiction of the limits of human meaning, limits beyond which politics may not trespass in its construction of political society.

The conceptual framework set forth in Patočka's work—one grounded in the "shaking of accepted meaning"—leads to a meaningfulness that is demanding but appropriate to our social being. This human meaningfulness constitutes a form of self-understanding that is coincident not only with the origin of philosophy but also with the origin of politics. What Patočka has sought to describe breaks new ground analytically and conceptually while appealing to symbolism long established. The Czech philosopher does not pretend to uncover a new human experience; rather, the experience is a familiar one, and the subject of human speculation throughout the ages. The radical questioning of naive meaning, which may be precipitated by a perceived loss of meaning, opens the individual up to the possibility of a "conversion" in the Platonic sense. It is the experience of the cave dweller in Plato's "Allegory of the Cave" who "turns" from a reality of shadows to one of truth experienced.[30]

Yet Patočka's work, we should recall, is undertaken in the context of a philosophy of history. The experience in question is precisely that which has been described as separating the "prehistoric" mentality from the "historic." Only in the light of a rejection of simply given meaning can human activity take on a character that is historically continuous with both past and future. The character of this activity, as I have stressed, is conducive not only to individual self-reflection, but also to the activity of politics. Thus it is not coincidental that the thematic differentiation of philosophy in Socrates took place in concert with an uncovering of a science of politics as a theme in human life. Patočka's work explicitly stresses this connection just as it implicitly leads toward the illumination of principles directly relevant to political thought.

> It is not only individual life which, if it passes through the experience of loss of meaning and if it derives from it the possibility and need for a wholly different self-relation to all that is, comes to a point of global "conversion." Perhaps the inmost nature of that rupture—which we sought to define as that which separates the prehistoric epoch from history proper—lies in that shaking of the naive certainty of meaning which governs the life of humankind up to that specific transformation which represents a nearly simultaneous—and in a more profound sense really unitary—origin of politics and philosophy.[31]

The "unitary origin" of politics and philosophy reflects the connectedness of the two. Politics is a mode of activity in which inheres the possibility to turn philosophy "into the practice of life itself."[32]

This is not to say, however, that politics as a realm of activity is to be ceded to philosophers. It is the insight inherent in philosophy as Patočka describes it—the understanding of freedom and problematicity—that he wishes to show is also crucial to our practice of the very human and problematic activities proper to the center of the polis. Patočka wishes to elevate the practice of politics to a level above that of reliance on slogan, dogma, and distortion, but he does not suggest a philosophical elevation of politics as a means to a solution of its problems. To the contrary, rather than elevate politics to a higher, philosophical plane, he seeks to bring philosophy back down to a human level. Patočka is acutely aware that the inconstant nature of human beings leads to unpredictability—an unpredictability that has not been eliminated by the advances of science and behavioral studies nor would be eliminated if philosophers were to rule. Rather, philosophy must accept the problematic nature of reality as something with which it much deal instead of try to overcome. In just the same way politics must deal with the problems that arise when humans attempt to live and act on a basis of freedom. "Just as in acting politically humans expose themselves to the problematic nature of action whose consequences are unpredictable and whose initiative soon passes into other hands, so in philosophy humans expose themselves to the problematic being and meaning of what there is."[33]

As a human endeavor, politics must resist the siren song of an objective metaphysics of meaning even as it strives for transcendence. Genuinely political activity transcends the particularities of present desires or physical needs. In doing so, it opens itself up to its greatest possibility, that of acting historically. Such activity is not arbitrary, it is invested with a meaningfulness that is both human and transcendental; it is the meaningfulness of a significant activity that unifies and expands human possibilities. As Patočka describes it:

> In the community, the *polis*, in life dedicated to the *polis*, in political life, humans make room for an autonomous, purely human meaningfulness, one of a mutual respect in activity significant for all its participants and which is not restricted to the preservation of physical life but which, rather, is a source of a life that transcends itself in the memory of deed guaranteed precisely by the *polis*. It is in many ways a more risky, dangerous life than the vegetative humility on which prehistoric humanhood depends.[34]

Politics is an activity "significant for all its participants" precisely because it is an activity that transcends itself. With this, Patočka provides a basis for the analysis and differentiation of political activity, a means of distinguishing political activity, activity proper to the polis, from the activities of life directed toward the physical or the ideological.

The model of politics, of the polis, that Patočka describes is grounded in an attitude of "mutual respect" guaranteed by the willingness of all participants to risk by giving up the security of naive meaning. Politics in this sense, like philosophy, is a matter of struggle. To conceive of it otherwise is to begin to hope for a solution that does not require risk, that is given rather than fought for. It is in this sense that, following on the work of Heidegger, Patočka evokes the name of Heraclitus and his symbol of *polemos*, or conflict, in bringing the *Heretical Essays* to a close. The spirit of the polis, and thus the spirit of politics, he argues, is conflict. Although Patočka evokes Heraclitus most distinctly in the final pages of the sixth and last "Heretical" essay, "War in the Twentieth Century and the Twentieth Century as War," this brief discussion does not adequately describe his understanding of the concept.[35] For this we should look to the consideration of *polemos* in the context of the polis, an analysis undertaken in the second "heretical" essay on "The Beginning of History."

The institutional model of the polis, Patočka writes, is a place of human unity and possibility that emerges from the insight that defines both philosophy and politics. That insight evokes struggle and problematicity and, in this chapter as throughout the *Essays*, Patočka argues decisively that this struggle is a unifying factor. It binds individuals rather than separates them. *Polemos* is the spirit of the polis, by which is meant not the spirit of the Greek polis as a historical event, but the spirit of free politics itself. Conflict, for Patočka, binds the activity of political life to philosophy as the struggle against the fall into an acceptance of given meaning. Struggle is a presupposition of life as problematic, and it manifests itself in the political community as conflict.

> The spirit of the *polis* is a spirit of unity in conflict, in battle. One cannot be a citizen—*polites*—except in a community of some against others, and the conflict itself gives rise to the tension, the tenor of the life of the *polis*, the shape of the space of freedom that citizens both offer and deny each other—offering themselves in seeking support and overcoming resistance.[36]

The conflict of which Patočka speaks is not a destructive force. To perceive it this way is to misunderstand the political intent of the *Heretical Essays*.

Polemos, in these essays, is constructive rather than destructive of community, and it is an appropriate symbol for Patočka's political thought; it stands with no contradiction beside the Socratic theme of care for the soul. Conflict is, for instance, the source of all collective will, and in turn, the source of all legislation. In the polis "*Polemos* is what is common. *Polemos* binds together the contending parties, not only because it stands over them but because in it they are at one. In it there arises the one, unitary power and will from which alone all laws and constitutions derive, however different they may be."[37] Common beliefs and ideologies passed intact from one individual to another, contrary to conventional wisdom, do not unite but divide. The unity of a free state is not founded on static ideology but on the struggle against its dominance. It is this commitment to struggle and acceptance of conflict that is the one force to which all parties may equally lay claim. Conflict and struggle make possible free thought and provide a stronger foundation for political unity than systems grounded in mere "coalitions of interests":

Thus *polemos* is at the same time that which constitutes the *polis* and the primordial insight that makes philosophy possible. Polemos is not the destructive passion of a wild brigand but is, rather, the creator of unity. The unity it founds is more profound than any ephemeral sympathy or coalition of interests; adversaries meet in the shaking of a given meaning, and so create a new way of being human—perhaps the only mode that offers hope amid the storm of the world: the unity of the shaken but undaunted.[38]

In this way, Patočka ties the appeal of "Wars of the Twentieth Century"—directed at his "shaken but undaunted" students—to an overall attempt to demarcate a philosophy that is inherently political. Thus the dramatic, quasi-Nietzschean appeal to the "solidarity of the shaken" and the references to war and the insight that originates in periods of "darkness," are shown to have a foundation in a more sober, broadly political analysis of conflict and the free polis.[39]

It is important, in concluding this chapter, to note that Patočka's use of *polemos* once again draws from a source in the work of Heidegger. This is, in fact, particularly important given that Heidegger made use of the concept in a text often cited as evidence of a proclivity toward political absolutism—evidence that Heidegger was, in a word, creating a philosophy that led toward the fascism he embraced in the 1930s. Heidegger's analysis of *polemos* is found in *An Introduction to Metaphysics*, the series of lectures he delivered in 1935 at the University of Freiburg.

In contrast to Patočka's use of the term, however, there is a difficult ambiguity in Heidegger's writings that results in problems. First of all, in *An Introduction to Metaphysics* Heidegger does not provide a sufficient analysis of *polemos*, and as a result leaves a degree of uncertainty that many are willing to resolve by referring to Heidegger's use of the term *Kampf* in his "Rectoral Address" infamous for its evocation of National Socialism.[40] This, of course, evokes a second and related problem. Heidegger's discussion of *polemos* comes in the context of his nationalistic writings of the thirties, making it difficult to disassociate from his ill-fated political involvement. Patočka's use of the symbol also had a political context. But in stark contrast to Heidegger, it was a context of an unambiguous struggle for truth and freedom, a struggle against totalitarianism that was explicit in its rejection of violence.

Though Patočka does not refer to Heidegger in his discussion of *polemos*, the reference is implicit. Heidegger had written in *An Introduction to Metaphysics* that "Conflict does not split, much less destroy, unity. It constitutes unity."[41] Patočka is taking a Heideggerean insight—but without a citation—and developing it in the direction of political thought. Interestingly, the argument has been made that if a political theory can be said to exist in Heidegger at all it is to be found in the not fully developed contention that Heraclitian conflict is the source of unity in the polis. In a 1981 article on Heidegger and community, Gregory Schufreider claims that it is Heidegger's use of *polemos* that enables him to express the formation of unity in the polis without abrogating difference or individualism. He writes:

> This struggle, which allows opposition while at the same time keeping the opponents unified, draws together as it sets apart, joins opponents together in their difference, while letting that difference prevail within unity. *Polemos* is, accordingly, thought [of] as a basic trait of being itself in that it unifies into unity what tends apart, and not in such a way that difference is annulled, which is why it remains that "hidden harmony" Heraclitus himself commends as superior (Fragment 54): the covert unity of opponents joining-together in their difference.[42]

As a trait of Heidegger's conception of being, then, *polemos* becomes part of a political theory, since community is "properly unfolded in a communication of struggle, a unification preserving difference, since we are then considering a community comprised of individuals."[43]

Though Schufreider states that this notion may point toward a "'political' philosophy" in Heidegger, he admits that there is "not much to go on" and that this certainly should not be construed as an attempt to suggest that Heidegger shows a "propensity toward democracy."[44] What I would like to suggest is that Jan Patočka takes a lead from Heidegger's analysis of *polemos* but does not follow the German philosopher toward a disdain for democracy. To the contrary, Patočka directly applies conflict to questions of democracy by conceiving of the polis as primarily a political unit, rather than the all-encompassing community described by Heidegger.

As a model for politics, the assumption of a freedom and equality among citizens at the center of the polis is the core of what Patočka envisions as a democratic state, infused with the insight of freedom and philosophy and accepting *polemos* as an animating and uniting force. This conclusion is the product of Patočka's phenomenological analysis; it does not appeal to a transcendent ideal acting as a source for our political values. Beyond the freedom and dignity inherent in the human as an ontologically aware being, there is little in the way of values that can be posited as natural to humanity in an ahistorical sense. This is to argue, in other words, that the values that inform our political self-organization are, like the political societies in which they exist, products of historical action. It makes little sense to speak of human rights based on a principle of freedom if the society with which you are concerned is what Patočka would term "prehistorical," that is, if the society is not grounded in a thematic understanding of freedom as a human possibility.

Politics, particularly the politics of Western states steeped in the democratic tradition, must recognize these limitations if they are to function effectively and humanly. It must understand, in sum, that its animating principle is problematicity. For democratic politics to seek to eliminate problematicity and conflict is for it to abandon freedom.

CONCLUSION

Patočka's discussion of the form of the Greek polis does not attempt to advocate the details of its institutional structures; his political thought is not directed at an analysis of competing forms of government or development of an ideal type of institution. The question is rather one of principles. In the movement from a discussion of Patočkan philosophy to one of politics, one notion stands out as fundamental to the ground on which a sustainable political life may be built. The notion, inherent in the use of *polemos* as a symbol of a unified democratic community, is roughly as follows: to the degree to which a state makes its goal the seeking of an objectified or systematic solution to the problems of social being—symbolized by Patočka in the dream of a "happy end"—it relinquishes its hold on freedom and ceases to care for its soul.

The goal in terms of democratic politics has been expressed succinctly by Ivan Chvatík, Patočka's student, who captures the spirit of Patočka's political thought when he concludes that: "The main trait of a functioning democracy is balance—something that should be supported so there will be no more 'better tomorrows' in democratic societies."[45] The promise of a "better tomorrow" was something with which Czechoslovakia was quite familiar during the years of communist rule. It was the false promise of a future utopianism that served to justify present repression. This is a promise also not foreign to Western ears, however.

Patočka understood with Husserl—better than Husserl, in fact—that the Greek notion of rationality was the guiding principle of Western life.[46] Yet he recognized, as Chvatík writes, that rationality is always "the rationality of finite beings who look at problems from particular viewpoints." While this does not imply relativism, as we have seen, it should be clear that it does not permit absolutism, whether in the name of a totalitarian or a democratic state. Because rationality is the rationality of finite beings, Chvatík continues, "it is impossible to ultimately reconcile their views, to resolve conflicts once and for all. Those who try to do so in the hope of attaining truth, justice and prosperity, no matter how deep their beliefs, capitulate to totalitarian traps inasmuchas [*sic*] they have yielded to the will to possess and live happily thereafter."⁴⁷ The dream of producing a "better tomorrow" is often the dream of overcoming the problematicity of today. It is the dream of answering Socratic questions, and is, in this sense, implicated in metaphysical speculation.

In his final completed work, a lengthy essay entitled "On Masaryk's Philosophy of Religion," Patočka summarizes the nature of the task before us in terms that bring his analysis of meaning together with his views on the polis. He writes:

> Man stands in front of an enormous task: not to reclaim meaning for itself, not to pick up the demand for the meaningfulness of the universe for reasons of his own advantage, but on the contrary to understand himself as a being existing out of meaning and for meaning, living therefore, in order for a meaningful world to originate, opening himself such that meaning, whose basis "is" outside of beings, settles and increases itself in it (the world). To understand himself as the recipient of an unshakable gift, to which nothing relative is comparable, as a being which cannot and may not call for an even happier end after a happy beginning, that "happyend" [*sic*] which philosophy construes from Plato to Kant.⁴⁸

Our task is not to search for meaning that will solve our problems for us, but rather to initiate meaning in the world. The result will not be an end to problematicity. There can be no such end to human striving. Our condition is inescapable. But insofar as we work to initiate meaning within the limits of our humanity, we extend those limits incrementally. We become more fully human, we maximize the potential of our nature, if you will, as we open ourselves to possibility via a self-reflective attitude and historical activity. The means toward this end, Patočka came to realize in his later works, was to understand the nature of the political unit most conducive to the pursuit of human possibility, and to illuminate its principles with the aim, not of a system designed to solve the problem of history, but of an institution geared toward truth and meaningful initiative in human life.

PERSPECTIVE

It is Jan Patočka's achievement in philosophy, in sum, to have offered a vision of human reality that represents, not only an internally consistent philosophy, but also a viable alternative to much of the political theory of the nineteenth and twentieth centuries. His work contains a direct response to the primary critique of postmodern thought, that is, the critique of the dominance of "metanarratives," including all forms of historical determinism. As a student of Heidegger and a victim of Marxism no less should have been expected of him. But Patočka was also a dedicated student of Platonic thought. He therefore rejected the alternative of a radical relativism of meaning. What he sought was a degree of consistency and a sense of meaningfulness, a ground on which it is possible to construct a polity.

In order to locate this perspective critically, it will be useful to consider the way in which this work is likely to be received by various interests in the field of political theory. Patočka's work is certainly relevant to all political theorists interested in the relation between the care of the individual soul and the illumination of the being of society; it is of particular relevance, however, to groups within contemporary theory who have a direct stake in the questions Patočka seeks to answer. Among these groups are, for instance, natural right theorists represented by Leo Strauss and his students, continental theorists in the tradition of either Husserlian phenomenology or Heideggerean ontology, postmodern liberals such as Richard Rorty, and continental postmodernists represented by Jacques Derrida among others. This list, of course, is by no means exhaustive; significant critique could come from within the traditions of Marxist thought and liberalism, and both common ground and critique could be elicited from the tradition of philosophy of history. But in terms of locating this work critically, it will be most useful to place it in its most immediate context, that is, in the context of theory that directly examines questions of the ultimate foundations of human social being.

For proponents of natural right in politics, it is likely that this body of work will be judged to have significant shortcomings. Primary will be the contention that Patočka's work, with its Heideggerean influences, verges on historicism, that there is an insufficient commitment to the notion of an ahistorical, or "natural," sense of right. For Patočka, human beings and the historical worlds they inhabit are wholly original, they are not naturally heirs to a meaning passed unchanged from age to age. A concept of right that does not take account of history, he would argue, is tantamount to a form of meaning accepted unreflectively. And Patočka is emphatic and consistent in his contention that genuine human possibility—and a genuine politics—can only emerge to the degree we are willing to shake ourselves free of the grip of such forms of meaning.

Patočka is clearly with natural right thinkers such as Leo Strauss, on the other hand, in his rejection of relativism as a solution to the problem of right.[49] Yet whereas Strauss frames the problem in terms that seem black and white, Patočka is explicitly interested in exploring the grayness of the situation—its problematicity. Strauss writes that "to reject natural right is tantamount to saying that all right is positive right, and this means that what is right is determined exclusively by the legislators and the courts of the various countries."⁵⁰ Patočka rejects such phrasing of the problem; it is not the case that we must choose between ahistorical truth or a relativism of right.⁵¹ His work explores a human reality that is too contingent and variable to admit to such a dichotomy. Human reality is far more of a problem than Western philosophy since Plato has generally been willing to admit.

Besides a challenge from theorists dedicated to solidifying the foundations of Western thought, Patočka's work is also subject to a challenge from those who wish to abandon foundations altogether. Patočka will not satisfy the committed antifoundationalist, for he consistently criticizes nihilist relativism and concludes that philosophy correctly—and necessarily—searches for foundations. Indeed, while postmodernist thinkers such as Richard Rorty and Jean-Francois Lyotard have argued that philosophy in a grand sense is no longer viable, that it can no longer function as a means to ground social activity,⁵² Patočka philosophizes in a classic, political style. He makes Socrates his model and uses the metaphor of "care for the soul" to embody his concerns.

Postmodern thinkers, then, will criticize this work for its reliance on classical thinking. One can argue that Patočka is, despite his "negative" Platonism, still something of a Platonist. Alternately, as with Jacques Derrida, one might build on Patočka's discussion of Christianity and find in him such reference to an Absolute Being as would make him, in the end, indistinguishable from a traditionally metaphysical thinker. As I indicate, however, these readings are inconsistent with Patočka's explicit discussion of foundationalism. A more defensible reading is that of Richard Rorty. Rorty, in contrast, reads Patočka as a true antifoundationalist. Yet even as he places him in the postmodern tradition, Rorty is troubled by the centrality of Socrates and Plato in the story. Patočka, he writes, "gave his heroes, Socrates and Plato, too much credit."⁵³ He is too much of a classical philosopher, too interested in speaking of the soul, truth, and absolute meaning to be welcomed by postmodernism without reservation.

It is in the middle of the divide between postmodern relativism and approaches that stress ahistorical foundations that Patočka can be most directly situated, then. As a means to navigate this divide, the Czech philosopher makes use of, first the phenomenology of Edmund Husserl, and second, the ontology of Martin Heidegger. Yet as I argued in chapter 2, students of these two schools will also be prompted to find fault with Patočka's work. He cannot be called a devotee of Husserl or of Heidegger because he is not a true follower of either. Patočka does not simply apply the methods and assumptions of either thinker.

For a phenomenologist, Patočka's work is insufficiently precise in terms of its conceptualizations. Above all it lacks the Husserlian commitment to mathematical rigor; when the Czech philosopher describes his work as "phenomenological philosophy,"[54] he means to say that his hope is not to replace philosophy with phenomenology—Patočka does not share the Husserlian goal of a philosophy that responds to the Cartesian hope for "apodicticity"—but rather to pursue philosophy on grounds informed primarily by phenomenological insight. The approach to Heidegger is similar, and the contemporary Heideggerean thinker will be dissatisfied. Patočka wishes to use Heideggerean insight, to explore the questions of being and history without seeking to definitively answer either one, but within the limits prescribed by attention to the "concrete human" in his "corporeal world." Thus he does not follow Heidegger into the depths of an exploration of ontological understanding, and he does not hold the Heideggerean line in avoiding Platonic symbolism or serious attention to the teaching of Socrates. Patočka is also willing to risk offending the scholar of Heidegger's work by mixing, for example, the early Heidegger of *Being and Time* with the later work on technology and the "fourfold" (*das Geviert*).

Patočka's approach can be characterized in this way: he believed that he was carrying on the philosophic enterprise in the wake of these two thinkers. He was taking their insight and developing it in ways that they did not envision, and perhaps may not have objected to. Patočka remains a true philosopher in his application of Husserl and Heidegger to the Socratic concern for the soul. Ontology is a philosophy of the soul. It is a philosophy which perceives that "authentic, transcendent being" in humans is something different from transient opinion. Following Socrates, Patočka situates his ontology, his care for the soul, in the polis. And in this way he concludes in the *Heretical Essays that "philosophy must be at the same* time care for the soul (*epimeleia tēs psuchēs*), ontology and theology—and all that in the care for the *polis*, for the optimal state."[55]

With this discussion it is possible to place the work of Jan Patočka on the critical map. I have attempted to show that Patočka's work presents us with a viable, and in many ways preferable, alternative to the approaches I have laid out. No one of the criticisms I have presented is fatal to this philosophy; Patočka adequately defends himself against each of them in the course of his work. In addition, he offers a benefit to which none of the other perspectives can attain.

The political theory of Jan Patočka is particularly deserving of attention for the seriousness with which it attempts to illuminate the murky ground between the more polarized alternatives on the scene. This is an internally consistent attempt to solve a primary dilemma of contemporary political thought. It seeks to bridge the divide between those wishing to shore up foundations and those wanting to tear them down. Patočka's work aimed at a conception of meaning that was neither relative nor nihilistic, yet did not amount to a new form of simple, given meaning or of "true" knowledge to be passed from one to another instead of achieved. The effect of this work was to demonstrate that the postmodern critique of foundationalism and metaphysics does not imply the impossibility of a coherent and consistent political ethics and democratic theory.

Although Patočka's work is not without its drawbacks, its relevance to contemporary political theory is evident. The political theorist, through this work, is able to speak of politics and ethics while remaining faithful to the contemporary descriptions of historicity, finitude, and contingency. He can, in other words, speak of concepts such as justice without anchoring those concepts to a single metaphysical narrative, or to the contrary allowing them to drift among an endless variety of particular meanings, thus stripping them of any coherency or power to bind together a society in an orderly fashion.

Yet Patočka's political philosophy, it must be recognized, is not entirely successful. There are shortcomings which, beyond the points of contention mentioned above, may stand in the way of a positive reception of this work on a large scale. First, and in direct contrast to the philosopher's contention that he seeks universal elements of human experience, there is a sense that this work is only narrowly applicable. Attendant to this is a larger and more significant point for Patočka's reception as a political theorist. This concerns the degree to which the Patočkan framework may be taken as a model, not for individual action in history, but for political action on a broader scale. Both points require some explanation.

Beginning with the first, it is significant that Patočka states explicitly that his work "should not be understood as an idealization of the Greek *polis*," despite its attribution of nothing less than "the very beginning of history in the proper sense of the word" to the rise of this institution.[56] While he does not idealize the historical development of the polis, he recognizes that it did not rise suddenly and out of selfless devotion to the common good, Patočka still places such importance on the event of the polis that it is difficult to see it as anything but an idealization. It is only in the age and the institution of the Greek city-state, he contends, that humans first dare to shake given meaning and take on the responsibility and understanding that meaning is a product of their living in both concreteness and transcendence, not a gift bestowed on them from without. And this is done in such a way as to attain "a universal significance."[57]

Patočka is, in this way, very much a political theorist, for his analysis locates the ontological categories that define humanity—freedom and the possibility of historical action—in the emergence of a political institution. Yet this analysis also has a reductive quality. When a single period and institution is held up as epitomizing human possibility, it denies such possibility to societies not that did not exist in the historical wake of Greek civilization. Patočka's philosophy of history has a quite explicit Eurocentric framework. Based on Husserl's work in his *Crisis of European*

Sciences, Patočka's outline of history makes it an entirely Western affair. Non-European civilizations, insofar as they did not benefit from the Hellenic experience, are most likely to be categorized as "prehistorical" societies. The spirit of history, Patočka argues, is the spirit of Europe and its descendants.

With this idealization of the polis, not merely as an institutional and spiritual model but as an historical event tied to a spirit that is particularly European, Patočka dismisses the possibility that experiences in non-Western cultures, to varying degrees, can be considered equivalent. In doing so he reduces unnecessarily the scope of his investigations and closes himself off to possibility. Patočka's work on the polis as a model for freedom and history is of such significance for political theory that it would be unfortunate to see it discounted for its neglect of comparative analysis. Patočka is right when he argues that there is something unique about the Western model of politics and philosophy, but he does himself a disservice when he frames his investigation in a way that precludes a truly comparative exploration of the universality of his ontological explanation of history.

It is when we consider the possibility of a positive application of this work to concrete political reality that the second question arises. Patočka is quite direct in the conclusion that his model of politics and philosophy can have a truly historical effect on Western civilization only at the point when we "turn from accidental rule to the rule of those who understand what history is about." In fact, he continues, those capable of understanding history would be subject to "tragic *guilt*" if they "failed to comprehend and grasp this opportunity,"[58] meaning the opportunity to rule. Clearly, if democratic politics in the contemporary situation is to be successful in a historical sense it will be because the "shaken" are able to act politically. If by this is understood that a certain group of individuals should organize a political order around themselves, then this philosophical perspective on democracy threatens to become a classical portrait of rule by Plato's Guardians, the undemocratic rule by the wise.

It is in light of this that the warning of Ivan Chvatík quoted above, to the effect that Patočka's work may not serve as a guideline for political action, is well taken. He is correct in pointing out that Patočka's ontological portrait of human being is not suitable as a straightforward guidepost for political activity—something that Patočka himself ultimately made clear at the end of his sixth and final *Heretical Essay*. He argued there, in the same breath as he spoke of the special role of those "who understand," that the 'solidarity of the shaken' "will not offer positive programs but will speak, like Socrates' *daimonion*, in warnings and prohibitions."[59] Patočka portrays his own political philosophy, here, as pointing to a "spiritual authority" that would not propose solutions to everyday problems but would instead become the spiritual power that could drive the political world toward the restraint it lacks. In doing so, in analyzing the nature of our being in society and leading the reader toward a reappraisal of the foundation on which his own understanding of politics is based, Patočka hopes that his work may help to render impossible the pernicious forms of ideological politics with which we are all too familiar from the century just past.

As I have argued, however, Chvatík is wrong to insist that a connection between this work and a science of political order cannot be established. Such a connection exists, but it is not without recognizable limitations. Patočka's analysis of the interrelationship between philosophy and politics leads, on the one hand, to principles that could be transformative for political theory as they persuasively illuminate the character of the soil on which the very concept of politics was built and continues to stand. It is insufficient, on the other hand, as a more traditional work of political theory; it cannot replace, but only supplement and act as a corrective to theory that aims at the construction of a framework for concrete activity or constitution building.

Patočka's work is directed toward an exploration of human possibility and the effect an understanding of our possibility could have on the realm of politics. It was his most famous student, Czech President Václav Havel, who noted that a politics of freedom and democracy will have its most universal appeal when it justifies its principles, not on foundations such as those implicit in the ideological positions of either liberalism or socialism, but on the basis of an ontological and phenomenological understanding of humanity that rejects abstraction and the pull of ideology. The end of communism on a worldwide scale does not ensure that dangerously radical versions of our contemporary supercivilization have ceased to be a real possibility. Human history has not been solved nor will it be solved. As political theory, the work of Jan Patočka is directed toward ensuring that we understand this reality, and that we create institutions based on that understanding.

Appendix

Patočka's Reception in the English-Language Literature

Jan Patočka remains a relatively unknown figure in the English-speaking world—nowhere more so than in the United States. His name is heard most often in relation to Václav Havel, who has regularly invoked the late philosopher in his writings and speeches. And though fundamental to an understanding of Havel's self-described "antipolitical" approach to politics,[1] Patočka's work has up to now received little attention from students of political thought in the West. Those studies that do exist, further, tend to share a particular trait: rather than read Patočka in terms of his stated philosophical aspirations, the more typical approach is to categorize him, to find the stream of already established philosophy into which his work can be placed. Yet when this approach is taken, the Czech philosopher inevitably appears to be inconsistent, as if he switches back and forth between different schools of thought. To read him in this way does not do justice to the content of Patočka's work; it fails to account for his intention to depict an approach to philosophy that is faithful, not to a particular method or school, but to a common insight into human reality.

Patočka's is a philosophy that inherently resists categorization. Though he is a contemporary thinker, his work does not conform to the categories of contemporary philosophy; it rather directly challenges them. There is disagreement, for instance, as to its status: classical or postmodern, conservative or radical, Platonic or Heideggerean? Many readers, having come to the work with their own preferences, will interpret Patočka accordingly. Yet in this act they betray the essence of his philosophical project: while the Czech thinker consciously remains open to the validity of a variety of philosophical approaches, he is uncompromisingly determined not to fall prey to the temptation of adopting the rigid outlines and limiting assumptions that define any one of them as a school or an "-ism."

The relatively little attention paid to Patočka has to do, most certainly, with the general unavailability of his work, particularly in English translation. Having spent most of his working life under fascist or communist governments, Patočka was unable to pursue his career at the university in Prague, let alone publish his philosophical work free of censorship. Many of the writings available today exist only through the efforts of his students, who painstakingly (and illegally) collected, transcribed, and cataloged his texts and lectures. It is a consequence of communist censorship that a good deal of his work has never been published, even in the original Czech. While great strides have been made since 1989, it is only recently that we have seen small steps toward a presentation of his work to the English-speaking public. Without doubt, the lack of a compendium of Patočka's works in English is the major factor behind the relative absence of a critical literature on the Czech philosopher. One aim of this work is to begin to make up for this shortcoming.

To the extent that Patočka is known in the academic world of the West, it is for two things: first, he is recognized to have been a phenomenologist of the first rank, a student of Husserl's and Heidegger's and an interpreter of the divide between them.[2] Second, he is remembered as an anticommunist dissident who paid a Socratic price for his involvement with Charter 77[3] and his defense of the unassailable moral foundation of politics. The two most ambitious interpretive studies of Patočka in English, by Erazim Kohák and Aviezer Tucker, focus primarily on these points and, in doing so, neglect the broader and, in my view, more significant issue of Patočka's engagement with the problem of a foundation for politics in a postmodern age. Other significant commentaries, from notable postmodern philosophers such as Jacques Derrida and Richard Rorty, for example,[4] focus more specifically on the question of foundations; yet in stressing the postmodern in Patočka, they misread, to differing degrees, the nature of the Czech philosopher's commitment to ethics. A brief look at the relevant texts at the way in which Western readers have received Patočka, will help to place the present study in a comparative context as well as into the context of current scholarship.

PATOČKA AS CONFLICTED HUMANIST

Prior to the publication of the present work, readers interested in Patočka could turn either to Erazim Kohák's "Jan Patočka: A Philosophical Biography" from 1989 or, more recently, to Aviezer Tucker's analysis of *The Philosophy and Politics of Czech Dissidence from Patočka to Havel*. Each work approaches the Czech philosopher from a distinctly different point of view, Kohák from the perspective of phenomenology and Tucker from that of dissidence. And yet both describe him in comparable terms. Broadly speaking, Kohák and Tucker argue that Patočka is best defined in terms of a humanism that displays itself in the concern for ethics and the human potential for authentic, transcendental morality that come through strongly in many of his texts. Other texts, such as those with a strong Heideggerean voice, for instance, contradict the image of Patočka as humanist and constitute a significant stumbling block to this reading. One has to contend either that Patočka should not be understood in terms of humanism, or that his work is simply inconsistent. For Kohák and Tucker, it is the latter argument that is closest to the truth. Since I have tried to portray a fundamental consistency in Patočka's work, it is important to look briefly at these arguments.

Without the dedication and commitment of Erazim Kohák, it is fair to say, Patočka would continue to be an anonymous figure in the English-speaking world. As a professor at Boston University, Kohák translated and published the vast majority of the texts currently available in English. A phenomenologist himself, Kohák has also written extensively about Patočka as one of the most significant of the successors of Edmund Husserl.[5] In his "Philosophical Biography," Kohák introduces a selection of Patočka's writings with an extensive, interpretive overview of the Czech philosopher. Kohák's book remains required reading for the English reader seeking a comprehensive overview of Patočka's philosophy and bibliography.

At the core of Kohák's reading of Patočka is the tradition of "Czech moral humanism," a tradition, he notes, in which "Husserl, a friend and fellow-student of Masaryk's, was also rooted."[6] Beyond Masaryk and Husserl, this tradition extends back to the figure of Comenius (Jan Amos Komenský), 1592–1670, the Czech philosopher known primarily for his pedagogical teachings. While it is true that Patočka wrote extensively about both Comenius and Masaryk—he spent more than a decade in the Masaryk Institute and Comenius Archive while he was barred from University teaching by the communists—and greatly appreciated the moral orientation of their philosophies, it does not follow that he is best described in terms of a "tradition" bounded by these two great figures. Kohák brings to his interpretation of Patočka a strong feeling for Christian humanism, a strong sense that the "moral maturity" of T. G. Masaryk and the harmony with the world of Comenius, grounded in love and blending a Protestant faith in God with an Enlightenment belief in humanity, is the appropriate response to the "crisis" of modern man described by Husserl. While this sense of a crisis certainly propelled the young Patočka into his academic vocation, it is debatable whether his philosophical response to the situation can be called a step in the path of Czech moral humanism.

Kohák's focus in this work is nearly exclusively on its phenomenological elements and their potential application toward a renewal of moral humanism in the world. Scant attention is paid, therefore, to the centrality of a concept of politics in Patočka's work. "Jan Patočka, after all, had never been . . . a political philosopher."⁷ And yet as I have shown, the political and the philosophical are inextricably intertwined in this work – the polis is the home of philosophy and its raison d'être is politics. Politics is the activity via which philosophy and freedom are made actual. Politics, then, is much more central to Patočka's overall project than Kohák is willing to recognize.

Erazim Kohák prefaces his philosophical biography by describing what he sees as "the basic tension underlying modernity": the tension between two contradictory traditions and conceptions of reality.⁸ In the Enlightenment tradition, to which Edmund Husserl belongs, reality is understood as familiar and accessible to understanding; the contending tradition, which he "superficially" designates as romanticism and associates with Martin Heidegger, finds reality to be essentially other, alien, and exceeding all understanding.⁹ Only in the context of medieval Christianity, of a God who allows for an intelligible world yet is radically beyond understanding, could both forms of understanding coexist, suggests Kohák. In the modern world, after the death of God, they can only contradict. Jan Patočka, as student and interpreter of both Husserl and Heidegger, has a foot in each tradition and he seeks to bridge the chasm beneath his feet.

Kohák presents this dichotomy in order to delineate two "basic insights," two modes of perceiving reality that are "irreducible yet irreconcilable."¹⁰ Patočka, he argues, moves between these two poles, seeking to synthesize them; his interpretation of Husserl and Heidegger forms the context of this synthesis. For Kohák, Patočka is most properly understood as situated somewhere in-between these poles, primarily oriented toward the Husserlian but also influenced (to different degrees in different historical circumstances) by the Heideggerean ontological critique. The use of Heideggerean, rather than Husserlian language represents a "shift" in Patočka's work that for Kohák is essentially a movement away from the Husserlian Enlightenment pole, which Kohák prefers, and toward the Heideggerean. Kohák is convinced that his dichotomy is appropriate and that its two poles are not reconcilable; and so he suggests that religion, conceived so as to allow room for an understandable world but a radically transcendent God, may provide the answer.

Although this description of a tension underlying modern thought—between a conception of reality as fundamentally comprehensible and one that sees in it only a nihilistic absence of meaning—is relevant, Patočka did not stress Husserl and Heidegger as representative of the two poles. The former pole, dominant in Western philosophy for two millennia, is exemplified not only by Enlightenment humanism but also, and more emphatically, by metaphysical constructions that posit a transcendental source of meaning that is objectively comprehensible, as in certain formulations of the concept of a divine Being. The latter pole is most commonly represented in Patočka's writings by the nihilistic prescriptions put forth by Nietzsche. Husserl and Heidegger, though they may err on either side of this dichotomy, represent for Patočka affirmative responses to the presence of this tension; they do not stand for the two poles themselves. Thus while Patočka is properly identified as an "interpreter of the dialogue between Husserl and Heidegger," this "interpretation" is not the center of gravity around which his thought, particularly his political thought, revolves. It is not Patočka's goal simply to find a way to bridge Husserl and Heidegger; his goal is greater—to renew in philosophy and politics an ancient insight by approaching it with the aid of contemporary phenomenological method, in its Husserlian and its Heideggerean varieties.

Kohák is clear to point out that Patočka is neither simply a Husserlian nor a Heideggerean thinker, but one who is genuinely heir to both.[11] As he interprets this dual legacy, however, Kohák consistently stresses the predominance of the Husserlian influence.[12] The persistent presence of Heidegger, then, leads Kohák to the conclusion that Patočka was a thinker of two "strands," one Husserlian and one Heideggerean. The latter strand surfaced during historical periods of discouragement and hopelessness, such as in the darkest days of Czechoslovak communist "normalization" in the 1970s. Yet "if we consider Patočka's work as a whole," Kohák concludes, "it is definitely the 'Husserlian' strand that is more consistent and dominant."[13] This claim comports with Kohák's own preference for the Husserlian.

As Kohák describes him, Patočka is an inconsistent thinker; the inconsistency shows itself in an unfortunate "shift" in Patočka's idiom and, more important, in his perception of reality. The "pronounced discontinuity in Patočka's thought" to which Kohák points explains the perceived difference between Patočka's stress on caring for the soul, living in truth and other ethical concepts on one hand, and his striking words in, for example, the last of his *Heretical Essays* on the other.[14] In these later writings, Kohák argues, the philosopher's perception of reality has been conditioned by the vicissitudes of the totalitarian situation in which he exists. Whereas he once perceived our human context, the world, to be supportive of human moral conduct, in periods of strife he altered his perception of the world, coming to see it as "hostile to human efforts," and "alien."[15] Effectively, then, there are two Patočkas, one a Husserlian or Masarykan humanist (whose thought is but a step away from a Christian solution), and a second, who has seen his hopes for moral advancement crushed and has turned to a more pessimistic and Heideggerean reading of being in stark contrast to his earlier work.

Such a reading, as I have tried to show, is flawed. It does not accord with Patočka's overall body of work, which is on the one hand inherently wary of the metaphysical content of "Enlightenment humanism" and on the other firmly insistent that elements of Heideggerean insight and symbolism are not incompatible with a goal of moral comportment.

Kohák does point, I should note, to a broad consistency in Patočka's writings, but he locates it in the philosopher's understanding of the "goals" of human striving, not in his description of the context of that striving. He defends Patočka, for example, against the misinterpretation of those who find in the later writings a 180-degree turn away from moral humanism and would accuse Patočka of becoming "a splenetic ultrarightist, glorying in orgiastic visions of war," a tragically erroneous interpretation which Kohák attributes only to "a number of Western readers, including Czech readers living in the West."[16] And yet Kohák's reading shares something in common with these readers'—the perception that Patočka's later, political writings are less a part of his true philosophy than a consolatory reaction written for his students, a striking out against the injustice of the historical situation in which he found himself.

Kohák's own preference, as he makes clear, is for those works that are more easily compatible with a Christian humanism. Yet while Patočka can express admiration for certain aspects and goals of the Christian worldview, he cannot embrace its dogmatic tenants. When he turns, in the *Essays*, to an explicit exhortation of struggle, Kohák is clearly disappointed. He seems to urge Patočka, and perhaps the reader, to "discover Being, in love rather than in strife." "[W]hy not the religious option?" he asks elsewhere, as a means to resolve the dilemma of a world simultaneously accessible to understanding and yet undeniably possessed of something that exceeds it.[17]

Kohák grudgingly recognizes that Patočka was not a believer, and that his reasons for this stance were fundamentally philosophical. Without rejecting the metaphors of Christian transcendence, Patočka resisted what he saw as a temptation to abandon philosophy for faith in the solidity of a divine Being. Instead, he sought to answer the dilemma by means of rigorous reflection, by philosophical means.

Erazim Kohák places Patočka in the tradition of Masarykan humanism, as I have noted. And yet Patočka is a critic of Masaryk, arguing that Masaryk's philosophy (and politics) is grounded in a fundamentally metaphysical view of the world. For Masaryk, "Democracy is not only a state form, but that theistic metaphysics which responds to the moral nature of human reality."[18] As such it is hampered by the lack of "independent philosophical thinking," meaning thinking able to free itself from dependence on assumptions that, whether positivistic or religious, rest on metaphysical foundations. Kohák's interpretive work is, in the end, subject to the same critique as that leveled against Masaryk. It seeks to rest on a metaphysical foundation to secure its deepest convictions and goals.

In contrast to Kohák, Aviezer Tucker focuses specifically on Patočka as a political philosopher, or, more precisely, as the philosopher whose work "united and shaped the Czechoslovak dissident movement."[19] His book, *The Philosophy and Politics of Czech Dissidence from Patočka to Havel*, describes the late philosopher as the guiding thread of Czech dissidence in the second half of the twentieth century. Its focus, then, is not Patočka, but Charter 77 and the twenty five years that have passed since its inception. And yet Patočka is the primary point of reference, the center of gravity of both Czech dissident activity in general and the politics of Václav Havel in particular. In three chapters devoted to the Czech philosopher, Tucker attempts to illuminate and clarify "the philosophical foundation for dissidence and political action"[20] that he locates in the philosophy of Patočka.

Tucker's examination of Patočka, as with Kohák's, encompasses a great deal and deserves careful consideration. Here I take up only one of its basic conclusions—that Patočka's political theory should be understood in terms of its invocation of a metaphysical theory of human rights. This conclusion, again like Kohák's, points to a fundamentally humanist perspective in Patočka, albeit an inconsistent one. Patočka's humanism is manifest in what Tucker calls his "universal ethics and political philosophy of human rights,"[21] a political philosophy that served as the basis, not only for Charter 77, but also for the politics of the future Czech president, Václav Havel. It is the search for this philosophy of human rights that determines Tucker's interpretation of the Czech philosopher.

Tucker is convinced, even more than Kohák, of the inconsistency of Patočka's work. Using Patočka's participation in Charter 77 as a baseline, he praises the Czech thinker as a humanist for those parts of his work that lend support to a concrete political ethics, and criticizes him as a reactionary for those parts (such as the later *Heretical Essays*) that lean away from ethics and toward Heideggereanism. Historical circumstances, he concludes, account for the variation in the material, arguing that the disappointments of the Communist era produced drastic changes in the substance and content of his writings.

It is Plato and Heidegger, here, who form the two poles of Patočka's philosophy. This is in contrast to Kohák, who reads Patočka as primarily a contemporary thinker trying to bridge the gap between Husserl and Heidegger. For Tucker, the contemporary pole of Patočka's thought seems dominated by Heidegger. While he accepts the "Heideggerean foundations" in Patočka's work, Tucker nonetheless argues that the Czech philosopher's humanism is "not Heideggerean." This is because Patočka pushes "the philosophy of *Being and Time* beyond where Heidegger intended it."[22] Tucker argues, almost without exception, that Patočka uses those Heideggerean concepts that figure prominently in his work differently than did Heidegger. "Patočka's 'care for the soul,'" for example, "also emphasizes the importance of recognizing finitude, but otherwise bears little resemblance to Heidegger's 'care.'"[23] It is much closer to Socrates than to Heidegger.

Tucker's focus is on Patočka as human rights activist; human rights are at the heart of his philosophy, the key to his "life in truth" and therefore to his politics. The argument proceeds from the claim that Patočka's work is fundamentally "metaphysical." The fulcrum of the analysis is the contention that Charter 77 sprung from metaphysical foundations in the philosophy of its spokesman, Jan Patočka. "Patočka's metaphysically founded ethical system," Tucker writes, "fully explains his involvement with Charter 77."[24] The Charter also helps to explain, conversely, the ground of Patočka's philosophy: a search for the human 'essence' that gives rise to absolute conceptions of right. "Since Patočka and the other Charter 77 dissidents supported universal and absolute human rights," Tucker writes, "they required an equally universal and absolute philosophical understanding of human existence that human rights should defend. Simply put, Patočka argued that human existence has an essence and that the realization of this essence is virtue."[25]

In Tucker's description, then, and in contrast to my conclusions in this book, Patočka is a metaphysical thinker with "no clear objection to foundations." Tucker recognizes, but only briefly, the attempt in "Negative Platonism" at a renewal of Platonic insight absent its reliance on foundational metaphysics—a rereading of Socrates and Plato through the eyes of Heidegger, in other words. "Patočka's negative Platonism," he writes, "adopted Plato's universalism and transcendence but attempted to do away with its ontology, with the separate, objective existence of the ideas. This is as near as Patočka ever got to synthesizing the platonic and Heideggerean elements in his thought."[26] Unfortunately, Tucker does not follow through with this line of inquiry; he reverts instead to the hypothesis that Patočka was, at one moment in time, Platonic and humanist, and at another, Heideggerean and reactionary.

Tucker's work, as I noted, shares Kohák's perception of two "poles" demarcating Patočka's work. Those poles are represented by a dominant humanism with Platonic roots, and a perspective that is reactionary in its Heideggereanism. The two faces of Patočka are exemplified in two main texts: *Plato and Europe* and the *Heretical Essays in the Philosophy of History*. The first exemplifies Patočka's humanism and his commitment to human rights, while the second text is pessimistic and Heideggerean.[27] As Tucker puts it,

> When Patočka held that the essence of the person is life in truth, and that truth is achieved by Platonic dialectic, he was a humanist, as in *Plato and Europe*. When he accepted from Heidegger that human authenticity is freedom from alienation, and that truth is involuntary disclosedness, he become [*sic*] a reactionary.[28]

Yet at the end of his life, Patočka chose at great risk to participate in Charter 77, to wager his safety in defense of his principles. And so Tucker concludes that it is the Platonic side of Patočka, the notion of "truth" as absolute, that not only defines Patočka's engagement with Charter 77, but also represents his core beliefs. This is the guiding thread, explained phenomenologically and with the help of Heideggerean terminology, that serves as a model for Czech dissident activity, most particularly that of Havel. It is the conclusion that the goal of philosophy, insofar as it relates to politics, is to construct a metaphysical system solid enough to support human morality. "Modern society," Tucker writes in his discussion of Havel, "requires an absolute moral foundation valid for all humans at all times, unconditional and independent of any circumstances, a nontechnological ethics. Human rights are the sacred, transcendental, and absolute moral principles."[29]

Tucker's reading of Patočka, on this point, is at odds with my own. As I argue in this book, Patočka remained consistent throughout his life in rejecting both relativism and its opposite, the assumption of an absolute perspective accessible to man. He was neither an anthropocentric humanist nor a reactionary, considering both to be forms of escape from the problematicity and historicity of human existence. Patočka felt that Enlightenment humanism, for example, reflected a metaphysical desire for harmony and surety, a desire that he criticized.[30] He could not, then, as I argue, even in his most Platonic of moments, have developed "an absolute and universal ethical system as a basis for political philosophy and action."[31]

Tucker's interpretation proceeds from a desire to explicate the connection between Charter 77's affirmation of transcendental ethics and the philosophy of its primary author, Jan Patočka. Yet as I have sought to show, the absolute morality of which Patočka speaks in the Charter documents is not expressible in a given set of rights or freedoms to which all societies must adhere in order to achieve authenticity.[32] The ethical politics sought by Patočka cannot be guaranteed through a metaphysical system; it is a more tentative and hard-won achievement that results from the commitment to freedom *from* ideology, never in support of it. It is freedom for others as well as for oneself. The freedom to which Patočka refers recognizes the transcendent, to be sure, but it is always a concrete and historically situated activity, and so never simply translatable into a universal, into a concept that itself stands beyond history.

PATOČKA AS POSTMODERN: ANTIFOUNDATIONALISM, THEOLOGY, AND LIBERALISM

Although Kohák and Tucker avoid the issue of foundations directly, each effectively argues for a foundation in humanism. It is with thinkers working in the postmodern tradition, however, that the question of foundations is raised directly. Patočka's work has been taken up by Richard Rorty and by Jacques Derrida, and both recognize that the question at the heart of his philosophy concerns a nonfoundational justification for moral and political activity. Derrida explores the theme of responsibility and the politics that accompanies it in Patočka's *Heretical Essays*, while Rorty reads the Czech's antifoundationalism in terms of his commitment to democracy.

Like Kohák and Tucker, Rorty and Derrida resist the notion that Patočka might be capable of forging a coherent path between traditional Western foundationalism and the antifoundationalism of contemporary, postmodern work. Both recognize Patočka's fundamentally contemporary outlook, but they characterize his work in distinctly different ways. While Derrida reads the Heretical Essays to contain a postmodern, yet messianic, theology, Rorty finds in those same texts a genuinely antifoundational position in the Heideggerean tradition. Both accounts, though, have significant flaws. Though broadly accurate, Rorty goes too far in depicting Patočka's antifoundationalism. Derrida, on the other hand, reaches conclusions that are explicitly contradicted by many of Patočka's other texts. For all of the iconoclastic qualities of their philosophies, Rorty and Derrida approach Patočka through standard philosophical categories, even if postmodern ones. Patočka's approach, though, starts from a position a step beyond the straightforward dichotomy between the traditional and the postmodern.

The theme of the foundation is presented most clearly in a short essay written for *The New Republic* by Richard Rorty. Rorty's short article is a book review of the collection of essays in English edited by Kohák, the *Heretical Essays*, and *Plato and Europe* (both in French translation), and it gives only a brief overview of Patočka as the model for Václav Havel and the other Czechoslovak dissidents of the sixties and seventies, yet it manages to elucidate what I see as the core issues in Patočka's thought in a way unmatched by other, longer analyses.

While Rorty agrees with Erazim Kohák that Patočka is most immediately significant as an interpreter of the dialogue between Husserl and Heidegger, he disagrees with him in a significant way: "Patočka," Rorty concludes, "is mostly on Heidegger's side."[33] For Rorty, it is the Heideggerean theme, the critique of metaphysics, that comes through most strongly. And yet he notes a fundamental difference between Patočka and Heidegger: while Heidegger, after his experience with National Socialism, abandoned his interest in politics and in resuscitating Western institutions, Patočka remained a political thinker who thought those institutions could be freed from their reliance on metaphysics and infused with freedom.

Heidegger found the difference between democracy and tyranny philosophically uninteresting, insignificant compared to the titanic drama of the self-destruction of metaphysics. Patočka threw himself, as soon as he was asked, into what turned out to be a mortal struggle for democratic freedom.[34]

Although he overstates the degree to which Patočka is on "Heidegger's side," Rorty is correct in pointing to this fundamental difference between the goals of the Czech philosopher and his German instructor.

In Rorty's reading, it is Patočka's critique of metaphysics that stands out, making him more of a Heideggerean than a Husserlian thinker. Though Patočka supported democratic values as a dissident, Rorty argues in distinct contrast to Tucker that he should not be thought of as a philosopher of human rights, meaning the "sort of philosopher who wants to give democratic institutions and hopes a 'firm philosophical foundation,'" for the simple reason that if one rejects metaphysics, one must reject all such foundations.[35] For Rorty, Patočka's critique of metaphysics makes him an antifoundationalist. In this, he stands quite apart from "Straussians like Allan Bloom" and others who "insist on metaphysical foundations for political choice," on a "moral reality" reflected in the institutions of democracy.[36] Still, Rorty does not ignore Patočka's moral language or his evocation of a moral foundation in the texts of Charter 77. He conceives of Patočkan moral sentiment as responding to an elemental and nonmetaphysical sense of human obligation; with this Rorty dismisses much of Patočka's ontological philosophy, implying that it is an overcomplication of a simple human reaction—the call of conscience.

The solution to the trap of choosing between "absolutism" and "relativism" (metaphysics and antifoundationalism) lies in understanding the term "absolute" in a different sense. For Rorty, Patočka is responding to a sense of absolute obligation, our conscience, that is in no way "objective." It lacks any kind of solid foundation, making it something of a "leap in the dark." "For Patočka," Rorty writes, "the unconditionality of the call of conscience has nothing to do with the notion of a moral demand being legitimated or underwritten by something factual, something 'out there.'"[37] Rorty thus reads Patočka to be thoroughly postmodern in his rejection of all metaphysical support for moral action. Conscience is directed simply by a shared humanity, a shared sense of dignity and resulting obligation. Any more solid grounding or understanding than this does not exist for Rorty. In a critique of Patočka, Rorty finds the seeds of the conditions for social conscience to be varied and widespread. As such, Patočka's focus on being and consciousness, on positive versus negative forms of Platonism, is superfluous and inordinate. Too much emphasis is placed on Socrates and Plato, on the position of philosophy in Patočka's thought as an absolutely central force in history.

Rorty's position is in sharp contrast to those of Kohák and Tucker. Kohák explicitly reads Patočka to allow "no facile escape into an 'anti-foundationalism.' Choose we must,"[38] he writes. While this choice to which Kohák alludes, judging by the content of his analysis, implies a certain metaphysical foundation, the point is nonetheless well taken. Patočka's moral and philosophical conviction seems incomparably more solid than Rorty's nonfoundational call of conscience. In reducing this philosophy to a simple call of conscience, Rorty leaves one with no conceptual apparatus to analyze, to compare against one's experience of reality.

The reality is that Patočka is never so simplistic in his rejection of metaphysics. It is not the concept of the ground, the foundation in and of itself, with which he takes issue, but the concept of the unproblematic, solid ground that we artificially posit in our desire for a simple answer to our most difficult questions. Patočka conceives of philosophy itself as the development of the theme of the problematic; within the boundaries of an understanding of problematicity, he argues, it *is* appropriate to philosophy to seek something permanent, but only as long as it is understood that the ground sought is never simple and concrete, but always problematic.[39] Rorty's antifoundationalism goes beyond the limits of what Patočka seeks, to the point that it verges on the relativism Patočka explicitly denies. This analysis provides an invaluable counterposition to those of Kohák and Tucker, but it does not adequately respond to Patočka himself.

Though his article is brief, Rorty clearly disagrees with the conclusion that *Plato and Europe* and the *Heretical Essays* represent contrary positions. Unlike Kohák and Tucker, Rorty sees no inconsistencies between these two texts, no significant distinction between the content or conclusions of one and the other. Here he is correct and so perhaps the most clear-sighted of Patočka's American interpreters. But rather than analyze and contest the fine points of Patočka's philosophy on its own merits, Rorty is content to be dismissive of it as an overcomplication of an apparently self-evident human faculty. Yet the faculty of conscience to which he refers and which, he must presume, is sufficient to serve as a stabilizing and ordering force in human society and politics, remains an undifferentiated concept in his account, not rigorously explained or defended. As such it is insufficient as a conceptual undergirding for a theory of politics.

The analysis of Patočka's work from a postmodern perspective continues with Jacques Derrida's *The Gift of Death*, which is dedicated largely to a consideration of the Czech philosopher and his perspective on responsibility. *The Gift of Death* is a reflection on the foundation of responsibility and its ethical and political contexts. This deconstructive analysis is conducted via an examination of two texts: Patočka's fifth "heretical" essay, entitled "Is Technological Civilization Decadent, and Why?" and Kierke-gaard's *Fear and Trembling* with its story of the sacrifice of Isaac by Abraham. The question of responsibility is a political question for Derrida as well as a philosophical one. "It concerns," he writes, "the very essence or future of European politics."[40]

Derrida is of course not searching for Patočka or Kierkegaard's con-cept of responsibility as much as for his own. As he deconstructs the con-cept, it becomes clear that his purpose is not to discount responsibility but to reinforce it. He seeks, in this as in much of his recent work, an "absolute" perspective on responsibility. To find it, Derrida looks to theol-ogy. He outlines a notion of responsibility grounded in a "messianic a priori," a ground for ethics that is messianic without being religious and ethical without being metaphysical.[41] With this, Derrida is trying to reestablish contact with the moral, the political, and even the religious, but without reverting to the metaphysical foundationalism that the Derridean practice of deconstruction has long aimed to subvert and decenter.[42] Responsibility, as Derrida evaluates it, becomes something "aporetic"; like his notion of justice, it is absolute and yet ever "undecidable."[43]

In the *Heretical Essays*, according to Derrida, Jan Patočka explores a genealogy of responsibility and religion from which a postmetaphysical sense of the responsible emerges—a heterodoxical and messianic responsi-bility which comes as a "gift," in mystery and secrecy, from a sacred Other. Supplementing this reading of Patočka with a consideration of the paradox of responsible ethics in Kierkegaard's story of Isaac and Abraham, Derrida ultimately develops a (nongrounding) groundwork for a version of respon-sibility he can call his own, and a portrait of God as the ultimate foundation for this absolute component of humanity.

Derrida is right to note the centrality of responsibility in Patočka's philosophy, and he recognizes a certain affinity between his own work and the Czech philosopher's. In both cases, the aim is a discourse open to ethics yet not subject to metaphysics. Drawing on a discussion from the *Heretical Essays* of the gift of faith from God to man that distinguishes Christianity, Derrida argues that the only genuine, and absolute, form of responsibility comes in absolute secrecy, in mystery, as a gift from the absolute other who is God. Philosophy, then, is not the appropriate means for distinguishing the responsible. Derrida seeks instead a form of theology, a picture of God that lacks any metaphysical attachment. Patočka's "genealogy" of responsi-bility is instrumental in this quest, even though the Frenchman concludes that the Czech is, in the end, not up to the task. It is Derrida, however, who is ultimately mistaken in his reading of Patočka.

In *The Gift of Death*, Derrida deconstructs responsibility in order to uncover its unconditionality and its paradox, making it beyond ethics and yet absolutely ethical. At its most profound level human responsibility is grounded in a relationship governed by mystery. As Derrida reads Patočka, the most profound responsibility was introduced to the West by Christianity, which is "intimately tied," writes Derrida, to the "terrifying mystery," the *mysterium tremendum*. In Kierkegaard, responsibility to God is absolute, such that it requires obedience without reason, even to the point of committing the irresponsible (unethical) act of murdering one's child. One responds to the "absolute request of the other" that is beyond knowledge and enters into a relationship of "absolute singularity" that is secretive and mysterious.[44]

Derrida's goal is a form of religion without the dogma, a "genealogy of thinking concerning the possibility and essence of the religious that doesn't amount to an article of faith." He seeks to think, rather than to philosophize, so as to be able to "repeat the possibility of religion without religion."[45] This formulation rests, to a large degree, on the distinction between thinking and philosophy. Philosophy is bound up in the metaphysical quest almost by definition. Derrida wants a form of thinking that frees itself from metaphysics, and so from philosophy and its heritage; it will be, in other words, an emancipation of European thought from Athens.[46] Philosophy would be subordinated to that which is to replace it, to a deconstruction that contains within itself an undeconstructable element: a quasi-messianic responsibility determined by one's relationship to the Other-as-God.[47]

The notion of the Other-as-God is the problem on which Derrida's exploration of responsibility ultimately comes to rest. God exists, it seems, but exists in what way? Beginning in *The Gift of Death* with what he sees as Patočka's "heretical" approach to Christianity, Derrida elaborates a perspective on God that represents his own, postmodern evocation of an ultimate, irreducible ground from which responsibility emerges. As David Goicoechea has put it, "Derrida gives his argument for faith in God's existence in *The Gift of Death*. God for him is the condition for the secret of responsibility."[48] A concept of God in and of itself, it is argued, does not imply a metaphysics; the type of metaphysics that Derrida excludes is metaphysics of presence. What is inadmissible is a concept of God as a presence independent of the self. In Derrida's version, God manifests himself as an interior structure of conscience, a presence only in ourselves.

> We should stop thinking about God as someone, over there, way up there, transcendent, . . . Then we might say: God is the name of the possibility I have of keeping a secret that is visible from the interior but not from the exterior. Once such a structure of conscience exists, . . . then what I call God exists, (there is) what I call God in me, (it happens that) I call myself God. . . . God is in me, he is the absolute 'me' or 'self,' he is that structure of invisible interiority that is called, in Kierkegaard's sense, subjectivity.[49]

In this undeconstructible construction, God is both the absolute Other with whom I interact in secrecy and from whom I receive the gift that is the source of my responsibility, and also that which is in me, my subjectivity. It is in recognizing the *mysterium tremendum* within myself, the possibility that my invisible interiority is both part of me (and subjective) and "absolutely invisible" to me (and absolute), that I open the possibility of an ethics that is subjective and yet independent. It is via this formulation that Derrida wishes to attend to moral and political questions without implicating himself in the metaphysics that his own project of deconstruction has been dedicated to undermining.

While *The Gift of Death* is not the only text in which Derrida presents this perspective, it is here, and via his reading of Patočka, that he takes on the question of responsibility most directly. His discussion of the Czech philosopher is crucial to his response to this question. Derrida's view of Patočka, in the end, is critical. Though the genealogy of responsibility and Christianity is recognized to be heretical, and thus of a kind with Derrida's own work, Patočka is not considered to be up to the task. The reason, quite simply, is that Derrida perceives his view of responsibility to ultimately rest on a metaphysics of presence. Patočka's perspective is said to be essentially Christian, and so dependent on the existence of a Supreme Being as the ultimate source of human responsibility. Patočka's Christianity may be heretical, concludes Derrida, but it is a Christianity nonetheless.

While Derrida is right to point to the sophisticated analysis of responsibility in the postmetaphysical world in Patočka's work, he is incorrect to enlist him in the cause of overcoming the legacy of Athens via a renewed Christianity. Derrida's argument is built on his reading of the analysis of responsibility and Western history in Patočka's fifth "heretical" essay. Here, the historical transition from Platonism to Christianity is considered in terms of its effect on responsibility. Through the explicit assumption of the *mysterium tremendum*, Patočka notes, Christianity effected a "deepening" of the human soul; it placed greater emphasis on the responsibility of the individual to care for the salvation of his soul. The content of the soul, bound to responsibility, is explicitly revealed. It is in this respect that Patočka writes:

> by virtue of this foundation in the abysmal deepening of the soul, Christianity remains thus far the greatest, unsurpassed but also un-thought-through human outreach that enabled humans to struggle against decadence.[50]

Based largely on this passage, Derrida concludes that for the Czech thinker, Christianity represented an advancement over Platonic thought in terms of its understanding of responsibility, an advancement that Patočka aims to see to its conclusion by "thinking through" Christianity and finally "emancipating" it from both Athens and Rome.[51] This emancipation of Christianity from Athens, of course, is an emancipation of theology from philosophy.

Derrida is right to depict Patočka as searching for an understanding of responsibility that recognizes its attachment to the mysterious and the ineffable, but he fails to recognize that the Czech sought that understanding through philosophy, not through religion: it was not a heretical form of Christianity that Patočka was after, but a heretical form of philosophy. In the *Heretical Essays*, Patočka links responsibility to a philosophical position: the human being's conscious acceptance of his or her life in freedom, absent any metaphysical anchor to act as ballast and deliver us from the full weight of its burden. This is an achievement, an "accomplishment" of life that is our coming to terms with it rather than seeking to escape or avoid it, and it defines Patočka's notion of responsibility.

Patočka was engaged in largely the same quest as Derrida—the quest to demarcate the nonmetaphysical bases for an ethical discourse and politics. His pursuit of that goal, however, was such that it obviated the need for the whole antiphilosophical, deconstructionist project. Patočka clearly saw the same impulses that led Derrida toward deconstruction, yet he responded to them in a way that would allow political and philosophical discourse to continue as before, but not to continue in error.

The basis for Derrida's portrayal of Patočka is his contention that the Czech philosopher relies on a metaphysics of presence that, for example, distinguishes him from Heidegger. While, in the second chapter of *The Gift of Death*, Derrida recognizes many connections between Patočka and Heidegger, he quickly distinguishes the two based on Patočka's "essential Christianity."[52] Whereas Heidegger analyzes Christian themes on an ontological level, Derrida writes, Patočka takes those same themes and re-Christianizes them.[53] By this he means that Patočka understands these themes, including the concept of responsibility, to rest on the foundation of a supreme being. Heidegger believes that "the origin of responsibility does not in any way reduce, originarily, to a supreme being," but Patočka "deliberately takes an opposite tack." He "is no doubt convinced," argues Derrida, "that there is no true binding responsibility or obligation that doesn't come from someone, from a person such as an absolute being who transfixes me."[54]

Appended to this interpretation of Patočka as Christian is a reading of the Czech philosopher's politics and analysis of the "crisis" of modern Europe. These politics, naturally, follow from the purported belief in an essentially Christian responsibility. Derrida concludes that, as Patočka speaks of the nexus between the *mysterium tremendum* and human responsibility, he has in mind a concrete political program. For Patočka speaks,

Derrida says, not of the Christian past but of the "promise" of a future event:

> One should understand that in saying that Christianity has not been thought right through Patočka intends that such a task be undertaken; not only by means of a more thorough thematization but also by means of a political and historical setting-in-train, by means of political and historical action; and he advocates that according to the logic of a messianic eschatology that is nevertheless indissociable from phenomenology. . . . What has not yet come about is the fulfillment, within history and in political history, and first and foremost in European politics, of the new responsibility announced by the *mysterium tremendum.* Only on this condition will Europe have a future, and will there be a future in general, for Patočka speaks less of a past event or fact than he does of a promise.[55]

Patočka's political philosophy, in this reading, would ground human responsibility in the specifically Christian *mysterium tremendum* and its "logic of messianic eschatology."

A look at Patočka's corpus shows that there is little basis for either of the above conclusions. Patočka's attitude toward Christianity, toward a supreme being, is not as Derrida depicts it. Rather than emancipating Europe from Athens through a messianic eschatology, the Czech philosopher tries to renew Europe's original philosophical spirit.

On three points, then, Derrida's account of Patočka requires clarification. There is, first of all, no conception of an absolute being as foundation in Patočka's work; second, he holds that philosophy is prior to theology, and never the reverse; and last, Patočka's politics, as we have seen, explicitly disavow the type of political activity that a Christianization of European politics would seem to imply. The historical action toward which Patočka aims consists in the transformation of individual souls along Socratic guidelines, not in the transformation of societies along messianic-religious guidelines.

Although Christianity represented a profound development by virtue of its plumbing of the depths of the human soul and its recognition of the problematicity of human life, it nevertheless provided for itself an escape into nonproblematicity, away from responsibility, in the figure of the supreme being. Patočka at one point describes Christianity as the "contemporaneous seeing of problematicity and attempt to escape it."[56] It is not merely the perception of a transcendental reality that constitutes the origin of metaphysics, therefore; this occurs only when the "living force of transcendence . . . is transformed, with a fatal inevitability, into a transcendent, supramundane reality, a transcendent deity."[57] The divine element of human life, which Patočka recognizes as a component of reality, is never viewed by him in objective terms, in the Christian figure of a supreme being.[58]

The *Heretical Essays*, which laid out the historical and political context of Patočka's approach to philosophy and sought to offer hope to young Czechs buffeted by the repression of Communist totalitarianism, speak not, as Derrida says, of a "promise" of a European future, but rather of a possibility. And it is a possibility tied, not to a "thinking-through" of Christianity, but to a genuine understanding of philosophy. Derrida wrongly concludes that the reference to Christian themes implies a longing for the Christian over the Greek. To the contrary, while recognizing a certain historical effectiveness in Christianity, Patočka links its practice to Platonism, which means he links it to the flaws of propositional metaphysics. What he proposes is not a thought-through Christianity, but rather a thought-through Platonism; he called it, already in his early discussion of the problem of the postmetaphysical world in 1955, a "Negative Platonism."[59]

Patočka is a critic of both Platonic metaphysics and dogmatic Christianity in terms of their effect on human responsibility; neither leads us to accept responsibility for our own lives because both rest to some degree on a supreme Idea and a supreme being, respectively. In suggesting that Christianity may need to be "thought-through," he anticipates Derrida's approach as a possibility. He does not endorse it, however. Christianity's profound historical effect on the suppression of decadence notwithstanding, the religious experience must remain secondary, in Patočka's thought, to the philosophical experience. For the Prague philosopher, the possibility opened up by philosophy is the possibility of freedom granted us by virtue of our interest in the ontological possibilities of our own being and its place in the whole. It is philosophy, and not religion, that most deeply probes these depths.

> Myth, religion, poetry do not speak out of an awareness of the problem but prior to it, our of fervor, enthusiasm—outright divine 'possession.' Philosophy speaks from an awareness of the problematic nature to a problematic awareness. Thus it cuts deeper into human life, into the realm of human possibilities. . . . Only here is life radically renewed because only here does it explicitly discover freedom as an other, our own, different from the common, accepted meaning and explicitly as something that is to be carried out, as a possibility we can accomplish, never just accept.[60]

Responsibility, if it is anything at all, is an accomplishment. The means to explore that accomplishment are available to us via philosophy purified of its metaphysical tendencies. Yet after this purification, this deconstructive critique, philosophy still remains. It need not relinquish its position as the preeminent human science to religion, or to a messianic form of deconstruction such as Derrida suggests.

Besides Derrida and Rorty, the postmodern elements in Patočka's work, and particularly their political implications, have been noted by two other analysts deserving of brief mention. Essays by Paul Ricoeur and Petr Lom give a more tempered, and thus more truthful, assessment of Patočka than either of the lengthier treatments already discussed. In this, despite their brevity, these essays are important additions to the English-language literature on the politics and philosophy of Jan Patočka.

Ricoeur, one of the most significant voices in contemporary philosophy, has long been an admirer of Patočka and his work in phenomenology and political thought. Though not the author of a major work on Patočka, Ricoeur's introduction to the French edition of the *Heretical Essays* (translated for the English edition) shows his appreciation for the Czech philosopher's goals and illustrates how European philosophy generally has for some time looked seriously at this work and found it to be eminently worthy of consideration. Ricoeur's essay exemplifies the twin concerns of many Continental analysts, the first being phenomenology, for which Patočka was well known, and the second being the political implications of his focus, in the later essays, on the role of history and politics within an overall philosophical approach to human existence.

In terms of his methodology, Ricoeur notes the influence of Husserl and Heidegger, as well as the degree to which Patočka's work is "heretical" with respect to theirs. Instead of pointing with other analysts to how he is "Husserlian" or "Heideggerean," Ricoeur sees an interpretive effort that moves in a direction independent of both of these philosophers. It is an effort, further, that he recognizes as inherently political. Patočka's *Heretical Essays* begin with an exposition of Husserl's concept of the "natural world," but then quickly proceed to critique Husserl for his lingering Cartesian idealism and his inability to reach the meaningful historicity of humans and their concrete action in the world.[61] Here Patočka is with Heidegger, finding the ontological concept of "openness" to being and to the world as a whole to be prior to the mental phenomenon of our consciousness. But Heidegger's preoccupation with the unconcealment of being proves also to be insufficient to the task of understanding humanity in its daily movement and pursuit of freedom, in its activity within a community. Human existence encompasses more than the movement toward a philosophical understanding of being, such as Heidegger undertakes. Our openness, Ricoeur notes, "exposes man and his freedom," it makes the history of philosophical mankind concurrent with a fundamental problematicity, a problematicity that is particularly relevant in the movement of man within the world and the community.[62]

Patočka's *Heretical Essays* aim to analyze the condition of European mankind in relation to all of its distinctively human activity, not simply its intellectual or its ontological strivings. Thus Ricoeur writes that these essays "trace the quasi-simultaneous origin in western Europe of *politics, philosophy,* and *history,*"[63] three topics that are inextricably intertwined in Patočka's explication of philosophy. Our humanity as philosophical or "historical" beings is in large part a measure of our understanding of and relation to the problematic nature of our own existence, our acceptance of life in its finitude, and its fundamental uncertainty. Ricoeur stresses both the philosophical and the political in Patočka's work. As individuals, we must face a process akin to *metanoia*, or conversion, in which we come to accept the loss of metaphysical meaning, but without falling into a nihilistic meaninglessness. In this way, we gain "access to the quality of meaning implied in the search itself," a meaning that accompanies the Socratic care for the soul, which is a "meaning within the condition of problematicity."[64] The properly political element comes, Ricoeur notes, with the reflection on the possibility of transferring "from the individual to the whole of European society the meditation on the relation between meaning, non-meaning, and searching."[65] It is relative to this transfer that Patočka discusses the "solidarity of the shaken," the phenomenon of Czechoslovak dissident life in which those individuals with a genuine understanding of their situation came together, amid persecution and uncertainty, to stand against the untruth around them.

A final essay in English, from the Summer, 1999 issue of *Political Theory*, deserves mention for its illuminating discussion of Patočka and the politics of liberalism. In Petr Lom's "East Meets West—Jan Patočka and Richard Rorty on Freedom: A Czech Philosopher Brought into Dialogue with American Postmodernism,"[66] the question of foundationalism is approached from a different angle, that of the justification of liberal political principles. Responding to Richard Rorty's well-known challenges to the traditional, metaphysical justifications, Lom points to Patočka as an example of an approach to liberalism that rescues metaphysics, rather than discards it.

Like Rorty, Patočka seeks to ground human freedom in a world that is postmetaphysical, to assess it as a philosophical concept in an age when philosophy has been discredited. Lom looks to Patočka, in this essay, primarily for the contrast he offers to Rorty's attempt to define freedom as "contingency." In an utterly contingent world such as Rorty proposes, metaphysics is disposed of, and with it all of the human "spiritual aspirations that feed it."[67] The moral responsibility that Rorty seeks is one that recognizes nothing above itself, it is grounded in an ultimately contingent and "thoroughly secular liberal culture."[68] Lom's critique of Rorty, in the aid of which he enlists Patočka, centers on the American postmodernist's abandonment of philosophical reflection, particularly reflection on the enigmatic nature of transcendent reality. Instead, Rorty expresses a dogmatic certainty as to the absence of transcendent reality, and seeks to ground his political responsibility and ethics elsewhere.

Lom doubts the wisdom of "trying to get rid of" the human urge toward the transcendent,[69] and he presents Patočka as offering an alternative that continues to recognize metaphysical limitations to human behavior, yet without falling back on an objectivized, metaphysical "keeper" of those limits. Rorty's postmetaphysical age, writes Lom, "does not recognize any limits to human capability."[70] Patočka, in contrast, recognizes limits in our freedom by pointing to our eternal relationship to the problematic nature of our own being. In relating, not to a caricature of being but to its enigmatic qualities, our freedom is preserved via a philosophical experience that includes the recognition of responsible limits to our humanity.

Lom has presented Patočka as a postmetaphysical alternative for contemporary liberalism—an alternative that recognizes contingency, but does not give itself up wholly to it. Patočka shows that the *experience* of metaphysics, or transcendence, can and should be preserved even as we recognize the flaws of absolute versions of it. Though its examination of the content of Patočka's "problematic" alternative to Rortian freedom is limited,[71] the application of Patočkan philosophy to questions of contemporary liberalism is valuable.

The essays by Ricoeur and Lom, though brief, show that the Czech philosopher can be profitably engaged without succumbing to the urge to categorize his work according to the divisions prevalent in contemporary discourse. What is primary is not whether, at bottom, he is best described as a humanist or a postmodernist, a classical philosopher or an antifoundationalist; more important is the ability of his philosophical work to stand on its own legs, to be persuasive in its attempt to wed a classical outlook with contemporary insight and to apply that perspective on the human condition not only academically, but in the concrete terms of a life in community, a political life.

Notes

CHAPTER 1. INTRODUCTION

1. See Jan Patočka, "What We Can and Cannot Expect from Charta [sic] 77," in *Jan Patočka: Philosophy and Selected Writings*, ed. Erazim Kohák (Chicago: University of Chicago Press, 1989), 346.

2. On Patočka's educational influences, see Ivan Blecha, *Jan Patočka* (Prague: Votobia, 1997), 22.

3. For a discussion of this theme, see Edmund Husserl, "The Vienna Lecture," in *The Crisis of European Sciences and Transcendental Phenomenology* (Evanston: Northwestern University Press, 1970), 269–299.

4. Patočka also took from Heidegger, and from Nietzsche, the contention that human historical reality precluded a foundation in an ahistorical, "metaphysical" reality such as a theory of a "true world" of which the human world is but a reflection. This is the basis of the critique of metaphysics that grounds much of contemporary thought.

5. Josef Novák, "Selected Bibliography of Jan Patočka's Writings," *Kosmas: Journal of Czechoslovak and Central European Studies* 5, no. 2 (winter 1986): 115–139.

6. Josef Moural, "The Question of the Core of Patočka's Work: Phenomenology, History of Philosophy, and Philosophy of History," *Report of the Center for Theoretical Study*, CTS-99–05, (Prague: Center for Theoretical Study, 1999), 1.

7. During the long periods when he was barred from university life, Patočka found stimulating refuge in archives dedicated to the works of the Czech philosophers Jan Amos Komenský (Comenius) and T. G. Masaryk. He wrote extensively on both thinkers during these periods, putting together what could be termed a history of the philosophy of each. The texts on Komenský alone will occupy three volumes of Patočka's Collected Works.

8. Moural, "The Question of the Core of Patočka's Work," 2.

9. Ibid., 3. Moural situates himself somewhere in-between these perspectives, pointing out that, while it would be wrong to contend that Patočka was not a phenomenologist, it is true that "he did relatively little of topically oriented phenomenological analysis, of doing phenomenology rather than speaking about it." Ibid., 4.

10. Ibid., 3.

11. Ivan Chvatík and Pavel Kouba, "Předmluva k souboru Péče o duši" (Preface to the Collection: Care for the Soul), in *Sebrané Spisy Jana Patočky, sv. 1* (The Collected Works of Jan Patočka, vol. 1), *Péče o duši I: Soubor statí a přednášek o postavení člověka ve světě a v dějinách* (Care for the Soul I: A Collection of Articles and Lectures on the Position of Man in the World and in History), eds. Ivan Chvatík and Pavel Kouba (Prague: OIKOYMENH, 1996), 10 (Hereafter *Péče o duši*).

12. Moural, "The Question of the Core of Patočka's Work," 8.

13. Jan Patočka, *Heretical Essays in the Philosophy of History*, trans. Erazim Kohák (Chicago: Open Court Press, 1996), 104.

14. Ibid., 154.

15. Ibid., 149.

16. Ibid., 154.

17. Patočka, *Body, Community, Language, World*, trans. Erazim Kohák (Chicago: Open Court Press, 1998), 97–98.

18. See, for example, Martin Heidegger, *An Introduction to Metaphysics*, trans. Ralph Manheim (New Haven: Yale University Press, 1987), 182–189.

19. Patočka, *Heretical Essays*, 118.

20. Hans Meyerhoff, introduction to *Man's Place in Nature*, by Max Scheler (Boston: Beacon Press, 1961), xiv.

21. Patočka, "The Spiritual Person and the Intellectual," unpublished translation by Edward F. Findlay, TMs. See also *"Duchovní člověk a intelektuál, in Péče o duši, Sv. 6: Kacířské eseje o filosofii dějin a texty k Chartě 77* (samizdat), eds. Ivan Chvatík and Pavel Kouba (Prague: Jan Patočka Archive, Center for Theoretical Study, 1988). Patočka uses the term *spiritual* knowing full well that it does not "sound pleasant today." "It sounds," he continues, "in some way spiritualist and we don't like such phrases nowadays; but does there exist a better expression for what I have in mind?" Ibid., 1.

22. The most complete biographical material on Patočka I have found is in Ivan Blecha's philosophical biography of the thinker published in Czech in 1997 and simply entitled *Jan Patočka*. My information here is largely based on this text.

23. On the relationship between Fink and Patočka, see the recently published collection of letters and documents exchanged between the two: Eugen Fink and Jan Patočka, *Briefe und Dokumente 1933–1977*, eds.

Michael Heitz and Bernhard Nessler (ORBIS PHAENOMENOLOGI-CUS Perspektiven und Quellen, Freiburg/München: Verlag Karl Alber and Prag: Verlag OIKOYMENH, 1999).

24. Several significant philosophical texts from this period do exist, however, such as "Negative Platonism" and "Supercivilization and Its Inner Conflict." Yet these texts could not be published in Patočka's lifetime, and are often unedited or even unfinished.

CHAPTER 2. "CONCRETE HUMANS IN THEIR CORPOREAL WORLD"

1. Jan Patočka, *Body, Community, Language, World*, 73.

2. Patočka calls his work "phenomenological philosophy," distinguishing it from phenomenology, in his *Plato and Europe* lectures. On this differentiation, see chapter 3, p. 59, below.

3. Karl Schuhmann, "Husserl a Patočka," trans. V. Hrubá, *Proměny* 24, no. 1 (spring 1987): 34; quoted in Erazim Kohák, *Jan Patočka*, 9.

4. In many ways, Fink was engaged in a similar effort to interpret Husserl with the aid of Heidegger as was Patočka. The latter's close contact with Fink in Freiburg was to result in a lifelong friendship. The recently published correspondence between the two sheds light on the importance of the relationship toward the development of Patočka's phenomenological perspective. See Eugen Fink and Jan Patočka, *Briefe und Dokumente 1933–1977*. See also Ivan Blecha, *Jan Patočka*, 27–28, on Patočka's relation to Fink and the latter's personal critique of Husserlian phenomenology.

5. Ivan Blecha, *Jan Patočka*, 29.

6. See David Carr, translator's introduction to *The Crisis of European Sciences and Transcendental Phenomenology*, by Edmund Husserl, xvi.

7. In a Preface to Parts I and II of the *Crisis*, Husserl wrote that "The work has grown from the development of ideas that made up the basic content of a series of lectures I gave in November, 1935, in Prague (half in the hospitable rooms of the German university, half in those of the Czech university), following a kind invitation by the *Cercle philosophique de Prague pour les recherches sur l'entendement humain.*" See David Carr, ibid., footnote 1, 3.

8. See also Erazim Kohák, "Philosophical Biography," in *Jan Patočka*, 24.

9. Carr, xxv.

10. Ibid., xxv–xxvi.

11. Husserl, "The Vienna Lecture," in *Crisis*, 270.

12. On this point, see also Kohák's explanation in "The Crisis of Rationality and the 'Natural' World," 88.

13. Husserl, "The Vienna Lecture," 290.

14. It is important to note that the term *Europe* is used here by Husserl, and later by Patočka as well, to refer to what would more commonly be called the West: "How is the spiritual shape of Europe to be characterized? Thus we refer to Europe not as it is understood geographically, as on a map, as if thereby the group of people who live together in this territory would define European humanity. In the spiritual sense the English Dominions, the United States, etc., clearly belong to Europe, whereas the Eskimos or Indians . . . do not. Hence the title 'Europe' clearly refers to the unity of a spiritual life, activity, creation, with all its ends, interests, cares and endeavors, with its products of purposeful activity, institutions, organizations." Ibid., 273.

15. Ibid., 276. Patočka explains Husserl's position in his Warsaw lecture of 1971: "As Husserl sees it, what makes Europe special is precisely the fact that reason constitutes the central axis of its history. There are numerous cultural traditions, but only the European places the universality of evidence—and so of proof and of reason—at the very center of its aspirations. The vision of living in truth, of living, as Husserl has it, responsibly, emerged only in Europe, and only here did it develop in the form of a continuous thought, capable of being universally duplicated and of being deepened and corrected through a shared effort." Patočka, "Edmund Husserl's Philosophy of the Crisis of the Sciences and His Conception of a Phenomenology of the *Life-World*," in Kohák, ed. *Jan Patočka*, 223.

16. Husserl, *Crisis*, 280.

17. This version of the "natural attitude," as David Carr points out, was a distinctly different approach than was taken in Husserl's early phenomenology. It is clearly "something other than the 'natural attitude' of *Ideen*, Vol. I." Carr, translator's introduction to *Crisis*, ibid., xxxix.

18. Husserl, ibid., 299.

19. Jan Patočka, "Masaryk's and Husserl's Conception of the Spiritual Crisis of Europe," in *Jan Patočka*, 146.

20. On Patočka's critique of Masarykan philosophy, see, for example, "An Attempt at a Czech National Philosophy and Its Failure," transl. Mark Suino, in *T. G. Masaryk in Perspective: Comments and Criticism*, Milič Čapek and Karel Hrubý, eds. (Ann Arbor: SVU Press, 1981).

21. Patočka, "Masaryk's and Husserl's Conception . . . ," 154.

22. Ibid.

23. Ibid., 155.

24. Patočka, "Edmund Husserl's Philosophy of the Crisis," in *Jan Patočka*, 226.

25. Ibid., 233.

26. Ibid.

27. Patočka, "Cartesianism and Phenomenology," in *Jan Patočka*, 315.

28. See Aristotle, *Nicomachean Ethics* VI. 6, trans. Martin Ostwald (New York: Macmillan Publishing, 1962), 154–155.

29. *The Collected Works of Jan Patočka (Sebrané spisy Jana Patočky)* in Czech, presently being published by OIKOYMENH Press in Prague, has allocated three volumes for Patočka's phenomenological writings.

30. Patočka, "Cartesianism and Phenomenology," in *Jan Patočka*, 293.

31. Ibid., 294.

32. Patočka, *Body, Community, Language, World*, 3.

33. Ibid., 4.

34. Patočka, "Martin Heidegger, myslitel lidskosti: Improvizovaná úvaha po zprávě o Heideggerově smrti" (Martin Heidegger, a Thinker of Humanity: An Improvised Reflection upon the News of Heidegger's Death), *Filosofický Časopis* 43, no. 1 (1995): 3–5.

35. Patočka, "Autorův doslov k Francouzskému vydání *přirozeného světa*" (The Author's Postscript to the French Printing of *The 'Natural' World*"), in *Přirozený svět jako filosofický problém (The Natural World as a Philosophical Problem)*, (Prague: Československý spisovatel, 1992): 256.

36. Kohák, "Philosophical Biography," in *Jan Patočka*, 83. See also, Jan Patočka, *An Introduction to Husserl's Phenomenology*, trans. Erazim Kohák, (Chicago and LaSalle, Illinois: Open Court Press, 1996).

37. Patočka's discussion of the "whole," it should be noted, draws from Husserl rather than Heidegger.

38. Patočka, *Přirozený svět jako filosofický problém*, 13.

39. Patočka, *Body, Community, Language, World*, 165.

40. Ibid.

41. See Kohák, "Philosophical Biography," 86.

42. Patočka, *Body, Community, Language, World*, 36.

43. Kohák notes that: "The grounding of (mathematical) objectivity in the subject is the achievement of Husserl's *Philosophy of Arithmetic*, the transcending of an arbitrary psychologism that of *Logical Investigations*." "Philosophical Biography," 88.

44. Patočka, *Introduction to Husserl's Phenomenology*, 102–103.

45. Kohák, "Philosophical Biography," 92.

46. Ibid.

47. Patočka, "The 'Natural' World and Phenomenology," *Jan Patočka*, 253.

48. "Asubjective" phenomenology refers to Patočka's desire to move beyond the Husserlian "quest for a ground of certainty in subjectivity,"as Kohák describes it, and toward an asubjective meaning of the whole. See Erazim Kohák, "Philosophical Biography," pp. 6-8 and 83-97. Corporeity is the explicit subject of *Body, Community, Language, World*, in which

Patočka extends the work on corporeity of among others, Merleau-Ponty (*Phenomenology of Perception*). See, for example, *Body, Community, Language, World*, pp. 47–50.

49. Patočka, *Body, Community, Language, World*, 33.

50. Edmund Husserl used the concepts of the "horizon" and the "world" in his *Crisis* writings, for example, in his Vienna Lecture: "Now natural life can be characterized as a life naively, straightforwardly directed at the world, the world being always in a certain sense consciously present as a universal horizon, without, however, being thematic as such." Husserl, "The Vienna Lecture," in *Crisis*, 281.

51. Patočka, *Body, Community, Language, World*, 34.

52. Ibid., 39.

53. Ibid., 35.

54. Ibid., 36.

55. Kohák, "Philosophical Biography," 100. The phrase "hardness of reality" is found in Patočka's *Body, Community, Language, World* where it is used in reference to the "grandiose optimism" of Hegel's philosophy, which, though it did not "mask the hardness of reality," understood the sorrows of life as mere stages on the way to a final peace (*Body, Community, Language, World*, 74).

56. Patočka, *Body, Community, Language, World*, 166.

57. Ibid., 166–167.

58. Ibid., 168.

59. On the concept of the phenomenological reduction, see Edmund Husserl, *Ideas: General Introduction to Pure Phenomenology*, trans. W. R. Boyce Gibson (London: Collier MacMillan Publishers, 1962), 101–103. The details of Patočka's response to Husserl's position can be found in his *Introduction to Husserl's Phenomenology*, 87–106.

60. Patočka, *Body, Community, Language, World*, 165-166.

61. Ibid., 165.

62. Ibid., 170.

63. Coming to the conclusion of his discussion of the whole in *Body, Community, Language, World*, Patočka asks if there is not a sense here of rehabilitating an ancient idea: *physis* as *archē*, which "rules in all particulars." This is an understanding first expressed in ancient fragments of Anaximander, of the whole in which all individuals come into being and perish. Ibid., 169.

64. Because the term "natural" world is somewhat ambiguous in English (though not in Czech), I will follow the example of Erazim Kohák and emphasize its specific connotation with quotation marks. In Patočka's usage, the "natural" world does not refer to the world of nature (*přírodní svět*) but rather to the world as it presents itself to us *naturally*, or simply, without our having reflected on it or studied it at all—the prereflective or

"pretheoretical" world. This meaning is adequately rendered in Czech by the term *přirozený svět*; English, however, has no equivalent and is limited to the term *natural* world. For Kohák's explanation of the same, see "Philosophical Biography," 22–23.

65. Patočka, "The 'Natural' World and Phenomenology," 245.

66. Husserl, *Crisis*, 121, 123.

67. This has been noted by several commentators. Paul Ricoeur, in his introduction to the *Heretical Essays*, wrote that while Husserl's "natural" world was prescientific, Patočka's was prehistorical, meaning that while the former thought theoretically, the latter had a significantly more concrete notion in mind. Erazim Kohák concurred with this diagnosis, writing that while the "natural" world was a "pre-human, neutral epistemological datum" for Husserl, for Patočka it is "*ab initio* a human world, a world of moral subjects living, again *ab initio*, in a network of moral relations, having to make decisions and to bear responsibility for them." Erazim Kohák, "The Crisis of Rationality and the 'Natural' World," *Review of Metaphysics* 40 (September 1986): 91.

68. Patočka, "Edmund Husserl's Philosophy of the Crisis," in *Jan Patočka*, 233.

69. Ibid., 237.

70. "By intuition here we need to understand a rational insight in the Husserlian sense, that is, the primordial presence of the intended object before the mental gaze of the subject." Ibid., 232.

71. Patočka writes that, "The Husserlian demand of the primordial givenness, the delving beneath all that is derivative to the primary source, takes from the world as a corelate [*sic*] of an intuition presenting things themselves . . . , toward a world that is first of all one of good (and of evil) and that, in virtue of this, deserves to be called the world of actual human existence." Ibid., 235. Patočka's conception of *good*, in this context, interestingly combines elements from Aristotle and Heidegger. The good is that toward which all things aim, yet it is not a metaphysical entity but rather described in terms of Heidegger's discussion of *das Worumwillen*, or that "*for the sake of which*" we act. See Ibid., 234–235. See also Heidegger, *Being and Time*, I. 3, pp. 118–122; I. 5, 184–187; I. 6, 235–240.

72. Ibid., 236.

73. Raymond Klibansky, for example, stresses the point that, in his opinion, Patočka's path is "totally different" from Heidegger's. Even Richard Rorty and Erazim Kohák, both of whom are respected as sober analysts who recognize the influence of both Husserl and Heidegger in Patočka's work, cannot resist voicing some opinion in the matter. Interestingly, while Rorty concludes that "[i]n the dialogue between Husserl and Heidegger, then, Patočka is mostly on Heidegger's side," Kohák comes to the opposite conclusion: considering Patočka as a whole,

he says, it is the Husserlian strand that is "dominant." See Raymond Klibansky, "Jan Patočka," in *La Responsabilite/Responsibility*, eds. P. Horák and J. Zumr (Prague: Filosofický ústav ČSAV, 1992), 17–35; Rorty, "The Seer of Prague," *The New Republic* 205 (July 1, 1991): 37; Kohák, "Jan Patočka's Search for the Natural World," 137.

74. Patočka, *Body, Community, Language, World*, 73.

75. See Patočka, *Heretical Essays in the Philosophy of History*, 45–46.

76. Ibid., 49.

77. Ibid., 46.

78. Patočka, *Body, Community, Language, World*, 97.

79. On the self-interestedness of *Dasein*, see the Introduction to Heidegger's *Being and Time*, trans. John Macquarrie and Edward Robinson (New York: Harper and Row, 1962).

80. Patočka, *Body, Community, Language, World*, 94.

81. Ibid., 95.

82. Ibid., 97.

83. Ibid.

84. Ibid.

85. Patočka, *Body, Community, Language, World*, 31. Czech, like German, allows for the easy distinguishing of "being" (*Sein* in German or *bytí* in Czech) from "beings" (*Seiende* or *jsoucno*). This is a problem in English that some have solved by rendering *Seiende* as "existents" or "what-is." I find that these solutions result in less rather than more clarity, so I prefer to render *Sein* or *bytí* traditionally, as "being," and to translate the various forms of *Seiende* or *jsoucno* as "a being," "beings," or, if the situation requires, "beings as a whole." Ralph Manheim, the translator of the Yale University Press edition of Heidegger's *An Introduction to Metaphysics*, argues that this solution, while essentially accurate, is to be avoided because it inevitably results in confusing formulations such as "Being is not a being." I disagree with this conclusion. In the end, if one hopes to read Heidegger and his students there is no alternative to developing a familiarity with the terminology sufficient to render such constructions comprehensible.

86. Heidegger's "existential analysis of death," or "being-towards-death," can be found in *Being and Time*, II. 1, 246–260.

87. Patočka, "Varna Lecture: The Dangers of Technicization in Science according to E. Husserl and the Essence of Technology as Danger according to M. Heidegger," in *Jan Patočka*, 334.

88. Patočka, *Body, Community, Lanaguage, World*, 73.

89. Ibid., 176.

90. Patočka, *Heretical Essays*, 105.

91. Ibid., 153.

92. See Heidegger, *Being and Time*, I. 6, 191–200.

93. Jacques Derrida, *The Gift of Death*, 13. That Heidegger does not quote the "canonical passage" from Plato's *Phaedo* in *Being and Time*, is, for Derrida, surprising.

94. Patočka, "Cartesianism and Phenomenology," 316.

95. Patočka, "Heidegger," trans. Edward F. Findlay, *Report of the Center for Theoretical Study*, CTS-98-06 (Prague: Center for Theoretical Study, 1998), 4.

96. Patočka, "Filosofie výchovy" (A Philosophy of Education), in *Péče o duši I* (Care for the Soul I), 377.

97. Patočka, *Body, Community, Language, World*, 49.

98. Ibid., 49-50.

99. Ibid., 31.

100. Ibid., 133.

101. Ibid., 138.

102. Ibid., 49–50.

103. Ibid., 50.

104. Ibid., 49.

105. Ibid.

106. Ibid., 153.

107. Ibid., 154.

108. Ibid., 79. Patočka notes that even inactivity, the holding back of movement, also belongs to the movements of the body.

109. Ibid., 80.

110. Ibid., 154. Patočka explains his interpretation of the Aristotelian concept as a "radicalization": "To understand the movement of human existence, for that we need to radicalize Aristotle's conception of movement. The possibilities that ground movement have no preexisting bearer, no necessary referent standing statically at their foundation, but rather all synthesis, all inner interconnection of movement takes place within it alone. All inner unification is accomplished by the movement itself, not by some bearer, . . . objectively understood." Ibid., 147. For Aristotle's concept of the "unmoved mover," see, for example, *Metaphysics* 3.8. 30–31.

111. Patočka, *Body, Community, Language, World*, 155.

112. Ibid., 155–156.

113. Ibid., 143.

114. Ibid., 148.

115. Ibid.

116. Patočka, "The 'Natural' World and Phenomenology," 264.

117. Patočka, *Body, Community, Language, World*, 149.

118. Ibid., 150.

119. Ibid.

120. See Patočka, *Heretical Essays*, 23. See also, Hannah Arendt, *The Human Condition*, (Chicago: University of Chicago Press, 1958), pp. 29–49.

121. It is important to distinguish the concept of the "Earth" from that of the "world," described earlier. Patočka is using the notion of the Earth, here, in a quasi-Heideggerean sense. It is not the literal earth, but rather the "unshakable ground" to which our movement relates. It is the referent of our movement, that which does not move when we do, that which is firm. The Earth symbolizes the power our corporeal nature exerts on and over us. For the Heideggerean perspective, see "The Origin of the Work of Art," in *Martin Heidegger: Basic Writings*, ed. David Farrell Krell (San Francisco: HarperCollins Publishers, 1993), 171–175.

122. Patočka, *Body, Community, Language, World*, 151.

123. Ibid.

124. Ibid.

125. Ibid., 160.

126. Ibid., 160–161.

127. Patočka writes that he follows Merleau-Ponty in his analysis of corporeity as the basis for a critique of Heidegger, and "On the basis of this criticism we demonstrated the possibility of interpreting existence as a triple movement. That we did using both an ancient and a modern idea. The modern idea was Heidegger's, that life is a life in possibilities characterized by a relation to our own being; we project that for the sake of which we are, that *for the sake of* is the possibility of our life; in the world a totality of possibilities is always open to us. The ancient idea—Aristotle's definition of movement as a possibility in the process of realization, not motion in Galileo's sense." Patočka, *Body, Community, Language, World*, 177.

128. Ibid., 161.

129. Ibid., 177.

130. Ibid., 178.

131. Ibid.

132. Ibid., 96-97.

133. Ibid., 97.

134. In the course of an underground seminar delivered on the occasion of the publication of the *Der Speigel* interview shortly after Heidegger's death, Patočka gives his students an insightful description of the difference between the early and the late Heidegger. The early Heidegger, he says, works from the conception that "*das Sein ist das Sein des Seienden*" (Being is the Being of beings), while the later Heidegger would say that "*das Seiende ist das Seiende des Seins*" *(beings are the beings of Being)*. In the former conceptualization Heidegger stresses that Being must not be thought of as "a" being, but rather as the ways in which beings appear, he emphasizes that fact that what we understand as Being comes

from us, from beings; in the latter formulation this is reversed. Heidegger shows himself to be no longer focused on beings so much as on their Being. This is the Heidegger of Hölderlin's poetry, of the fourfold of earth, sky, divinity, and mortals. (See Patočka, "Documenta Philosophiae: Diskuse k Heideggerovi," *Filosofický časopis* 43, no. 2 (1995): 218.

135. On the "saving power," see Heidegger's evocation of Hölderlin in "The Question Concerning Technology," *Basic Writings*, 333–334.

136. Kohák, "Philosophical Biography," 134.

137. James Dodd, introduction to *Body, Community, Language, World*, xxxi.

CHAPTER 3. PHILOSOPHY AFTER THE DEATH OF METAPHYSICS

1. See, for example, Plato's discussion of the "divided line" in *The Republic*, 510A–511E. *Great Dialogues of Plato*, trans. W. H. D. Rouse (New York: Penguin Books, 1984), 310–311.

2. Patočka, "Negative Platonism," 205.

3. Plato, "Apology," in *Great Dialogues of Plato*, 27D–29E, 436.

4. See Martin Heidegger, *An Introduction to Metaphysics*, trans. Ralph Manheim (New Haven: Yale University Press, 1959) 179–188. Patočka's thought is dominated by the phenomenologically inspired rejection of abstract theory as interfering in the direct and true experience of a particular phenomenon. For a phenomenon to be examined free of distortion, we must abstain from speculation about it, simply let it appear. Starting from this phenomenological principle, it was but a short step for Patočka to the critique of metaphysics offered by Heidegger—the contention that all of European thought since Plato suffers from the distortion wrought by metaphysics, the systematization of Platonic thought into ideal essences serving as objective, transcendental models for earthly phenomena.

5. None of these texts have as yet appeared in English translation, although a translation of *Plato and Europe* is soon to be published by Stanford University Press. *Europe and the Post-European Age* and *Plato and Europe* have recently been published in the Czech volume *Péče o duši II*, the second volume of Patočka's collected works, published in 1999 by OIKOYMENH publishers and the Jan Patočka Archive. In addition to these texts, the four published volumes of Patočka's university lectures on Socrates, Plato, Aristotle, and the Presocratics during the years 1945–1949 also belong in the category of significant texts on Greek philosophy.

6. See Husserl, "The Vienna Lecture," 276–277.

7. Patočka, *Platón a Evropa* (Plato and Europe), in *Sebrané Spisy Jana Patočky*, sv. 2 (The Collected Works of Jan Patočka, vol. 2), *Péče o*

duši II: Soubor statí a přednášek o postavení člověka ve světě a v dějinách (Care for the Soul II: A Collection of Articles and Lectures on the Position of Man in the World and in History), eds. Ivan Chvatík and Pavel Kouba (Prague: OIKOYMENH, 1999), 149 [Hereafter *Plato and Europe*].

8. Ibid.

9. Ibid.

10. Patočka, "Filosofie výchovy" (Philosophy of Education), in *Péče o duši I*, 367.

11. See, for example, "Filosofie výchovy," 434; this is the same phrase that Václav Havel has made famous as a symbol for his own "antipolitical" approach to politics. See Václav Havel, "Politics and Conscience" and "The Power of the Powerless," in *Open Letters* (London: Faber and Faber, 1991).

12. See Martin Heidegger, *An Introduction to Metaphysics*, 125–145.

13. For the discussion of truth as freedom, see Patočka, "Problém pravdy z hlediska negativního platonismu" (The Problem of Truth from the Perspective of Negative Platonism), in *Péče o duši I*, 460; Martin Heidegger, "On the Essence of Truth," in *Basic Writings*, 115–138. Heidegger writes that "The openness of comportment as the inner condition of the possibility of correctness is grounded in freedom. *The essence of truth is freedom.*" Ibid., 123.

14. Patočka, "Nadcivilizace a její vnitřní konflikt" (Super-civilization and its Inner Conflict), in *Péče o duši I*, 289.

15. Patočka, Plato and Europe, 227.

16. Ibid., 313.

17. Ibid.

18. Ibid., 159.

19. Ibid., 156.

20. Ibid., 157.

21. See essay six of *Heretical Essays in the Philosophy of History*, entitled "Wars of the Twentieth Century and the Twentieth Century as War."

22. Patočka, *Plato and Europe*, 228. Though arresting, this analysis is insufficiently backed by argumentation; it is asserted but not defended with historical evidence, making it a shortcoming in Patočka's work. In contrast, see Eric Voegelin's multi-volume *Order and History*, in which the author conducts an equally in-depth analysis of Judaism and Christianity in regard to the source of conceptions of order in the Western world.

23. Patočka, *Plato and Europe*, 159–160.

24. Ibid., 177.

25. Ibid., 162.

26. See ibid.

27. Ibid., 181.

28. Ibid., 180.

29. Ibid.

30. Patočka, *Europe and the Post-European Age*, 30.

31. Patočka, *Plato and Europe*, 181.

32. See Heidegger, *Being and Time*, I. 6, 225–241.

33. Jacques Derrida, *The Gift of Death*, 13. See also Plato, "Phaedo," in *Great Dialogues of Plato*, 484–485.

34. Patočka, *Heretical Essays*, 105.

35. Patočka, *Plato and Europe*, 172.

36. Patočka, *Čtyři semináře k problému Evropy* (Four Seminars on the Problem of Europe), in *Péče o duši, Sv. 3. Soubor statí, přednášek a poznámek k problematice postavení člověka ve světě a v dějinách* (Care for the Soul, Vol. 3: Collection of Essays and Notes on the Problems of the Situation of Man in the World and in History), (samizdat), (Prague: Jan Patočka Archive, Center for Theoretical Study, 1988) 319.

37. See chapter 2, above, pp. 61–65.

38. Patočka, *Sokrates*, eds. Ivan Chvatík and Pavel Kouba (Prague: Státní pedagogické nakladatelství, 1991), 109.

39. Plato, *Phaedrus* 245C-E, trans. Alexander Nehamas and Paul Woodruff (Indianapolis: Hackett Publishing Company, 1995), 29–30.

40. Patočka, *Europe and the Post-European Age*, 72.

41. Ibid., 72–73.

42. See chapters 3 and 4 of "Plato and Europe" for a discussion of the relationship between myth and philosophy. On Greek tragedy, see *Sokrates*, 19-23.

43. Ibid., 211.

44. See Husserl, *Ideas: General Introduction to Pure Phenomenology*, trans. W. R. Boyce Gibson (London: Collier MacMillen Publishers, 1962), 48–50.

45. Patočka, *Plato and Europe*, 197.

46. Patočka, *Europe and the Post-European Age*, 68.

47. Ibid., 69.

48. Patočka, *Plato and Europe*, 229.

49. Patočka, *Europe and the Post-European Age*, 67.

50. Ibid.

51. Patočka, *Plato and Europe*, 229.

52. Ibid., 224.

53. Ibid.

54. See "Negativní platonismus," "Věčnost a dějinnost" (Eternity and Historicity), and "Problém pravdy z hlediska negativního platonismu" (The Problem of Truth from the Perspective of Negative Platonism), in *Péče o duši I, (Care for the Soul, vol. I)*.

55. *Péče o duši I* "Negative Platonism," 175.

56. Ibid., 178.

57. Ibid., 175.

58. Ibid., 179–180. In referring to "protophilosophy," Patočka has in mind such pre-Socratic philosophers as Heraclitus, Parmenides, and the Pythagoreans.

59. As to the question of whether Socrates was a historical reality, Patočka writes: "Whether Socrates the philosopher is a literary myth or a historical reality—personally, I continue to favor the second possibility—it seems certain that in the figure of Socrates we have before us, in Plato's writings, a special active, anthropologically oriented version of this philosophical protoknowledge." Ibid. In addition, a chapter of Patočka's volume of university lectures on Socrates bears the title "What we know about Socrates's life," and consists of a detailed reconstruction of ancient references to Socrates, further demonstrating the conviction that Socrates was in fact a historical character. See Patočka, *Sokrates.*

60. Patočka, "Eternity and Historicity," in *Péče o duši I (Care for the Soul, vol. I)*, 142.

61. The basic outline of this critique of metaphysics, Patočka argues, emerged separately and for different reasons in two disparate disciplines, theology and the philosophy of existence, and precisely at the time when anthropocentric humanism was reaching its height. It arose in theology "seeking to free itself from the metaphysical and so also the anthropological habit," and in existentialism "insofar as it [was] an expression of a revolt against anthropologism, against integral humanism." Patočka, "Negative Platonism," 188.

62. Ibid.

63. Ibid., 180.

64. Ibid.

65. Ibid.

66. Ibid., 181.

67. Ibid., 195.

68. Ibid. In Plato, see, for example, the discussion of the "divided line" in *The Republic* 508E–511E.

69. Ibid.

70. Ibid.

71. Ibid., 182. Note: in those instances where the translator, Erazim Kohák, uses the terms "existents" and "what-is" to refer to different forms of the Czech "*jsoucno,*" I have noted the alternate translation of "beings" or "beings as a whole." See footnote 85 in chapter 2.

72. Ibid.

73. Ibid., 188.

74. Patočka, *Heretical Essays,* 117.

75. Patočka, "Negative Platonism," 192.

76. Ibid., 180.

77. Ibid., 196.
78. Ibid., 197.
79. Ibid.
80. Ibid., 205–206.
81. Patočka, "Ideology and Life in the Idea," trans. Eric Manton, *Report of the Center for Theoretical Study*, CTS-96–09 (Prague: Center for Theoretical Study, 1996).
82. Patočka, "Negative Platonism," 198. The reference to a *chorismos* draws upon Heidegger's analysis in his *An Introduction to Metaphysics*, 106. This analysis, which is brief and dismissive of the Platonic experience, forms the basis for much of "Negative Platonism." Heidegger writes that via Platonism,

> [a] chasm, *chorismos*, was created between the merely apparent essent here below and real being somewhere on high. In that chasm Christianity settled down, at the same time reinterpreting the lower as the created and the higher as the creator. These refashioned weapons it turned against antiquity (as paganism) and so disfigured it. Nietzsche was right in saying that Christianity is Platonism for the people.

Unlike Heidegger, Patočka discerns an important difference between Socrates and later Platonism and so interprets the *chorismos* differently. For Patočka, the *chorismos* does not represent metaphysics (Heidegger) but freedom. Heidegger's analysis of the *chorismos* and the separation of being, or Idea, from appearance leads to a distinction between being and thinking. Here the contrast with Patočka is strongest, for Heidegger finds *this* distinction to represent the spirit of the West, and he stands against it. "In the seemingly unimportant distinction between being and thinking we must discern the fundamental position of the Western spirit, against which our central attack is directed." (117)
83. Ibid., 198–199.
84. Ibid., 199.
85. In articulating what could be called a "philosophy of freedom," Patočka takes care to distinguish his own endeavor from that of German Idealism. The interpretation of the Idea presented here has the advantage of avoiding subjectivism:

> The philosophy of freedom is usually identified with the doctrines of German idealism; undoubtedly, it is most closely linked to them historically, yet German idealism is a philosophy of an absolute, sovereign subjectivity, of the supremacy of the humanly historical 'I' to whom it attributes the significance of absolute substance. As a subjectivism, German idealism is metaphysical. . . . By contrast,

> the Idea . . . has the advantage that, if stripped of metaphysical encrustations, it stands above both subjective and objective existents.

Ibid., 200.

86. Husserl, _Ideas_, 118.

87. Patočka, "Negative Platonism," 204.

88. Ibid., 203.

89. See Patočka, _Heretical Essays_, chapter 6, "Wars of the Twentieth Century and the Twentieth Century as War," 119–137.

90. Patočka, "Negative Platonism," 204–205.

91. Patočka, "Eternity and Historicity," in _Péče o duši I_ (Care for the Soul, Vol. I), 144.

92. Ibid., 146.

93. Ibid.

94. See note 41, above.

95. Patočka, "Eternity and Historicity," 147.

96. Ibid., 146.

97. Patočka, "The Problem of Truth from the Perspective of Negative Platonism," in _Péče o duši I_, 447.

98. Ibid., 458.

99. Ibid., 459.

100. Ibid., 461.

101. See ibid., 460.

102. Ibid., 465.

103. Patočka, "Historicity and Eternity," 145.

104. Ibid.

105. Patočka, Sokrates, 115–116.

CHAPTER 4. A PHILOSOPHY OF HISTORY AND A THEORY OF POLITICS

1. Paul Ricoeur, Preface to the French Edition of Jan Patočka, _Heretical Essays in the Philosophy of History_, viii.

2. See Patočka, _Heretical Essays_, 69.

3. Ibid., 92.

4. Ibid.

5. Ibid., 93.

6. Ibid., 118.

7. See Kohák, Jan Patočka, 26.

8. Jan Patočka, "Some Comments Concerning the Concept of a 'World History,'" unpublished translation by Erazim Kohák, TMs (photo-

copy), 9. See also the original "Několik poznámek o pojmu 'světových dějin,'" *Česká mysl* 31 (1935), 86–96.

9. Patočka, "Negative Platonism," 191.

10. Ibid.

11. Ibid.

12 Patočka, *Heretical Essays*, 44.

13 See Patočka, "Několik poznámek k pojmům dějin a dějepisu" (Some Comments Concerning the Concepts of History and Historiography), in *Péče o duši I*, 43–44. See also Erazim Kohák, "A Philosophical Biography," 28; and Heidegger, *Being and Time*, "Division One: Preparatory Fundamental Analysis of Dasein."

14. Patočka, "Some Comments Concerning the Concept of a 'World History,'" 1.

15. Patočka, *Heretical Essays*, 45.

16. Ibid., 46.

17. Ibid.

18. Ibid., 51.

19. Ibid. "The reflections that follow," he writes, "will attempt to explicate several problems of older and contemporary history in light of motifs taken over from it [Heidegger's philosophy]. The author alone, to be sure, must bear responsibility for his deductions."

20. A similar critique of Husserl was made by Eric Voegelin, also a Central European scholar on whom Husserl's *Crisis of European Sciences* made a significant impression. Voegelin writes of his shock at Husserl's search for an *apodiktische Anfang*, an "apodictic beginning" to a final philosophy. Philosophy can never, Voegelin argued, have the character of apodicticity. Eric Voegelin, *Anamnesis*, trans. and ed. by Gerhart Niemeyer (Columbia, Missouri: University of Missouri Press, 1990), 9–10.

21. Patočka, "Cartesianism and Phenomenology," in *Jan Patočka*, 315.

22. Patočka, *Heretical Essays*, 27.

23. Ibid. 103.

24. Ibid., 44.

25. Patočka writes, "At first glance this conception seems to revive the naive rationalism of the eighteenth century for which enlightenment, light, is the sole source of life. In truth, it is integral to the entire cast of Husserl's phenomenology and phenomenological philosophy." Ibid., 44–45.

26. Ibid., 45.

27. The content of other philosophical traditions or cultural symbols should also be analyzed in order to uncover commonalities in the experiences that underlie them. On this point, see Eric Voegelin's discussion of the concept of "equivalences of experiences" in, for instance, "Equivalences of Experience and Symbolization in History," in *The Collected Works of*

Eric Voegelin, Vol. 12: Published Essays 1966–1985, ed. Ellis Sandoz (Baton Rouge: Louisiana State University Press, 1990), 115–133.

28. Patočka, *Plato and Europe*, 228.

29. Patočka, "Some Comments Concerning the Concept of a 'World History,'" 4.

30. Ibid., 5-6.

31. Ibid., 5.

32. Patočka, *Heretical Essays*, 10.

33. Ibid., 11. On the question of the "movements" of life, see chapter 2 of this work, pp. 42–48, above.

34. See Kohák, "A Philosophical Biography," 120.

35. Patočka, *Heretical Essays*, 12.

36. Ibid., 13.

37. Ibid., 14.

38. On this point see, for example, the 1953 text "Negative Platonism."

39. Patočka, *Heretical Essays*, 14. See also Hannah Arendt, *The Human Condition* (Chicago: The University of Chicago Press, 1958).

40. Patočka, *Heretical Essays*, 15.

41. Ibid., 16.

42. Ibid., 23. See also Arendt, *The Human Condition*, 38–49.

43. Ibid.

44. Ibid., 25.

45. Ibid.

46. Ibid., 29.

47. Ibid., 37–38.

48. Ibid., 40.

49. Ibid., 41.

50. Patočka, *Europe and the Post-European Age*, 30.

51. Patočka, *Heretical Essays*, 41.

52. See Chapter Three, pp. 72-74, above.

53. Patočka, *Heretical Essays*, 48.

54. Ibid., 49.

55. Ibid.

56. Patočka, "The Problem of Truth from the Perspective of Negative Platonism," 461.

57. Patočka, "Negative Platonism," 194.

58. Ibid.

59. Patočka, "Filosofie výchovy" (The Philosophy of Education), in *Péče o duši I* (Care for the Soul, Vol. I), 434.

60. Ibid., 435.

61. Patočka, "The Spiritual Person and the Intellectual," 2.

62. Ibid., 2.

63. "I think that the world spiritual does not sound pleasant today, it sounds in some way spiritualist and we don't like such phrases nowadays; but does there exist a better expression for what I have in mind?" Ibid., 1. See also chapter 1, above, note 21.

64. Ibid., 3.

65. Ibid., 4.

66. Ibid.

67. Patočka, *Heretical Essays*, 39.

68. Ibid., 39–40.

69. Ibid., 39.

70. Ibid.

71. Ibid., 47.

72. This is evident in the works of the 1930s. For example, in "On the Essence of Truth," Heidegger makes an analysis on which Patočka builds, concluding that "the essence of truth reveals itself as freedom," which in turn is defined as disclosure or unconcealment. In "The Origin of the Work of Art," however, the questions of freedom—or unconcealment—and history are examined, not in terms of how they play themselves out in the realm of the social or political, but rather in terms of art. It is art and poetry, not politics, that dominate Heidegger's later philosophy. Art attains to history through its founding activity, and so relates most directly not to beings in their practical manifestations, but to beings as a whole: "Art as poetry is founding, . . . Always when beings as a whole, as being themselves, demand a grounding in openness, art attains to its historical essence as foundation. This foundation happened in the West for the first time in Greece. What was in the future to be called Being was set into work, setting the standard." Martin Heidegger, "The Origin of the Work of Art," in *Basic Writings*, 201.

73. This is in contrast with the opinion of Erazim Kohák, who wrote that, "Jan Patočka, after all, had never been . . . a political philosopher." Kohák, "A Philosophical Biography," 3.

74. Patočka, "Platonism and Politics," in *Two Articles by Jan Patočka*, trans. Eric Manton, CTS-96–09, (Prague: Center for Theoretical Study, 1996), 2.

75. Patočka, *Europe and the Post-European Age*, 69.

76. See Plato, *The Republic*, 368c–d.

77. Patočka, "Author's Glosses to the *Heretical Essays*," in *Heretical Essays*, 139.

78. Ibid., 142–143.

79. Here I would note David Easton's definition of politics as the "authoritative allocations of values for society as a whole," or Harold Lasswell's more pithy "who gets what, when, and how."

80. Ibid., 148.

81. Ibid., 149.

82. Patočka, *Heretical Essays*, 77.

83. Patočka, "An Attempt at a Czech National Philosophy and its Failure," in *T. G. Masaryk in Perspective*, ed. M. Čapek and K. Hrubý (New York: SVU Press, 1981), 1.

84. Rorty, "The Seer of Prague," 36, 37.

85. Patočka, *Plato and Europe*, 220.

86. Patočka, *Heretical Essays*, 64.

87. The "controversial tone" of the last of the *Heretical Essays* has been noticed by numerous commentators, among them Paul Ricoeur, who noted in his introduction to the *Essays* the "strange, frankly shocking passages" about darkness and war.

88. Patočka, *Heretical Essays*, 67.

89. Ibid., 66–67.

90. Ibid., 67.

91. Ibid., 68–69.

92. See Karl Löwith, *Meaning in History: The Theological Implications of the Philosophy of History* (Chicago: University of Chicago Press, 1949).

93. Patočka, Heretical Essays, 69.

94. Ibid., 70.

95. Ibid., 69.

96. Ibid., 72. Further discussion of the critique of Marxian materialism may be found in *Four Seminars on the Problem of Europe*, Patočka's unpublished series of underground seminars from 1973. Here Patočka notes that the Marxian pretense of the dialectic to totality and absoluteness is destructive of the historicity of being See *Čtyři semináře k problému Evropy* (Four Seminars on the Probem of Europe), 327.

97. Ibid. On Hegel and Sartre see Patočka's comments in *Body, Community, Language, World*, p. 53 and p. 60, respectively.

98. Patočka, *Heretical Essays*, 73.

99. Ibid., 74.

100. Ibid.

101. Ibid., 93

CHAPTER 5. POLITICS AND ETHICS IN THE TWENTIETH CENTURY

1. Patočka, *Heretical Essays*, 118.

2. Ibid.

3. Ibid.

4. Patočka refers to the possibility of a *"metanoesis"* in his *Heretical Essays*, 75.

5. See, for instance, Kohák, "A Philosophical Biography," 3.

6. See the remark of Josef Novák in Chapter One, p. 5.

7. Edmund Husserl, "The Vienna Lecture," in *Crisis*, 299.

8. Patočka, "Několik poznámek o mimosvětské a světské pozici filosofie" (Some Comments on the Worldly and the Extra-worldly Posture of Philosophy), 66.

9. See. Ibid., 62–65; Idem, "Životní rovnováha a životní amplituda" (Life in Balance and Life in Amplitude), *Kritický měsíčník* (Critical Monthly) 2, no. 3 (1939): 101-106.

10. Patočka, "Titanism," in *Jan Patočka*, ed. Erazim Kohák, 140.

11. Ibid., 142.

12. Ibid., 143.

13. Kohák, "A Philosophical Biography," 17.

14. "The Doubtfulness of Existentialism," a brief essay from 1947, laid to rest any questions as to whether Patočka's own philosophy pointed in this direction.

15. Patočka, "Some Comments on . . . Philosophy," 64.

16. Patočka, "European Culture," trans. Paul Wilson, *Cross Currents* no. 3 (1984): 4.

17. Ibid., 6.

18. Blecha, 100.

19. Jan Patočka, "Nadcivilizace a její vnitřní konflikt" (Supercivilization and its Inner Conflict), in *Péče o duši I* (Care for the Soul, Vol. I), 249.

20. Ibid., 251.

21. Ibid., 253.

22. Ibid., 256.

23. Ibid., 256–257.

24. Ibid., 257.

25. Ibid.

26. As opposed to the political religions characteristic of radicalism, Patočka notes that Christianity belongs with moderate versions of civilization. Christianity, he says, "in its consciousness that the empire of God is not of this world, *structurally* belongs today in connection with moderate (even when *factually* this is not always so).". Ibid., 260.

27. Ibid.

28. Ibid., 259–260.

29. Ibid., 258.

30. Ibid., 285.

31. Ibid., 292.

32. See Blecha, 104.

33. Patočka, "Supercivilization . . . ," 295.
34. Ivan Blecha, *Jan Patočka*, 100.
35. Ibid., 98.
36. Recollection of Zdeněk Urbánek, in Jan Vladislav, *Vzpomínky a pocty: na paměť Jana Patočky* (Recollections in Honor of the Memory of Jan Patočka) (samizdat) (Prague: 1980), 116, quoted in Ivan Blecha, *Jan Patočka*, 99.
37. See Eric Voegelin, *The New Science of Politics*, 107–132.
38. Radim Palouš, "Patočka and the Community of the Shaken," TMs, Jan Patočka Archive, Center for Theoretical Study, Prague, 3.
39. Blecha, 100.
40. Palouš, 7.
41. Insightful analysis of the ideological nature of rule during normalization can be found in the essays of Václav Havel. See "The Power of the Powerless" and "Politics and Conscience" in *Open Letters: Selected Prose 1965–1990*, ed. Paul Wilson (London: Faber and Faber, 1991).
42. Patočka, "Two Charta 77 Texts," in *Jan Patočka*, 341.
43. Ibid.
44. Ibid.
45. Ibid., 342.
46. On Strauss's notion of exoteric writing, see for example, Kenneth L. Deutsch and Walter Nicgorski, "Introduction" to *Leo Strauss: Political Philosopher and Jewish Thinker* (Lanham, Maryland: Rowman & Littlefield, 1994), 8.
47. Patočka, *Heretical Essays*, 118.
48. Ibid., 97.
49. Ibid.
50. Ibid., 95.
51. The very field of modern sociology, Patočka points out, is "basically an outgrowth of an awareness of the danger, or even of a sense of the pathological nature, of the development of the industrial civilization up to now." Ibid., 96.
52. See the reference to Heidegger in Ibid., 117. See also Martin Heidegger, *Being and Time*, 126–30, 176–80.
53. Patočka, *Heretical Essays*, 114–115.
54. Ibid., 115.
55. Ibid.
56. Ibid., 116.
57. Ibid., 117.
58. Ibid., see pp. 98–103, 113–115.
59. Ibid., 118. Note: here Patočka makes use of the symbol of a "turn," prefiguring the discussion of the individual capable of "conversion," or "*metanoia*," with which he concludes the *Heretical Essays*.

60. Ibid., 118.

61. Ibid., 117.

62. See, for instance, Erazim Kohák and Aviezer Tucker, discussed in the Appendix to this work, below.

63. Paul Ricoeur, "Preface to the French Edition of Jan Patočka's *Heretical Essays*," in *Heretical Essays*, viii.

64. Patočka, *Heretical Essays*, 124.

65. Ibid., 121.

66. Ibid.

67. Ibid., 122. Patočka adds that "[t]he revolution taking place here had its deep driving force in the conspicuous scientification which all prewar experts on Europe and on Germany saw as the chief trait of its life: a scientification which understood science as technology, actually a positivism." Ibid., 123.

68. Ibid.

69. Ibid., 124.

70. Ibid., 125.

71. Ibid., 133.

72. Ibid., 120.

73. Ibid., 128.

74. See Pierre Teilhard de Chardin, "La nostalgie du front," in *Ecrits du temps de la guerre* (Paris: Grasset, 1965), and Ernst Jünger, *Die Arbeiter: Herrschaft und Gestalt and Die totale Mobilmachung*, in *Sämtliche Werke*, Zweite Abteilung, vol. 7–8 (Stuttgart: Klett Cotta, 1980).

75. Patočka, *Heretical Essays*, 126.

76. Ibid., 130.

77. Ibid., 129.

78. Ibid., 134.

79. Ibid., 133–134.

80. Ibid., 134.

81. Ibid.

82. Ibid.

83. Ibid.

84. Ibid., 136.

85. Ibid., 135.

86. Plato does not stress *polemos*, as does Heraclitus, but it is worth noting that he speaks of an "immortal battle" among good and bad things in heaven that requires of us an "amazing guard." See Plato, *The Laws of Plato* 906a–b, trans. Thomas L. Pangle (Chicago: University of Chicago Press, 1980), 306.

87. See Patočka, *Heretical Essays*, 136–137. See also Heidegger, *An Introduction to Metaphysics*, 62–63.

88. Erazim Kohák writes in his biography of Patočka that "a number of Western readers" have in fact read the essay in this light. He is correct in responding that such an interpretation is "totally and tragically erroneous." Kohák, "A Philosophical Biography," 129.

89. Martin Heidegger, *An Introduction to Metaphysics*, 62.

90. Patočka, *Heretical Essays*, 42.

91. Ibid., 43. On *polemos* as constitutive of unity in the polis, see pp. 173–177, below. The Heraclitian perspective, it should be noted, is not only explored in the *Heretical Essays*, but also in *Plato and Europe*, where Patočka makes an analogy to Sophocles' Oedipus and the harmony that comes to exist through struggle and through an examination of the ambiguity between good and evil. See *Plato and Europe*, pp. 191–192.

92. Patočka, *Four Seminars on the Problem of Europe*, 315.

93. Ibid., 329.

94. Light is a prominent symbol of the highest good in Christian and Enlightenment thought; peace is also considered the highest of goals for rational thought: see, for example, Immanuel Kant's "On Eternal Peace." See also Plato's treatment of light and reason in the Divided Line in *The Republic*.

95. Patočka, "The Spiritual Person and the Intellectual," 6.

96. See *Heretical Essays*, 39.

97. See ibid., 134–135. For a discussion of the "conversion" in the context of its source in Plato's "Allegory of the Cave," see ibid., 60–61.

98. Ibid., 134. In distinct contrast to "Wars of the Twentieth Century," Patočka's individual possessed of understanding is not a soldier, here, but a "spiritual person" (*duchovní člověk*). Far from evoking a glorified image of war, this title seems to do the opposite, calling to mind a religious sentiment that is also foreign to modern ears.

99. Patočka, "The Spiritual Person and the Intellectual," 5.

100. Patočka, *Plato and Europe*, 223–224.

101. Patočka, "The Spiritual Person and the Intellectual," 6.

102. Patočka, *Plato and Europe*, 269.

103. Patočka, "The Spiritual Person and the Intellectual," 8.

104. Ibid.

105. Patočka, "The Dangers of Technicization in Science," in *Jan Patočka*, 327–339.

106. Ibid., 336.

107. Ibid., 337.

108. Ibid., 336.

109. On the idea of "negative" freedom, see Isaiah Berlin, "Two Concepts of Liberty," in *Four Essays on Liberty* (Oxford: Oxford University Press), 1969.

110. Patočka, "Four Seminars on the Problem of Europe," 340.

111. On this point, see the analysis by Ivan Chvatík in his essay, "Solidarity of the Shaken," in *Telos* 94 (New York: 1993): 164–165.

112. Patočka, *Heretical Essays*, 135.

113. See Ibid., 98–102; "Four Seminars on the Problem of Europe," 336–337.

114. Patočka, *Heretical Essays*, 153.

115. "A Philosophy of Education" (*Filosofie výchovy*), 435. "The work, which a certain artist or theoretician performs apparently for himself alone, is in actuality work for all possible, work for a possible society, enriching not only himself, but man in general. The free person thus comes to understand this relation of his own actions to society as a necessary assumption, and he experiences it as a feeling of responsibility."

116. Patočka, "The Dangers of Technicization in Science," 339.

117. See my review of Tucker's work in the Appendix to this study, below.

118. Patočka, "Two Charta 77 Texts," in *Jan Patočka*, 341. Note: In Erazim Kohák's translation of these two short texts, he leaves the title "Charter 77" in its Czech form, which is "*Charta 77.*"

119. While Charter 77 is often considered to be a "human rights" document or to represent a human rights movement, it actually does not presume or enumerate any particular human rights. It contends, instead, that "[t]he idea of human rights is nothing other than the conviction that even states, even society as a whole, are subject to the sovereignty of moral sentiment: that they recognize something unconditional that is higher than they are, something that is binding even on them, sacred, inviolable, and that in their power to establish and maintain a rule of law they seek to express this recognition." Ibid.

120. Ibid.

121. Patočka, "Two Charter 77 Texts," in *Jan Patočka*, 342.

122. Patočka, "Four Seminars on the Problem of Europe," 336.

123. Ibid.

124. Patočka, "Opposition and Intellectuals," trans. Edward F. Findlay, *Report of the Center for Theoretical Study*, Prague. CTS-98–07 (July 1998), 5.

125. Patočka, "The Spiritual Person and the Intellectual," 5.

126. Ibid., 6.

127. Ibid.

128. Ibid.

129. Ibid. Even as a young man, when his view of philosophy was as a *heroic* enterprise and he could have been justifiably criticized for a rhetoric that tended toward "titanism," that is, a deification of man in the wake of the death of God, Patočka was never tempted by the Nietzschean solution. In commenting on the task of philosophy in 1934, the young philosopher

already sees a connection between, for example, Nietzsche's Superman and Marx's dreams of the socialist man to come, characterizing both as seeking a substitute for a lost meaning. While Nietzsche viciously condemns Socrates the philosopher for standing in the way of the creator, still naively seeking understanding, Patočka argues that philosophy is not, as Nietzsche characterized it, a naive intellectualism. To the contrary, Patočka's vision of philosophy sees it as relinquishing all recourse to salvation. See Patočka, "Some Comments on the Otherworldly and Worldly Position of Philosophy," in *Péče o duši I*, 58–67.

130. Patočka, "*Harmonismus moderních humanistů: Mravní problémy a hlediska současné filosofie*" (The Harmonism of Modern Humanists: Moral Problems and the Perspective of Contemporary Philosophy), in *Péče o duši I*, 356.

131. Ibid. In addition to Masaryk, Patočka refers to Fourier, Comte and Herder as examples of this type of thought.

132. Ibid., 362.

133. Patočka, "Negative Platonism," 176.

134. Ibid., 178.

135. Ibid., 186. Note: the Kohák translation of this passage contains what I assume to be a typographical error—a period between the words *God* and *myth*—that I have corrected based on the Czech original.

136. Patočka, *Europe and the Post-European Age*, 73

137. Patočka, *Four Seminars on the Problem of Europe*, 336.

138. See Martin Heidegger, "Being and Time: Introduction," in *Basic Writings*, 46–50.

139. Patočka, *Four Seminars on the Problem of Europe*, 336.

140. Patočka, *Europe and the Post-European Age*, 72.

141. Ibid.

142. Ibid., 73.

CHAPTER 6. CONCLUSION

1. On (anti)foundationalism as a theme in contemporary thought and its relation to political theory, see the essay, "What difference does anti-foundationalism make to political theory?," by Michael Brint, William G. Weaver, and Meredith Garmon, *New Literary History* 26, no. 2 (Spring 1995) 225–238. The authors note that foundationalism as a theme has penetrated numerous academic disciplines and is central to the thought of such figures as Heidegger, Gadamer, Derrida, Richard Rorty, Stanley Fish, and W. V. Quine.

2. Patočka, *Heretical Essays*, 38.

3. The phrase "happy end" appears in contemporary Czech philosophy as a concept. Rather than attempt a translation, the English phrase—sometimes even written as one word, "happyend"—is used in Patočka and elsewhere to depict a utopian longing, an eschatological hope. A political lesson of Patočka's thought, as Ivan Chvatik has expressed it, must be the realization that democracy should abandon the hope for such a "happy end," recognizing instead that history is ruled by struggle and problematicity. Ivan Chvatík, "Solidarity of the Shaken," 166.

4. Richard Rorty, "The Seer of Prague," 38.

5. Patočka, *Europe and the Post-European Age*, 39.

6. Ibid.

7. Ibid., 38.

8. Ibid., 39.

9. Patočka, "Supercivilization," 302.

10. Patočka, *Heretical Essays*, 118.

11. Patočka, "Osnova dějin" (The Pattern of History), in *Europe and the Post-European Age*, 100.

12. Patočka, *Heretical Essays*, 59.

13. Ibid., 61.

14. Ibid., 56.

15. Of values, for example, Patočka writes the following: "Values mean nothing other than that being is meaningful, and they indicate what 'gives' it meaning: truth means that beauty is intelligible and accessible to understanding and explanation; beauty means that the emergence of being in the human world manifests the mystery of being as something perennially enchanting; goodness that the world may include an unselfconscious or self-forgotten favor and grace. So it is with the entire infinite variety of values that constantly address us." Ibid., 55.

16. Ibid., 56–57. Note: The term *what is* designates "beings," including "things."

17. Ibid., 57.

18. Ibid.

19. Ibid.

20. Heiddeger's analysis of anxiety is helpful here, as is Plato's Parable of the Cave. They are comparable on at least one level: both entail the possibility or necessity of return from a confrontation with a loss of immediate meaning. A new type of meaning, Patočka argues, emerges from this confrontation. He characterizes that meaning as "wonder," as the discovery that there is being beyond mere beings, albeit being that appears as *no thing*—as nothing. See Ibid., p. 60.

21. Ibid.

22. Ibid., 60-61.

23. Ivan Chvatík, "Kacířství Jana Patočky v úvahách o krizi Evropy," A Report for the Center for Theoretical Study, CTS-96-02, (January 1996), 11.

24. Ibid.

25. Patočka, *Heretical Essays*, 77.

26. Ibid., 59.

27. Ibid., 75.

28. Ibid.

29. Ibid., 77.

30. See Plato, *The Republic*, Book VII, 514A–519D.

31. Patočka, *Heretical Essays*, 61.

32. Ibid., 143.

33. Ibid., 63.

34. Ibid.

35. Here, we should recall, Patočka is speaking directly to his discouraged students, and the Nietzschean tone he adopts does not well reflect the tenor of his understanding either of *polemos*, or of the goal of philosophy in general. See my argument on the provocative tone of Essay Six above, pp. 142–146.

36. Ibid., 41–42.

37. Ibid., 42.

38. Ibid., 43.

39. Patočka's discussion, in the sixth essay, of the "great phenomenon of *fighting for peace*" as something akin to an "eschatological" longing can be read as a commentary on Nietzsche's controversial suggestion to "love peace as a means to new wars—and the short peace more than the long" in *Thus Spoke Zarathustra*. Rather than evoking violence, both Patočka and Nietzsche seem to evoke struggle as a means to prevent the atrophy of the spirit that is most directly to blame when totalitarian or fascist movements are able to take hold.

40. Richard Wolin, for example, after condemning Heidegger's use of the term *Kampf* in his "Rectoral Address," concludes that Heidegger's later explanations of *Kampf* as *polemos* amount to "transparent, post fetum apologetics." Richard Wolin, *The Politics of Being: the Political Thought of Martin Heidegger* (New York: Columbia University Press, 1990), 90.

41. Martin Heidegger, *An Introduction to Metaphysics*, trans. Ralph Manheim (New Haven, Yale University Press, 1959), 62.

42. Gregory Schufreider, "Heidegger on Community," *Man and World* 14 (1981): 35.

43. Ibid., 36.

44. Ibid., 36, 50.

45. Ivan Chvatík, "Solidarity of the Shaken," 166.

46. Patočka understood that Husserl's conception of reason, as with his ideal for philosophy, was overly determined by his desire to develop a philosophy capable of a Cartesian certainty. Patočka therefore pursued a renewal of a more authentically Greek understanding of reason, centered in his commitment to the differentiation of the Platonic symbolism of "care for the soul."

47. Chvatík, "Solidarity of the Shaken," 166.

48. Patočka, "Kolem Masarykovy filosofie náboženství" (On Masaryk's Philosophy of Religion), in *Tři studie o Masarykovi* (*Three Studies on Masaryk*), ed. Ivan Chvatík and Pavel Kouba (Prague: Mladá Fronta, 1991),117.

49. "Humans cannot live in the certitude of meaninglessness" presupposed by genuine relativism, Patočka writes. See *Heretical Essays*, 75.

50. Leo Strauss, *Natural Right and History* (Chicago: University of Chicago Press, 1953), 2.

51. Strauss does exhibit, however, some particular affinities with the Patočkan approach, nowhere more so than when he characterizes the Socratic vision in terms very reminiscent of Patočkan phenomenology. Strauss writes that: "All knowledge, however limited or 'scientific,' presupposes a horizon, a comprehensive view within which knowledge is possible. All understanding presupposes a fundamental awareness of the whole: prior to any perception of particular things, the human soul must have had a vision of the ideas, a vision of the articulated whole" (Ibid., 125). The images of the "horizon" and the "awareness of the whole" prior to the perception of individual things seem to betray the continental, Husserlian influence that is at the heart of Patočka's work. Yet the development of a theory of natural right based on a perception of a horizon of human knowledge, Patočka would claim, is tantamount to offering an answer to the Socratic question, which is the question of the whole.

52. This argument is made by Nancy Fraser and Linda Nicholson in their essay "Social Criticism without Philosophy: An encounter between feminism and postmodernism," in *Postmodernism: A Reader* (New York: Columbia University Press, 1993), 415–432.

53. Richard Rorty, "The Seer of Prague," 40. See also my discussion of this essay in the Appendix, below, pp. 194-196.

54. See footnote 24 in chapter 3, above.

55. Patočka, *Heretical Essays*, 104.

56. Ibid., 40–41.

57. Ibid., 41.

58. Ibid., 118.

59. Ibid., 135.

APPENDIX

1. On Havel's "antipolitical" politics, see his essay "Politics and Conscience," in *Open Letters: Selected Prose 1965–1990*, ed. Paul Wilson (London: Faber and Faber, 1991), 249–271.

2. See Erazim Kohák, preface to *Jan Patočka*, xii–xiii.

3. It was Patočka's involvement with the human rights protest *Charter 77* that led to his arrest and interrogation, at age sixty nine, and to the brain hemorrhage that cost him his life.

4. Jacques Derrida, *The Gift of Death*, trans. David Wills (Chicago: University of Chicago Press, 1995); Rorty, "The Seer of Prague," 37.

5. In "Jan Patočka's Search for the Natural World," *Husserl Studies* 2 (Dordrecht, the Netherlands: Martinus Nijhoff Publishers, 1985): 129–155, Kohák notes that, at the time of his death, Patočka was "one of Europe's most respected, most loved, and least known philosophers" (129). Future scholars, he adds, should come to regard Patočka as "the most persistent of Husserl's successors" (130).

6. Ibid., 134. Kohák notes that Husserl had been born in Moravia and on numerous occasions "writes of Czechoslovakia as his homeland."

7. Kohák, "A Philosophical Biography," 3.

8. Kohák, preface to *Jan Patočka*, xii.

9. Ibid.

10. Ibid.

11. Patočka, preface to *Jan Patočka*, xii.

12. "Though in the course of his philosophical career Patočka was to deal intensively with Plato, with Aristotle and his heirs, with Comenius, Herder, Kant, Hegel, and especially Heidegger, as well as with numerous other thinkers, he remained throughout a critical heir of Husserl—and of Masaryk, two men who, for all their differences, were, as Husserl recognized at the end of his life, rooted in the same philosophical tradition." Kohák, "A Philosophical Biography," 10.

13. Patočka, "Jan Patočka's Search for the Natural World," 137. This conclusion is by no means unanimous. Richard Rorty comes to precisely the opposite conclusion, writing that: "In the dialogue between Husserl and Heidegger, then, Patočka is mostly on Heidegger's side." Rorty, "The Seer of Prague," 37.

14. Kohák speaks of this "discontinuity" in ibid., 109.

15. Kohák, "A Philosophical Biography," 113. The Soviet invasion of Czechoslovakia in 1968 effectively crushed all existing hope. With the loss of hope and the onset of depression, Kohák argues that Patočka assumed the role of consoler for his discouraged students: the *Heretical Essays*, with its invocation of struggle, "follows the ageless strategy of all consolatory

writings, giving up all worldly hope and calling up internal sources of strength." Ibid., 103.

16. Ibid., 129.

17. Patočka, "A Philosophical Biography," 134; "The Crisis of Rationality and the 'Natural' World," 105. In fact, Patočka does not consider love and strife mutually exclusive. Life in wakefulness and mutual strife, he argues in "The 'Natural' World and Phenomenology," actually results in a form of unconditional love for others. "That is not love as sympathy," however, "as fellow feeling for a destiny of the same suffering, but of the same glory, of the same victory—the victory over the self-destructive self-centeredness." Patočka, "The 'Natural' World and Phenomenology," 268.

18. Jan Patočka, "An Attempt at a Czech National Philosophy and its Failure," trans. Mark Suino, in *T. G. Masaryk in Perspective: Comments and Criticism*, ed. M. Čapek and K. Hrubý (Ann Arbor: SVU Press, 1981), 8.

19. Aviezer Tucker, *The Philosophy and Politics of Czech Dissidence from Patočka to Havel*, (Pittsburgh: University of Pittsburgh Press, 2000), 3.

20. Ibid.

21. Ibid., 14.

22. Ibid., 33.

23. Ibid.

24. Ibid., 43.

25. Ibid., 19.

26. Ibid., 52.

27. Tucker goes farther than Kohák in his charge that Patočka was "reactionary." While Kohák defends Patočka, albeit haltingly, from this charge, Tucker replies: "I disagree with Kohak's claim that such an interpretation would be 'tragically erroneous.'" He continues, "I think that Patočka changed his views. For a time, perhaps following the Soviet invasion, Patočka was indeed toying with reactionary ideas." Tucker, *Philosophy and Politics of Czech Dissidence*, 70.

28. Ibid., 71.

29. Ibid., 157.

30. In an early essay entitled "The Harmonism of Modern Humanism," only recently published in the original Czech, Patočka is critical of secular humanism. This modern form of thought, he argues, aims perpetually toward human harmony; it is, as he calls it, a "harmonism" that conceives of ethics as, for example, a system of moral postulates. For Patočka, however, ethics, or "moral striving," must be understood as "the striving of concrete, historical people." Ethics are to be uncovered in the

"actual history of the engaged person." The modern humanist, in seeking harmony and uninterrupted growth, is a "man of harmonism," and "a closed, ready being, simple and entirely transparent." See Jan Patočka, "Harmonismus moderních humanistů: Mravní problémy a hlediska současné filosofie" (The Harmonism of Modern Humanists: Moral Problems and the Perspective of Contemporary Philosophy), in *Péče o duši I*, 354, 362.

31. Tucker, 16.

32. See chapter 5 of this work, pp. 131–133.

33. Rorty, "The Seer of Prague," 37. Rorty adds, by way of summarizing the difference between the two, that "Patočka was a philosopher of groundless hope and Heidegger a philosopher of grounded hopelessness."

34. Ibid.

35. Ibid.

36. Ibid.

37. Ibid., 39.

38. Kohák, "The Crisis of Rationality and the 'Natural' World," 89.

39. In his essay "The Spiritual Person and the Intellectual," Patočka argues that, "[e]ssentially, all of philosophy is nothing other than the development of this problematicity, in the way that great thinkers have grasped and expressed it. The battle to extract out of this problematicity something that emerges from it; to find a solid shore, but to again problematize that which emerges as that shore." Patočka, "The Spiritual Person and the Intellectual," 202. For my discussion of the concept of problematicity, see chapter 4 of this study.

40. Jacques Derrida, *The Gift of Death*, 33.

41. See Jacques Derrida, "Remarks on Deconstruction and Pragmatism," in Deconstruction and Pragmatism, ed. Chantal Mouffe (London: Routledge, 1996), 82, 86. Quoted in Simon Critchley, "Metaphysics in the Dark: A response to Richard Rorty and Ernesto Laclau," *Political Theory*, 26, no. 6, December 1998: 808.

42. On this recent direction in Derrida's thought, see, for example, Derrida's *Specters of Marx* (London: Routledge, 1994); see also David Goicoechea's comments on the "stages" of Derrida's thinking in "The Moment of Responsibility (Derrida and Kierkegaard), *Philosophy Today* 43 (1999), 224.

43. See Critchley, 806–807.

44. Jacques Derrida, *The Gift of Death*, 77.

45. Ibid., 49.

46. Ibid., 29.

47. This element of Derrida's recent thought has received considerable attention in the critical literature. See, for example, David Goicoechea,

"The Moment of Responsibility," Simon Critchley's "Metaphysics in the Dark," and David Wood's "Much Obliged."

48. Goicoechea, 218.

49. Derrida, *The Gift of Death*, 108–109.

50. Patočka, *Heretical Essays*, 108. Note: I cite the English translation of the *Essays* rather than the French quoted by Derrida because of a difference in verb tense that may have encouraged Derrida in his analysis. The Czech *uschnopnil* is the third person past tense of the English verb "to enable," correctly translated in the passage cited above. In the French translation cited by Derrida, however, Christianity is portrayed as the "most powerful means . . . by which man is *able to* struggle against his own decline" (*Gift of Death*, 28). The use of the present tense is, in my view, misleading, for it implies that Patočka's statement looks to the future of Christianity, rather than simply to the historical past and present.

51. "What is implicit yet explosive in Patočka's text can be extended in a radical way, for it is heretical with respect to a certain Christianity and a certain Heideggerianism but also with respect to all the important European discourses. Taken to its extreme, the text seems to suggest on the one hand that Europe will not be what it must be until it becomes fully Christian, until the *mysterium tremendum* is adequately thematized. On the other hand it also suggests that the Europe to come will no longer be Greek, Greco-Roman, or even Roman." Derrida, *Gift of Death*, 29.

52. Derrida, *Gift of Death*, 22.

53. Derrida writes that "Heideggerean thinking often consists, notably in *Sein und Zeit*, in repeating on an ontological level Christian themes and texts that have been 'de-Christianized'. . . . Patočka makes an inverse yet symmetrical gesture, which therefore amounts to the same thing. He reontologizes the historic themes of Christianity and attributes to revelation or to the *mysterium tremendum* the ontological content that Heidegger attempts to remove from it." Ibid., 23.

54. Ibid., 32.

55. Ibid., 28–29.

56. Patočka, "The Spiritual Person and the Intellectual," 210.

57. Patočka, "Negative Platonism," 182.

58. Kohák, the author of a philosophical biography of Patočka, is also clear in noting that Patočka "was not and could not be a believer." Kohák, "A Philosophical Biography," 16.

59. Patočka, "Negative Platonism," 175–206.

60. Ibid., 141–142.

61. Paul Ricoeur, preface to *Heretical Essays*, by Jan Patočka, x.

62. Ibid., xi.

63. Ibid., viii.

64. Ibid., xiv. Ricoeur contrasts distinctly here with Derrida, adding that "[a]ccess to this meaning requires nothing less than a *metanoia*, a conversion, but in the philosophical sense rather than the religious."

65. Ibid.

66. Petr Lom, "East Meets West—Jan Patočka and Richard Rorty on Freedom: A Czech Philosopher Brought into Dialogue with American Postmodernism," *Political Theory* 27, no. 4, August 1999: 447–459.

67. Ibid., 457.

68. Ibid., 450.

69. Ibid., 456.

70. Ibid.

71. There is no discussion here, for instance, of the phenomenological groundwork for Patočka's discussion of transcendence and problematicity. Absent this, it is difficult to distinguish the "metaphysical spirituality" to which Lom refers from the foundational metaphysics rightly criticized by Rorty.

Works Cited

PATOČKA, JAN

1935.   "Několik poznámek o pojmu 'světových dějin'" (Some Comments Concerning the Concept of a 'World History'). *Česká mysl* 31: 86–96.

1938.   "Myšlenka vzdělanosti a její dnešní aktuálnost" (The Idea of Liberal Education and Its Contemporary Relevance). *Kritický měsíčník* 1, no. 6: 241–253.

1939.   "Životní rovnováha a světské pozice filosofie" (Life in Balance and Life in Amplitude). *Kritický měsíčník* 2, no. 3: 101-106.

1979.   *Platón a Evropa* (Plato and Europe). Prague: (samizdat). Jan Patočka Archive, Center for Theoretical Study.

1981.   "An Attempt at a Czech National Philosophy and Its Failure." In *T. G. Masaryk in Perspective.* Edited by M. Čapek and K. Hrubý. New York: SVU Press.

1984.   "European Culture." Translated by Paul Wilson. *Cross Currents* no. 3: 3–6.

1988a. *Čtyři semináře k problému Evropy* (Four Seminars on the Problem of Europe). In *Péče o duši, Sv. 3. Soubor statí, přednášek a poznámek k problematice postavení člověka ve světě a v dějinách* (Care for the Soul, Vol. 3: Collection of Essays and Notes on the Problems of the Situation of Man in the World and in History). Prague: (samizdat) Jan Patočka Archive, Center for Theoretical Study.

1988b. "Duchovní člověk a intelektuál" ("The Spiritual Person and the Intellectual"). In *Péče o duši, Sv. 6. Kacířské eseje o filosofii dějin a texty k Chartě 77* (Care for the Soul, Vol. 6: Heretical Essays in the Philosophy of History and Charter 77 Texts). Prague: (samizdat) Jan Patočka Archive, Center for Theoretical Study.

1989a. "Titanism" (1936). In *Jan Patočka: Philosophy and Selected Writings*, ed. Erazim Kohák. Chicago: University of Chicago Press.

1989b. "Masaryk's and Husserl's Conception of the Spiritual Crisis of European Humanity" (1936). In *Jan Patočka: Philosophy and Selected Writings,* ed. Erazim Kohák. Chicago: University of Chicago Press.

1989c. "Two Senses of Reason and Nature in the German Enlightenment: A Herderian Study" (1942). In *Jan Patočka: Philosophy and Selected Writings,* ed. Erazim Kohák. Chicago: University of Chicago Press.

1989d. "Negative Platonism: Reflections concerning the Rise, the Scope, and the Demise of Metaphysics—and Whether Philosophy Can Survive It" (circa 1955). In *Jan Patočka: Philosophy and Selected Writings,* ed. Erazim Kohák. Chicago: University of Chicago Press.

1989e. "The *Natural World* and Phenomenology" (1967). In *Jan Patočka: Philosophy and Selected Writings,* ed. Erazim Kohák. Chicago: University of Chicago Press.

1989f. "Edmund Husserl's Philosophy of the Crisis of the Sciences and His Conception of a Phenomenology of the 'Life-World'" (Warsaw Lecture, 1971). In *Jan Patočka: Philosophy and Selected Writings,* ed. Erazim Kohák. Chicago: University of Chicago Press.

1989g. "The Dangers of Technicization in Science According to E. Husserl and the Essence of Technology as Danger according to M. Heidegger: Varna Lecture, 1973." In *Jan Patočka: Philosophy and Selected Writings,* ed. Erazim Kohák. Chicago: University of Chicago Press.

1989h. "Two Charta 77 Texts" (1977). In *Jan Patočka: Philosophy and Selected Writings,* ed. Erazim Kohák. Chicago: University of Chicago Press.

1990. *Kacířské eseje o filosofii dějin* (Heretical Essays in the Philosophy of History). Prague: Academia.

1991a. "Kolem Masarykovy filosofie náboženství" (On Masaryk's Philosophy of Religion). In *Tři studie o Masarykovi* (Three Studies on Masaryk), ed. Ivan Chvatík and Pavel Kouba. Prague: Mladá Fronta.

1991b. *Sokrates.* Edited by Ivan Chvatík and Pavel Kouba. Prague: Státní pedagogické nakladatelství.

1992a. *Evropa a doba poevropská* (Europe and the Post-European Age). Prague: Lidové Noviny.

1992b. *Přirozený svět jako filosofický problém* (The Natural World as a Philosophical Problem). Prague: Československý spisovatel.

1995a. "Documenta Philosophiae: Diskuse k Heideggerovi." *Filosofický časopis* 43, no. 2: 206–218.

1995b.   "Martin Heidegger, myslitel lidskosti: Improvizovaná úvaha po
         zprávě o Heideggerově smrti" (Martin Heidegger, a Thinker of
         Humanity: An Improvised Reflection upon the News of Heideg-
         ger's Death). *Filosofický časopis* 43, no. 1: 3–5.
1996a.   *Heretical Essays in the Philosophy of History.* Translated by
         Erazim Kohák. Chicago and LaSalle, Illinois: Open Court Press.
1996b.   "Ideology and Life in the Idea." In *Two Articles by Jan Patočka.*
         Translated by Eric Manton. *Report of the Center for Theoretical
         Study* CTS-96-09. Prague: Center for Theoretical Study.
1996c.   *An Introduction to Husserl's Phenomenology.* Translated by
         Erazim Kohák. Chicago and LaSalle, Illinois: Open Court Press.
1996d.   "Platonism and Politics." In *Two Articles by Jan Patočka.*
         Translated by Eric Manton. *Report of the Center for Theoretical
         Study* CTS-96-09. Prague: Center for Theoretical Study.
1996e.   *Sebrané spisy Jana Patočky: Svazek 1* (The Collected Works of Jan
         Patočka). Edited by Ivan Chvatík and Pavel Kouba. Vol. 1, *Péče o
         duši I: Soubor statí a přednásek o postavení člověka ve světě a v
         dějinách. První díl: Stati z let 1929–1952, Nevydané texty z
         padesátých let.* (Care for the Soul I: A Collection of Articles and
         Lectures on the Position of Man in the World and in History. First
         Part: Manuscripts from the Years 1929–1952, Unpublished Texts
         from the Fifties). Prague: OIKOYMENH.
1997.   *Bibliografie 1928–1996: Jan Patočka.* Prague: OIKOYMENH.
1997b.   *Sebrané Spisy Jana Patočky* (The Collected Works of Jan Patočka).
         Edited by Ivan Chvatík and Pavel Kouba. Vol. 9, *Komeniologické
         studie I* (Comeniological Studies I). Prague: OIKOYMENH.
1998a.   *Body, Community, Language, World.* Translated by Erazim Kohák.
         Chicago and LaSalle, Illinois: Open Court Press.
1998b.   "Heidegger." Translated by Edward F. Findlay. *Report of the
         Center for Theoretical Study* CTS-98-06. Prague: Center for
         Theoretical Study.
1998c.   "Opposition and Intellectuals." Translated by Edward F. Findlay.
         Report of the Center for Theoretical Study CTS-98-07. Prague:
         Center for Theoretical Study.
1998d.   *Sebrané Spisy Jana Patočky* (The Collected Works of Jan Patočka).
         Edited by Ivan Chvatík and Pavel Kouba. Vol. 10, *Komeniologické
         studie II* (Comeniological Studies II). Prague: OIKOYMENH.
1999.   *Sebrané Spisy Jana Patočky* (The Collected Works of Jan Patočka).
         Edited by Ivan Chvatík and Pavel Kouba. Vol. 2, *Péče o duši II:
         Soubor statí a přednásek o postavení člověka ve světě a v dějinách.
         Druhý díl: Stati z let 1970–1977, Nevydané texty a přednásky ze
         sedmdesátých let.* (Care for the Soul II: A Collection of Articles
         and Lectures on the Position of Man in the World and in History.

First Part: Manuscripts from the Years 1970–1977, Unpublished Texts and Lectures from the Seventies). Prague: OIKOYMENH.

SECONDARY LITERATURE

Arendt, Hannah. *The Human Condition*. Chicago: University of Chicago Press, 1958.

Aristotle. *Nicomachean Ethics*. New York: Macmillan Publishing, 1962.

Bednář, Miroslav. "Ethics and Politics in Plato, Tomáš Garrigue Masaryk and Jan Patočka as a Topical Issue," in *Traditions and Present Problems of Czech Political Culture*, Czech Philosophical Studies I. Edited by Miroslav Bednář and Michal Vejražka. Vol. IVA.3, *Cultural Heritage and Contemporary Change: Central and Eastern Europe*. Washington, D.C.: The Council for Research in Values & Philosophy, 1994.

——. "Platonism in the Czech Philosophy of Politics," in *Symposium: Greek Philosophical Tradition and Czech Thought*. Athens: Municipality of Athens-Cultural Organization, 1997: 141–151.

Berlin, Isaiah. "Two Concepts of Liberty." In *Four Essays on Liberty*. Oxford: Oxford University Press, 1969.

Blecha, Ivan. *Jan Patočka*. Prague: Votobia, 1997.

Brint, Michael, William G. Weaver, and Meredith Garmon. "What Difference Does Anti-foundationalism Make to Political Theory?" *New Literary History* 26, no. 2 (spring 1995): 225–238.

Carr, David. Introduction to The *Crisis of European Sciences and Transcendental Phenomenology*, by Edmund Husserl. Evanston, Ill.: Northwestern University Press, 1970.

Chvatík, Ivan. "Solidarity of the Shaken." *Telos* 94 (1993): 163–166.

——. "The Guarantee of Death (The Importance of Being Mortal), Report of the Center for Theoretical Study, CTS-96-10 (November 1995): 24–27.

——. "Kacířství Jana Patočky v úvahách o krizi Evropy" (The Hereticism of Jan Patočka in Reflections upon the Crisis of Europe), Report of the Center for Theoretical Study, CTS-96-02 (January 1996).

Critchley, Simon. "Metaphysics in the Dark: A Response to Richard Rorty and Ernesto Laclau." *Political Theory* 26, no. 6 (December 1998): 803–817.

Derrida, Jacques. *Specters of Marx*. London: Routledge, 1994.

——. *The Gift of Death*. Translated by David Wills. Chicago: University of Chicago Press, 1995.

Deutsch, Kenneth L., and Walter Nicgorski, eds. Introduction to *Leo Strauss: Political Philosopher and Jewish Thinker*. Lanham, Maryland: Rowman & Littlefield, 1994.

Dodd, James. Introduction to *Body, Community, Language, World*, by Jan Patočka. Chicago and LaSalle, Illinois: Open Court Press, 1996.

Elshtain, Jean Bethke. "A Man for This Season: Václav Havel on Freedom and Responsibility," *Perspectives on Political Science* 21, no. 4 (fall 1992): 207–211.

Fink, Eugen and Jan Patočka. *Briefe und Dokumente 1933–1977*. Edited by Michael Heitz and Bernhard Nessler. ORBIS PHAENOMENOLOGICUS Perspektiven und Quellen, Freiburg/München: Verlag Karl Alber and Prag: Verlag OIKOYMENH, 1999.

Fraser, Nancy, and Linda Nicholson. "Social Criticism without Philosophy: An Encounter between Feminism and Postmodernism." In *Postmodernism: A Reader*. New York: Columbia University Press, 1993.

Goetz-Stankiewicz, Marketa, ed. *Good-bye, Samizdat: Twenty Years of Czechoslovak Underground Writing*. Evanston, Ill.: Northwestern University Press, 1992.

David Goicoechea's. "The Moment of Responsibility (Derrida and Kierkegaard)." *Philosophy Today*: 211–225

Hammer, Dean C. "Václav Havel's Construction of a Democratic Discourse: Politics in a Postmodern Age." *Philosophy Today* (summer 1995): 119–130.

Havel, Václav. *Living in Truth*. Edited by Jan Vladislav. London: Faber and Faber, 1987.

———. *Letters to Olga*. Translated by Paul Wilson. London: Faber and Faber, 1990.

———. *Disturbing the Peace: A Conversation with Karel Hvížďala*. Translated by Paul Wilson. New York: Alfred A. Knopf, 1990.

———. *Open Letters: Selected Prose 1965–1990*. Edited by Paul Wilson. London: Faber and Faber, 1991.

———. "Politics and Conscience." In *Open Letters*. London: Faber and Faber, 1991.

———. "The Power of the Powerless." In *Open Letters*. London: Faber and Faber, 1991.

———. "A Call for Sacrifice: the Co-responsibility of the West." *Foreign Affairs* 73, no. 2 (March-April 1994): 2–6.

———. "Post-Modernism: The Search for Universal Laws." *Vital Speeches of the Day*. LX:20, (August 1, 1994): 613–615.

———. "Transcending the Clash of Cultures: Democracy's Forgotten Dimension." *Journal of Democracy* 6, no. 2 (April 1995): 3–10.

——. "Europe at the *fin de siecle.*" Interview by Maximilian Schell. *Society.* 32:6, (September-October 1995): 68–73.

——. A statement delivered by H.E. Václav Havel, The President of the Czech Republic. Conference FORUM 2000: Prague, Czech Republic. (September 4, 1997).

Heidegger, Martin. *An Introduction to Metaphysics.* Translated by Ralph Manheim. New Haven: Yale University Press, 1959.

——. *Being and Time.* Translated by John Macquarrie & Edward Robinson. New York: Harper & Row, 1962.

——. *Basic Writings,* Edited by David Farrell Krell. San Francisco: HarperCollins, 1993.

——. "The Question Concerning Technology." In *Basic Writings,* edited by David Farrell Krell. San Francisco: HarperCollins, 1993.

Hejdánek, Ladislav. "Nothingness and Responsibility. The Problem of 'Negative Platonism' in Patočka's Philosophy." In *La Responsabilite/Responsibility,* Edited by P. Horák and J. Zumr, 36–41. Prague: Filosofický ústav ČSAV, 1992.

Husserl, Edmund. *Ideas: General Introduction to Pure Phenomenology.* Translated by W. R. Boyce Gibson. London: Collier MacMillan Publishers, 1962.

——. *The Crisis of European Sciences and Transcendental Phenomenology.* Translated by David Carr. Evanston, Ill.: Northwestern University Press, 1970.

Kahn, Charles H. *The Art and Thought of Heraclitus: An Edition of the Fragments with Translation and Commentary.* Cambridge: Cambridge University Press, 1979.

Klibansky, Raymond. "Jan Patočka." In *La Responsabilite/Responsibility,* edited by P. Horák and J. Zumr, 17–35. Prague: Filosofický ústav ČSAV, 1992.

Kohák, Erazim. "Jan Patočka's Search for the Natural World." *Husserl Studies* 2, (1985): 129-139.

——. "The Crisis of Rationality and the *Natural World.*" *Review of Metaphysics* 40 (September 1986): 79-106.

——. *Jan Patočka: Philosophy and Selected Writings.* Chicago: University of Chicago Press, 1989.

Kriseová, Eda. *Václav Havel: The Authorized Biography.* Translated by Caleb Crain. New York: St. Martin's Press, 1993.

Lawler, Peter Augustine. "Havel on Political Responsibility." *The Political Science Reviewer* XXII (1993): 20–55.

——. "Havel's Postmodern View of Man in the Cosmos." *Perspectives on Political Science* 26, no. 1 (winter 1997): 27–34.

Lom, Petr. "East Meets West—Jan Patočka and Richard Rorty on Freedom: A Czech Philosopher Brought into Dialogue with

American Postmodernism." *Political Theory* 27, no. 4 (August 1999): 447–459

Löwith, Karl. *Meaning in History: The Theological Implications of the Philosophy of History*. Chicago: University of Chicago Press, 1949.

Matustik, Martin. "Towards an Existential Politics: A Conversation with Martin Matustik." Interview by Bernard Murchland. *The Civic Arts Review* 9, no. 1 (winter 1996): 4–9.

McKenna, Andrew J. "Derrida, Death, and Forgiveness." *First Things* 71, (March 1997): 34–37.

Meyerhoff, Hans. Introduction to *Man's Place in Nature*, by Max Scheler. Boston: Beacon Press, 1961.

Moural, Josef. "The Question of the Core of Jan Patočka's Work." *Report of the Center for Theoretical Study* CTS-99-05. Prague: Center for Theoretical Study: 1–8.

Nietzsche, Friedrich. *Beyond Good and Evil*. Translated by Walter Kaufmann. New York: Vintage Books, 1989.

———. *Thus Spoke Zarathustra. In The Portable Nietzsche*, ed. Walter Kaufmann. New York: Penguin Books, 1982.

Novák, Josef. "Selected Bibliography of Jan Patočka's Writings." *Kosmas: Journal of Czechoslovak and Central European Studies* 5, no. 2 (winter 1986): 115–139.

Palouš, Martin. "Jan Patočka versus Václav Benda." In *Civic Freedom in Central Europe: Voices from Czechoslovakia*, edited by H. Gordon Skilling and Paul Wilson, 121–128. New York: St. Martin's Press, 1991.

———. "Post-Totalitarian Politics and European Philosophy." *Public Affairs Quarterly*. 7, no. 2 (April 1993): 149–164.

———. *Beyond Politics: Sixteen Exercises in Political Thought*. Habilitazionsschrift, Univerzita Karlova, 1999.

Palouš, Radim. "Patočka and the Community of the Shaken." TMs (photocopy). Jan Patočka Archive, Center for Theoretical Study, Prague.

Plato. *The Laws of Plato*. Translated by Thomas L. Pangle. Chicago: The University of Chicago Press, 1980.

———. *Phaedrus*. Translated by Alexander Nehamas and Paul Woodruff. Indianapolis: Hackett Publishing Company, 1995.

———. *The Republic*. In *Great Dialogues of Plato*. Translated by W. H. D. Rouse. New York: Penguin Books, 1984.

Ricoeur, Paul. Preface to the French Edition of *Heretical Essays in the Philosophy of History*, by Jan Patočka. Translated by Erazim Kohák. Chicago and LaSalle, Illinois: Open Court Press, 1996.

Rorty, Richard. *Contingency, Irony, and Solidarity*. Cambridge: Cambridge University Press, 1989.

——. *Objectivity, Relativism, and Truth: Philosophical papers I.* Cambridge: Cambridge University Press, 1991.

——. "The Seer of Prague." *The New Republic* 205 (July 1, 1991): 35–40.

Scheler, Max. *Man's Place in Nature.* Translated by Hans Meyerhoff. Boston: Beacon Press, 1961.

——. *Selected Philosophical Essays.* Translated by David R. Lachterman. Evanston: Northwestern University Press, 1973.

Schufreider, Gregory. "Heidegger on Community." *Man and World* 14 (1981): 25–54.

Schuhmann, Karl. "Husserl a Patočka." Translated by V. Hrubá. *Proměny* 24, no. 1 (spring 1987): 34. Quoted in Erazim Kohák, *Jan Patočka: Philosophy and Selected Writings*, 9. Chicago: University of Chicago Press, 1989.

Scruton, Roger. "Masaryk, Patočka and the Care of the Soul." In *On Masaryk*, edited by Josef Novák, 111–128. Amsterdam: Rodopi, 1988.

Skilling, H. Gordon and Wilson, Paul, eds. *Civic Freedom in Central Europe: Voices from Czechoslovakia.* New York: St. Martin's Press, 1991.

Strauss, Leo. *Natural Right and History.* Chicago: University of Chicago Press, 1950.

Szakolczai, Arpad. "Thinking Beyond the East-West Divide: Foucault, Patočka, and the Care of the Self." *Social Research* 61, no. 2 (summer 1994): 297–320.

Tucker, Avizier. "Václav Havel's Heideggerianism." *Telos* 85, (1990): 63–78.

——. "Patočka vs. Heidegger: The Humanistic Difference." *Telos* 92, (1992): 85–98.

——. "Shipwrecked: Patočka's Philosophy of Czech History." *History and Theory.* 35:2, (May 1996): 196–217.

——. *Fenomenologie a Politika: od J. Patočky k V. Havlovi* (Phenomenology and Politics: from J. Patočka to V. Havel), translated by Klára Cabalková. Prague: Votobia, 1997.

——. *The Philosophy and Politics of Czech Dissidence from Patočka to Havel.* Pittsburgh: University of Pittsburgh Press, 2000.

Voegelin, Eric. *The New Science of Politics: An Introduction.* Chicago: University of Chicago Press, 1952.

——. "Equivalences of Experience and Symbolization in History." In *Published Essays 1966–1985*, Vol. 12, *The Collected Works of Eric Voegelin.* Edited by Ellis Sandoz. Baton Rouge: Louisiana State University Press, 1990.

———. *History of Political Ideas Vol. VIII: Crisis and the Apocalypse of Man*, Vol. 26, *The Collected Works of Eric Voegelin*. Edited by David Walsh. Columbia: University of Missouri Press, 1999.

Wolin, Richard. *The Politics of Being: The Political Thought of Martin Heidegger*. New York: Columbia University Press, 1990.

Wood, David. "Much Obliged." *Philosophy Today* (Spring 1997): 135–140.

Index